Bernhard Schandl

From Files to Siles

Bernhard Schandl

From Files to Siles

An Infrastructure for the Development of Semantic Desktop Applications

Südwestdeutscher Verlag für Hochschulschriften

Impressum/Imprint (nur für Deutschland/ only for Germany)
Bibliografische Information der Deutschen Nationalbibliothek: Die Deutsche Nationalbibliothek verzeichnet diese Publikation in der Deutschen Nationalbibliografie; detaillierte bibliografische Daten sind im Internet über http://dnb.d-nb.de abrufbar.

Alle in diesem Buch genannten Marken und Produktnamen unterliegen warenzeichen-, marken- oder patentrechtlichem Schutz bzw. sind Warenzeichen oder eingetragene Warenzeichen der jeweiligen Inhaber. Die Wiedergabe von Marken, Produktnamen, Gebrauchsnamen, Handelsnamen, Warenbezeichnungen u.s.w. in diesem Werk berechtigt auch ohne besondere Kennzeichnung nicht zu der Annahme, dass solche Namen im Sinne der Warenzeichen- und Markenschutzgesetzgebung als frei zu betrachten wären und daher von jedermann benutzt werden dürften.

Verlag: Südwestdeutscher Verlag für Hochschulschriften Aktiengesellschaft & Co. KG
Dudweiler Landstr. 99, 66123 Saarbrücken, Deutschland
Telefon +49 681 37 20 271-1, Telefax +49 681 37 20 271-0
Email: info@svh-verlag.de
Zugl.: Wien, Universität Wien, Dissertation, 2009

Herstellung in Deutschland:
Schaltungsdienst Lange o.H.G., Berlin
Books on Demand GmbH, Norderstedt
Reha GmbH, Saarbrücken
Amazon Distribution GmbH, Leipzig
ISBN: 978-3-8381-1360-9

Imprint (only for USA, GB)
Bibliographic information published by the Deutsche Nationalbibliothek: The Deutsche Nationalbibliothek lists this publication in the Deutsche Nationalbibliografie; detailed bibliographic data are available in the Internet at http://dnb.d-nb.de.

Any brand names and product names mentioned in this book are subject to trademark, brand or patent protection and are trademarks or registered trademarks of their respective holders. The use of brand names, product names, common names, trade names, product descriptions etc. even without a particular marking in this works is in no way to be construed to mean that such names may be regarded as unrestricted in respect of trademark and brand protection legislation and could thus be used by anyone.

Publisher: Südwestdeutscher Verlag für Hochschulschriften Aktiengesellschaft & Co. KG
Dudweiler Landstr. 99, 66123 Saarbrücken, Germany
Phone +49 681 37 20 271-1, Fax +49 681 37 20 271-0
Email: info@svh-verlag.de

Printed in the U.S.A.
Printed in the U.K. by (see last page)
ISBN: 978-3-8381-1360-9

Copyright © 2010 by the author and Südwestdeutscher Verlag für Hochschulschriften Aktiengesellschaft & Co. KG and licensors
All rights reserved. Saarbrücken 2010

Abstract

The extent to which our daily lives are digitized is continuously growing. Many of our everyday activities manifest themselves in digital form; either in an explicit way, when we actively use digital information for work or spare time; or in an implicit way, when information is indirectly created or manipulated as a consequence of our action. A large fraction of these data volumes can be considered as personal information, that is, information that has a certain class of relationship to us as human beings.

The storage and processing capacity of the devices that we use to interact with these data has been enormously increasing over the last years, and we can expect this development to continue in the future. However, while the power of physical data storage is permanently increasing, the development of logical data organization power of personal devices has been stagnating since the invention of the first personal computers.

Still, hierarchical file systems are the de-facto standard for data organization on personal devices. File systems represent information as a set of discrete data units (files) that are arranged as leaves on a tree of labeled nodes (directories). This structure, on the one hand, can be easily understood by humans, since the separation into small information units supports the manual manageability of the personal data space, in comparison to systems that employ continuous data structures. On the other hand, hierarchical structures suffer from a number of deficiencies which have negative impact on the quality of personal information management, and it lacks of expressive mechanisms which in turn would help to improve information retrieval according to user needs.

Significant research effort has been invested in order to improve the mechanisms for personal information management. The resulting works represent potential alternatives or supplements for systems in place, but sometimes run the risk of over-formalizing information management; a problem that is especially apparent in situations where a non-expert end user is the direct consumer of such services.

The contribution of this thesis is to present an alternative organizational model for management of personal data that strikes a balance between the unstructured nature of file systems and the highly formal characteristics of logic-based systems. After a comparative analysis of the current situation and recent research effort in this direction, it describes this organizational metaphor on three levels: First, on a conceptual level, it discusses an abstract data model, a corresponding query algebra, and a set of abstract operations on this data model. This formal framework is suitable to represent common data structures and usage patterns that can be found in personal information management, but on the same time does not enforce a complete paradigm shift away from established systems. Second, on a representation level, it discusses how this model can be efficiently processed, stored, and exchanged between different systems. Third, on an implementation level, it describes how concrete realizations of this data model can be built and used in various application scenarios.

Zusammenfassung

In einem permanent wachsenden Ausmaß wird unser Leben digital organisiert. Viele tagtägliche Aktivitäten manifestieren sich (auch) in digitaler Form: einerseits explizit, wenn digitale Informationen für Arbeitsaufgaben oder in der Freizeit entstehen und verwendet werden; andererseits auch implizit, wenn Informationen indirekt, als Konsequenz unseres Handelns, erzeugt oder manipuliert wird. Ein großer Teil dieser Informationsbestände ist persönlicher Natur, d.h., diese Information hat einen bestimmten Bezug zu uns als Person.

Die Speicher- und Rechenleistung der Geräte, mit denen wir üblicherweise mit solchen persönlichen Daten interagieren, wurde in den letzten Jahren kontinuierlich erhöht, und es besteht Grund zur Annahme, dass sich diese Entwicklung in der Zukunft fortsetzt. Während also die physische Leistung von Datenspeichern enorm erhöht wurde, hat deren logische und organisatorische Leistung seit der Erfindung der ersten Personal Computer praktisch stagniert.

Nach wie vor sind hierarchische Dateisysteme der de-facto-Standard für die Organisation von persönlichen Daten. Solche Dateisysteme repräsentieren Daten als diskrete Einheiten (Dateien), die Blätter eines Baums von beschrifteten Knoten (Verzeichnisse) darstellen. Die Unterteilung des persönlichen Datenraums in kleine Einheiten unterstützt die Handhabung solcher Strukturen durch den Menschen, allerdings können viele Arten von Organisationsinformation nicht adäquat in einer Baumstruktur dargestellt werden. Dies wirkt sich negativ auf die Qualität der Datenorganisation aus.

Aktuelle Forschung im Bereich Personal Information Management liefert zwar mögliche Ansätze, um hierarchische Systeme zu ersetzen, tendiert jedoch manchmal dazu, die Arbeit mit Information überzuformalisieren. Dies ist insbesondere kritisch, weil der durchschnittliche Anwender von PIM-Systemen über keine Erfahrung mit komplexen logischen Systemen verfügt.

Diese Arbeit präsentiert ein alternatives Organisationsmodell für persönliche Daten, die darauf abzielt, eine Balance zwischen der unstrukturierten Charakteristik von Dateisystemen und den formalen Eigenschaften von logik-basierten Systemen zu finden. Nach einer vergleichenden Studie der aktuellen Forschungssituation im Bereich Semantic Desktop und Personal Information Management wird dieses Modell auf drei Ebenen vorgestellt. Zunächst wird ein abstraktes Modell sowie eine Abfrage-Algebra in Form von abstrakten Operationen auf dieses Modell vorgestellt. Dieses Modell erlaubt die Abbildung von im Personal Information Management gebräuchlichen Daten, aber erfordert keine völlige Umstellung auf Seiten des Benutzers. Anschließend wird dieses abstrakte Modell in konkreten Repräsentationen übergeführt, und es wird gezeigt, wie diese Repräsentationen effizient bearbeitet, gespeichert, und ausgetauscht werden können. Schließlich wird die Anwendung dieses Modells anhand von konkreten prototypischen Implementierungen gezeigt.

Acknowledgements

I would like to thank my supervisor, Prof. Dr. Wolfgang Klas, who thoughtfully guided and helped me throughout the work on this thesis, and my second advisor, Prof. DDr. Gerald Quirchmayr, for his kind support and encouragement.

I gratefully thank my parents who supported me throughout my years of study in every aspect of life, and who encouraged me to start this thesis.

I would like to express my special appreciation to my former colleagues Stefan, Diman, and Arash, who did a great job in implementing parts of the work presented in this thesis, and always provided a strong wall to reflect my ideas and fallacies. I would like to thank my colleagues Stefan, Wolfgang, Bernhard, Niko, and Stefan, with whom I had the pleasure to work with during the past years, and who provided not only excellent ideas and input, but made work really fun. Equally I would like to thank Jan, Peter, Manuela, Diana, and Ramona for keeping the department running.

Finally, from the deepest of my heart I thank my love Anna, who endured life with a PhD researcher without any complaints throughout the years. I dedicate this work to my beloved son Laurin, who constantly reminds me that there are much more important things in life than a PhD thesis.

Contents

1 Introduction   1
   1.1 Motivating Scenarios 3
   1.2 Research Methodology 5
   1.3 Contributions 6
   1.4 Organization 7

I Background and Related Work   9

2 A Comparative Study on Technologies for Desktop Data Management   11
   2.1 File Systems 12
   2.2 The Semantic Web: Expressing Knowledge about Resources 34
   2.3 Semantic Technologies for the Desktop 44

II Concepts   63

3 Siles: An Abstract Model for Semantic Representation of Data Assets on the Desktop   65
   3.1 Design Considerations 65
   3.2 Data Model 75
   3.3 A Query Framework for Siles 82
   3.4 Summary 90

4 An Application Programming Interface for Siles   93
   4.1 API Specification 94
   4.2 Usage Examples 108
   4.3 Summary 112

III Implementation   115

5 Digital Manifestation of Siles   117
5.1   A Core Ontology for the Sile Model 118
5.2   Representation of Sile Data as RDF 122
5.3   Transforming Sile Filters to SPARQL Queries 128
5.4   Discussion of Alternative Representations 139
5.5   Summary 144

6 Serializing Sile Data   145
6.1   Silepacks: Transportable Sile Containers 146
6.2   Sile Systems as Part of the Web of Data 150
6.3   Distributing Sile Systems via XML-RPC 153
6.4   Enriching WebDAV with Sile Annotations 165
6.5   Summary 172

7 Case Studies of Sile Repository Implementations   173
7.1   The SemDAV Server: A Triple Store-based Sile Repository 174
7.2   silefiles: A Semantic File System Extension 180
7.3   SileMail: Semantic Extensions to E-Mail 183
7.4   Summary 184

8 The Semplorer: A User Interface for Sile Management   185
8.1   Design Considerations 186
8.2   Interface Design 189
8.3   Summary 197

IV Conclusions   199

9 Discussion and Experimental Results   201
9.1   Comparison and Differentiation 201
9.2   Experimental Results 205

10 Conclusions and Future Directions   213
10.1 Summary and Conclusions 213
10.2 Future Research Directions 215

Chapter 1

Introduction

> *The quality of an organization can never exceed the quality of the minds that make it up.* —
> Harold R. McAlindon

Personal computing devices are permanent companions in our daily lives, for both private and professional activities. Many aspects of our lives involve the usage of such devices, including personal desktop computers and notebooks, mobile phones, multimedia or navigation devices. Communication is largely done via e-mail or instant messaging; videos, audio, and pictures are digitally recorded and stored; financial transactions are carried out online; discussions are conducted via mailing lists or in web forums; work groups and projects are coordinated using digital calendars; and so forth.

In addition to their original purpose, computing, *storage* has become a most important service of said devices. With the increasing availability and decreasing cost of digital memory capacity, a trend towards keeping every piece of information in digital form can be observed. With the introduction of digital signatures and encryption it has become even more easy and safe to transfer and store content in digital form, and the need to delete information is constantly reduced.

In the field of personal information management, the effects of increased storage capacity are even more obvious: the size of a typical digital music collection can easily go into the thousands, quite often a mail account holds a 7-digit number of messages, and a typical home directory of a research assistant contains up to 100,000 files. Facing such numbers, the need emerges for management mechanisms that allow humans to cope with such amounts of data, and to search and retrieve information if demanded. *Metadata*, i.e., descriptive information about data, can be used to organize a person's information space; however efficient metadata management requires infrastructures in the form of data models, meta data models, and corresponding access algorithms.

Hierarchical file systems have been the de-facto standard for personal data management since the invention of the first personal computers in the late 1970s. For decades, hierarchical directory structures have been used to organize, describe, and retrieve files, especially in the domain of personal information management. One reason for this wide spreading lies in the fact that files are highly generic storage containers: they are capable of storing basically any kind of data in any kind of format. However, current file systems do not provide means for representing the *semantics* of files, although such functionality would greatly increase the quality of data organization and, consequently, usability of desktop systems.

There exist facilities to annotate files in all current file systems, but these suffer from their lack of a common agreement on their syntax and semantics. This renders it difficult to exchange annotations between systems, and to implement applications that utilize these features in a way that is helpful to end users. The recent development of Semantic Web technologies, i.e., generalized mechanisms to convey meaningful information in distributed systems, is a promising approach towards such information exchange. The main building block of the Semantic Web, the Resource Description Framework (RDF), is a graph-based meta model to represent arbitrary kinds of information, and a number of languages exist that can be used to describe the vocabularies used in these representations. However, we identify two main problems with respect to the applicability of Semantic Web technologies to the problem of information management on the desktop: *(1)* the inherent complexity of semantic technologies requires application developers and users to adopt to new paradigms of information representation; and *(2)* Semantic Web technologies do not comprise the representation of actual content; instead they restrict themselves to the description of abstract resources whose actual contents are not further specified. This leads to two main problems: first, desktop application developers are forced to adopt new modeling paradigms; and second, desktop resources and their semantic annotations cannot be seamlessly processed. Both problems put additional effort on developers, which hinders a widespread adoption of semantic technologies in desktop environments.

In this thesis, we aim to solve these problems by considering storage and retrieval of content and descriptive metadata in an unified manner, and to integrate elements from semantic technology and elements from file systems into a single information representation model. Such an expressive data model may serve as a common basis for desktop applications to store and manage their data. Similar to the currently observable extension of the World Wide Web from a web of documents to a web of data, desktop systems will shift from heaps of unrelated binary objects (e.g., hierarchical file systems) to *miniature semantic webs*; i.e., structurally rich information meshes that are present on every computing device. It is the goal of this thesis to discuss such a data model, to convey it to actual artifacts that can be used by application developers, and to show the feasibility of these artifacts by the means of a number of example implementations.

1.1 Motivating Scenarios

The potential application scenarios for semantic information systems are manifold: starting from the possibility to exchange semi-structured information between heterogeneous applications and systems, via the integration of data from unknown sources, over modeling application domains as ontologies and validating data structures, to the full exploitation of reasoning, rules, and inference of implicit knowledge. Several works have described possible use cases and scenarios where semantic technologies bring additional benefit in comparison to other technologies[1].

In the following we describe three application scenarios by which we indicate the need for, and the benefits of a semantic infrastructure for the desktop, as outlined above. These scenarios are neither complete nor representative for every possible situation: as the initial position of computer users differs, so do their requirements, and so do the applications they are working with. However we think that this list covers a significantly large spectrum of applications, ranging from non-expert end users, who are not willing or able to intensively engage in semantics, to high-end knowledge workers who are able to define their own, highly complex personal ontologies. Of course, none of these scenarios are realizable by only instantiating the semantic infrastructure described in this thesis: in all cases, the infrastructure must be utilized by specialized applications that are developed for specific usage scenarios, and must be customized by appropriate domain ontologies.

---

[1]A number of references can be found at `http://www.w3.org/2001/sw/sweo/public/UseCases/`.

1.1.1 Scenario 1: Enhanced Electronic Communication

An increasing extent of personal communication is carried out via electronic channels, the most popular of which are e-mail and instant messaging (IM). Increasingly, Voice-over-IP (VoIP) services integrate the formerly analogous world of telephony with other digital services. A typical user of these services owns multiple mailboxes (professional and private), several IM accounts for different providers, and regularly uses VoIP services. Most of these services and applications are used via the personal computer or laptop; some of them may be used on mobile devices. However, currently these services and applications do not integrate: there exists no materialized digital connection between a received mail and a subsequently issued phone call. Neither do these services connect themselves to other information already present: current desktop infrastructure does not provide mechanisms to model that a document has been discussed during an IM conversation, and thus it is not possible to easily retrieve the transcript of this conversation when the document is revised.

A semantic infrastructure, if supported by the respective communication applications, could allow the user to formulate such simple relationships and therefore create memory hooks for later retrieval. Many such relationships could also be generated automatically: an e-mail application could annotate files sent as attachments with the corresponding recipient and subject, or it could send an updated version of a document via e-mail to all participants of the previous conference call, where the document was discussed, with only a few mouse clicks.

1.1.2 Scenario 2: Wiki-driven Personal Information Management

Wikis are powerful tools for knowledge capture. Large data sources have been created using wiki technology (e.g., Wikipedia[2]), and different approaches how to merge the wiki world and the semantic world have been proposed: DBpedia [ABK+07], for instance, exports contents from Wikipedia as RDF and thus enables applications to use these data, and Semantic Wikis [VS06] extend the structure and syntax of wikis so that articles can be semantically annotated and related seamlessly within the editing process. Additionally, it has been shown that the usage of (semantic) wikis can enhance not only collaborative, but also personal information management [OVBD06].

A semantic personal wiki that uses a shared, desktop-wide infrastructure could help users to manually annotate information items: for instance, unstructured items like

---
[2]http://www.wikipedia.org

images, videos, or plain text notes that are stored in a semantic file system are accessible by the wiki instance and can be further described within wiki articles. Also it allows the user to directly relate textual artifacts (e.g., short notes or large documents) to other resources on her desktop.

1.1.3 Scenario 3: Semantic Software Development

Software development is a complex process and involves large numbers of resources of different kinds. This includes design artifacts, source code documents, mock-ups, bug issues, referenced libraries, team-internal communication, and so forth. During the development process it is hard to track the relationship between these different information items: these may be distributed across the members of the development team and across different services and platforms, and it is often difficult to maintain different versions of artifacts and the relationships between them.

A semantically enhanced suite of development tools could automatically relate and annotate artifacts with corresponding information and thus help the team of developers to keep track of the project progress. When stored in shared repositories, information becomes available to all project members. Developers could, based on a domain ontology, be notified about new tasks, artifacts, or patches to be applied, and thus keep up-to-date with the co-developers. Similarly, project management resources (e.g., deadlines, work package management, or resource planning) can be directly integrated into the development environment.

1.2 Research Methodology

In this thesis we apply the *design-science research method* as described in [HMPR04]:

> *The design-science paradigm seeks to extend the boundaries of human and organizational capabilities by creating new and innovative artifacts. [...] IT artifacts are broadly defined as constructs (vocabulary and symbols), models (abstractions and representations), methods (algorithms and practices), and instantiations (implemented and prototype systems).*

We build our model definition on the requirements derived from an analysis of current approaches in desktop information management. From this model, we derive further artifacts; namely, a concrete application programming interface, a concrete representation of the model using the RDF framework, and several methods to serialize the data model. We show the feasibility of the model and its derived artifacts by discussing a number of reference implementations, which include data storage components based on different data backends, as well as a prototypical user interface.

1.3 Contributions

To reach these aims, we make the following contributions in this thesis:

1. We carry out a comprehensive analysis on the existing mechanisms for data organization on the personal desktop. The scope of considered subjects ranges from hierarchical file systems, which are the predominant metaphor for personal data management, via lightweight extensions to files and the Semantic Web technology family, which seeks to enable the formulation and exchange of machine-meaningful information on the Web, to a number of approaches that apply these semantic technologies to the desktop and the personal information management domain.

2. From this analysis we draw a number of conclusions and requirements for a data model, which we call the *sile model*, that is capable of representing a wide range of personal information in a semantically enriched way. We present this model and a corresponding query framework on an abstract, conceptual level.

3. To build a solid basis for implementations of our model, we specify a generic, language-independent application programming interface that covers static and dynamic aspects of our model and its query algebra. This specification allows for the implementation of the envisioned data model in a number of common programming languages.

4. We further anticipate implementations of our models by defining rules that specify how the elements of our data model can be mapped to concrete representations, namely, the Semantic Web technology family around RDF and SPARQL. Through the application of these rules, we provide directions for implementations of our data model, and we enable sile data to seamlessly integrate with other data sources on the Web of Data.

5. We outline alternative serialization rules for our data model which can be used to distribute sile systems, and to transport data in the form of self-contained files. These serialization rules help users to work with data represented as siles even if they are not working with specialized, model-aware applications.

6. To show the feasibility of our approach, we discuss three prototypical implementations that store data according to the sile model, using different storage back-ends and exposing varying functionalities. These implementations also show how data sources that are relevant for personal information management can be wrapped and interpreted as semantically rich objects.

7. Finally, we present a user interface implementation that allows users to work with our data model using interaction metaphors similar to these found in typical file browsers. With this prototype we enable end users to experience the benefits of semantic information modelling without the need to cope with the exact details of the data model, its physical representation, or storage implementations.

1.4 Organization

This thesis is structured as follows. In Chapter 2 we give a comprehensive analysis on the current state of the art in the field of organization mechanisms for desktop data. We analyze the capabilities of the currently predominant storage structure, the file system, as well as approaches that aim to enrich file system with semantic features. Finally, we analyze recent research effort in the area of the semantic desktop.

From this analysis, we derive a number of requirements and design goals for our envisioned data model (Chapter 3). We propose a formal model for the representation of personal information that is sufficiently generic to represent content together with structured, semi-structured, and unstructured annotations. In addition to the static data model, we describe an abstract framework for modelling queries on this data model, which can be used to retrieve information objects that fulfill certain criteria.

Chapter 4 introduces a concrete manifestation of this data model in the form of an application programming interface (API). This API establishes a common language for developers of desktop applications and represents the elements of the sile data model in a way that allows them to easily implement it in common programming languages.

One of our goals is to enable data interoperability between the desktop and the Semantic Web; thus Chapter 5 describes how sile data can be represented by the *lingua franca* of the web of data, RDF. Using this representation, sile data can be published on the Semantic Web and can be queried using standardized query languages like SPARQL, for which transformation rules for filter expressions are discussed. This chapter also introduces a formal ontology that represents the core model elements of the sile model, and gives directions for the mapping between the sile model and other modelling paradigms.

Chapter 6 describes three methods how sile data can be serialized in order to exchange sile data between agents, each of which targets different application scenarios and requirements.

Prototypical implementations of the sile model are discussed in Chapter 7, while in Chapter 8, we present the requirements for, and the design and implementation of a generic user interface for sile data. Preliminary experience with this user interface, as well as a discussion regarding the quantitative performance of our system implementation can be found in Chapter 9.

Finally, in Chapter 10 we conclude our work with a qualitative analysis of our approach and discuss future research directions based on the results of this thesis.

Part I

Background and Related Work

Chapter 2

A Comparative Study on Technologies for Desktop Data Management

Honest criticism is hard to take, particularly from a relative, a friend, an acquaintance, or a stranger. —
Franklin P. Jones

In this section we analyze the current state of the art in the field of data management for desktop data. We start this analysis by discussing the capabilities of current desktop file systems, as well as typical file system user interfaces. Second, we introduce the Semantic Web technology family and discuss its suitability for the representation of personal information. Finally, we give an overview and a comparative analysis of recent research projects that apply semantic technologies to the problem of personal information management.

2.1 File Systems

File systems, as they are available in common desktop operating systems, provide the underlying foundation for data management on the user desktop. Files and file systems are highly generic which makes them applicable for a manifold of usage scenarios. In the following we analyze the data management mechanisms that typical file systems provide, and discuss proposed extensions in terms of data models and user interfaces that aim to increase the expressivity and usability of file collections.

2.1.1 Nomenclature

In the following we will give definitions of terms to clarify the meaning that we assume in this work. These terms are often used in literature although they are only weakly defined. The IEEE Standard 1003.1 [JCS+04] (informally called *Portable Operating System Interface*, POSIX) gives an informal definition of files and file systems that serve as common agreement on file interoperability, and many desktop operating systems are fully or mostly compliant to this standard.

However this standard does not cover aspects of file metadata management. Thus we give our own definitions in the following, for which we restrict ourselves to the context of this chapter, management of file metadata on the user desktop. Hence we skip all terms that deal with the physical layer (e.g., distribution of file system data on physical storage devices) and concentrate on the parts of the file system that are visible to end users.

File A file is a collection of contextually related data or information, expressed in machine-processable digital form, and read- and/or writeable by applications. Usually, a file is considered as a single, self-contained unit by a processing entity, e.g., an application or a human user.

File Type A file usually adheres to a file type which describes a schema for its internal data structure, i.e., it describes how the file content is to be interpreted and processed. The file type may be formally specified (e.g., by a published standard like XHTML or JAR) or implicitly defined through the applications that create, read, and modify such files, as it is often the case with proprietary file types.

File Contents The data that are stored within a file, in a format that conforms to the structure and rules alleged by the file type. File systems do not cope with the inner structure of file contents, since files are treated as atomic data units. As there may exist an arbitrary number of file types, processing functionalities for file contents is however often provided through a system-wide plugin framework, e.g., for content analysis and metadata extraction.

File Metadata The set of information that is associated with a file but not represented within the file contents. Typical representatives of file metadata are the file name, its path, its type, the date of creation and last update, and access permissions. Mostly, the file metadata is used by the file system to manage files and directories. Many file systems provide designated mechanisms for handling user- and application-defined metadata.

File System A file system consists of a collection of files that are organized within a single organizational entity, as well as the logical and physical methods used to read and write files and their associated metadata on this medium. Usually the services of file systems are exposed to applications via defined interfaces that are part of the operating system's API, and make use of services provided by drivers for physical devices.

Overlay File System A layer that extends the upper interface of a file system with additional services, e.g., for the management of additional metadata. Often these additional services are implemented by reusing or adapting facilities that are present in the underlying file system and are therefore dependent on its features.

File System User Interface (File System UI) The paradigms and concepts that render the elements of file systems to the user (i.e., a human being) and allow her to access the data stored in the file system, in particular the file metadata. Typical file system user interfaces are graphical file browsers and command line interfaces. Often, graphical file system user interfaces are referred to as *file browsers* or *file managers*.

File System Application Programming Interface (File System API) The means and methods that a file system provides to applications, enabling them to make use of files, file contents, and file metadata. The file system API may provide more sophisticated features than the file system UI because the latter must be oriented towards the human being, which makes it more difficult to reflect and manipulate complex data structures.

2.1.2 Metadata Support in Current File Systems

The file system is an integral part of every operating system for desktop computers. In the file system the most relevant components for information management are those that deal with file metadata. The numerous other file system components (e.g., basic I/O management, distribution of data blocks onto physical devices, and so forth) are of secondary relevance in the context of this paper; consequently we describe only file systems that provide explicit support for semantic features or file metadata. We also restrict ourselves to general-purpose file systems that can be found on consumer desktops; an overview of all analyzed file systems is given in Table 2.1.

File Allocation Table (FAT)

The standard file systems of MS-DOS-based operating systems (FAT) supports file metadata only in a very restricted manner. Files are identified by the combination of the hierarchical path name and a name, plus an extension. In the FAT system the file system metadata structure consists of *directory entries* that are 32 bytes long. In the original version, file names can have a length of up to 8 characters plus a 3-character extension. FAT was later extended to support longer file names: depending on the implementation, long file names may be stored in additional directory entries, and an additional mechanism links them to the file system entry they actually belong to. File metadata are limited to a fixed set of attributes (including archived, hidden, read-only, and time and date of creation and last modification), and there exists no search index and no system-wide means of breaking the strictly hierarchical structure. With FAT32, an extension to FAT introduced in 1996, larger files can be managed than with FAT, but no additional features with respect to file metadata are provided.

New Technology File System (NTFS)

The NT File System was introduced together with Windows NT in 1993 and has since become the standard file system of the Windows operating system, including the recent XP and Vista releases. Besides many improvements in comparison to FAT (including advanced security, support for quotas, compression, sparse files, and encryption) the storage strategy for files was fundamentally changed: NTFS stores all file data and metadata, as well as the file system structure itself, in the form of file attributes, and it also provides means to attach user- or application-defined attributes to files. *Alternate*

	FAT / FAT32	NTFS	HFS	HFS+	ext3
File names and paths					
Year of Publication	1987	1993	1985	1998	1999
Native OS	MS-DOS	Windows NT	Mac OS	Mac OS	Linux
File names and paths					
Max. File Name Length	255	254	31	255	255
Max. Path Length	80 / 260 (1)	32.767	unlimited (2)	unlimited (2)	unlimited (2)
Case Sensitive	no	no	no	optional	yes
Case Preserving	partial	yes	?	yes	yes
Predefined Metadata					
File Owner	-	✓	-	✓	✓
Creation Time	✓	✓	✓	✓	-
Last Access Time	✓	✓	-	✓	✓
Last Modification Time	✓	✓	-	✓	✓
Extensible Metadata					
Extended Attributes	-	✓	-	✓	✓
Multiple Streams / Forks	-	✓	2 forks	✓	✓
Links	-	✓	✓	✓	✓
Other Features					
Encryption	-	✓	-	-	-
Compression	-	✓	-	-	-

(1) depending on OS implementation
(2) drivers and OS implementations may impose limits

Table 2.1: Comparison of file system characteristics

Data Streams (ADS) [BB04] are a special form of such attributes: each file in NTFS may have—in addition to its *primary data stream* that holds the file contents—an arbitrary number of such alternate streams. These may be used to store additional, application- or operating-system-specific metadata, and are invisible when the actual file content is accessed. In principle, an ADS is a file that is attached to another file. To access an alternate data stream, the file name of the primary stream is extended by adding an arbitrary sub-file name.

However, there are no restrictions or formalisms on the syntax and semantics of the naming and contents of attributes and alternate data streams, and no system-wide index for their contents exists. Moreover, the file system utilities of the operating systems using NTFS (including, for example, Windows Explorer and Windows Task Manager) have not been designed to support ADS, thus they are hard to detect and use for the end user [BB04]. This fact may not be the only reason for the non-usage of ADS in practice, but also for severe security problems: for instance, private information that is stored in alternate data streams may be imparted to others by accident.

WinFS

The announce of WinFS[1] marked a change in paradigm for Windows-based operating systems: with WinFS, Microsoft aimed to implement a purely database-based, semantically enriched file system that should overcome the drawbacks of hierarchical systems. The original design for WinFS incorporated a database-like architecture and access methods oriented towards relational query languages; examples for such queries are given, e.g., in [Gri04]. Instead of files, WinFS was designed to operate with typed *items* that could be arranged in multiple folders and exposed attributes according to their type schema. An application could register itself for notifications on file system changes, and WinFS instances could synchronize themselves with other instances [NHT+06]. It was also planned to include components into WinFS that analyze the content of files and make the extracted metadata available to desktop search engines.

However, it is difficult to estimate how WinFS would have looked like, and whether it would have paved the way for a new data management paradigm on Windows-based desktop systems: the development of WinFS has been postponed or even cancelled, and it is currently not clear which features will be implemented and when and how WinFS will be available. The lack of a proper, stable implementation of WinFS makes it

---

[1]WinFS Team Blog: http://blogs.msdn.com/winfs/

difficult to analyze possible impacts on applications and its usability both for application developers and end users of this system.

HFS Plus (HFS+) / Mac OS Extended

HFS+ [App00], which is often referred to as *Mac OS Extended*, supports the concepts of multiple streams to various extents: in HFS, files are limited to one *data fork* that holds the actual file contents, and one *resource fork* for additional, structured metadata [App93], while HFS+ theoretically supports an arbitrary number of forks for one single file. Originally, the GUI of Mac OS stored metadata regarding the presentation of the file system to the user (e.g., icons, positions, etc.) directly within the file. HFS+ additionally uses an *attribute file* in the form of a B-tree to store additional descriptive information (e.g., the identifier of the application that created a file) in the form of attribute/value pairs, which can also be accessed by applications and users. Usage scenarios and further details about compatibility with other file systems are given in [Sir05]. With Mac OS X version 10.4, Apple introduced a system-wide index of file system contents called *Spotlight*[2]. Spotlight is able to index files using application-specific metadata importer plugins and can therefore be extended to search previously unknown file types and metadata records. Siracusa [Sir05] analyzes the indexing and search performance of Spotlight, as well as potential sources of user confusion which originate from the inconsistent integration of Spotlight's user interface into the operating system and the file manager.

UNIX and Linux File Systems

Depending on the configuration of the respective operating system kernel, common UNIX und Linux file systems provide support for file system metadata described in the POSIX standard [JCS+04], including access rights and modification timestamps. Additionally, it is possible to store *extended attributes* in implementations of ext2, ext3, and XFS systems. Extended attributes are pairs of an attribute identifier and a value, where the attribute identifier is separated into a namespace and a name part which allows the definition of attribute classes for various reasons. Standard namespaces for extended attributes are `user`, `trusted`, and `system`. *Beagle*[3] is an example for a search engine tool that supports system-wide indexing of file contents and extended attributes.

---

[2] http://developer.apple.com/macosx/spotlight.html
[3] http://beagle-project.org

Reiser File System

Version 3 of the Reiser file system is the default file system in many UNIX/Linux based operating systems. It is based on a strictly object-oriented architecture, where interaction with objects (i.e., files) is delegated to *file plug-ins*. ReiserFS 4 made major changes to the way the file system manages metadata: while in ReiserFS 3 file attributes could be attached to a file, in ReiserFS 4 attributes are implemented as self-contained files, similar to Alternate Data Streams. This allows for orthogonal handling of a variety of file metadata (permissions, timestamps, other attributes): the same mechanisms that are also used to manage files are used to manage file metadata.

Be File System

The Be File System [Gia99] is used as the native file system in the Be operating system (BeOS). It is a hierarchical file system where files can have arbitrary numbers of attributes (i.e., pairs of names and values). Attribute values may be data typed (int, float, double, string), or may consist of raw data of any size. For typed attribute values, BeFS automatically indexes the values using B+-Trees; these values can subsequently be queried by applications using a variety of operators.

2.1.3 Content-Inherent Metadata

Many file types define storage structures for metadata stored within the file contents. Although this contradicts our definition of file metadata (cf. Section 2.1.1) which requires file metadata to be stored distinct from the file contents, this has proved to be a passable strategy: since the interpretation of file contents requires knowledge of its file type, metadata stored by such a mechanism does not interfere with the file contents. Instead, file-inherent metadata has the big advantage that is preserved when the file is stored in, or transmitted across, file systems that are incompatible in terms of their metadata structures.

Specifications for inherent metadata fields exist for a variety of file types. A number of standards exist for image metadata: for instance, EXIF [JEI02] defines how to integrate metadata about images (like the camera model, the date and time of taking, and illumination conditions) into image formats like *TIFF* and *JPEG*. In the music domain, MP3 files can contain ID3 tags describing a piece of music's artist, song title, year, genre, and so forth. The standard format for web pages, HTML, provides a facility to include describing information via special `META` elements.

A significant effort towards integrating metadata descriptions into files is carried out by Adobe with the *eXtensible Metadata Platform (XMP)* specification [Ado05]. Unlike the mechanisms described before, XMP can be regarded as a generic framework for inclusion of metadata in files of various types. The XMP data model is based on a subset of the RDF language (see Section 2.2.1; thus every valid XMP document is also a valid RDF document. In addition to its data model, XMP defines a number of metadata schemas for various file types, including paged text, dynamic media (video), and images; and application scenarios, including rights management and media management. Additionally guidelines describe how to include XMP descriptions into files of different types, including TIFF, JPEG, PNG, HTML, PDF, and more. XMP can be regarded as a cross-platform framework for the storage and transport of file-inherent metadata, and it is currently supported by the majority of Adobe's own products. Because the standard is freely available and is built on top of RDF one can expect further adoption within other products.

2.1.4 Ontological Use of File Systems

The limited expressivity of the file system can nevertheless be used to pseudo-classify files. On the one hand, a user who creates folders and sub-folders, names them, and arranges their files into them, performs a sort of classification task on the files. Although there exists no formalized class vocabulary, there are often regularities found in such folder hierarchies: a teacher may store lecture files in folders arranged per semester; or an account manager may create a folder for each of her customers. Such pseudo-classification schemes are often not appropriate for machine processing because they lack a formal definition, but are still of use for direct, manual retrieval by the user. The same applies for file names: to the best of our knowledge there exist no systematic studies about the structure of file names or how they could be used; with the exception of domain-specific procedures like software engineering [AL98].

On the other hand, applications may store internal data (i.e., data that is not directly exposed to the user) by utilizing file system metaphors for annotation or organization. An example of where such a pattern is applied to user data can be found in the audio domain: many music library utilities use directories to organize audio files by artist and by album, and use the file name to store the track title (cf. Figure 2.1). However, this usage may be partially redundant with file-internal metadata (cf. Section 2.1.3).

Similar mechanisms can be found in operating systems: for example, the files and

Figure 2.1: Pseudo-ontological use of file names and directories in a media library

subdirectories located under `C:\WINDOWS` on a Windows machine follow certain predefined conventions and must be named correctly; otherwise the operating system will not be able to locate them and hence will not work. The same applies to files and directories for application-internal files: a Mac OS X application bundle, for example, consists of a directory hierarchy wherein files and directories must follow specific naming conventions in order to be correctly interpreted by the operating system.

2.1.5 Semantic File Systems

Many traditional file systems provide support for file annotations, but still rely on directory hierarchies as their main method for file organization; hence the additional metadata mechanisms do not overcome most of the problems of file hierarchies. *Semantic file systems* go one step further and consider file metadata (in whatever form) as core instrument for file management; however they still are denoted as "file systems" because to the outside—i.e., to end users and applications—they expose the same elements as known from really hierarchical file systems: files and directories. Usually this is accomplished by algorithms that establish a mapping between these elements and the metadata used to describe files.

	Hard/Symbolic Links	Tags/Keywords	Attributes	Orthogonal Categories	Internal Relationships	External Relationships	Multiple Streams/Forks	Full Read+Write Support	Virtual File Hierarchy	API	Structured Query Language
SFS	✓	-	✓	-	-	-	-	-	✓	-	✓
AttrFS	✓	✓	✓	-	-	-	-	✓	✓	-	-
Presto	-	-	✓	-	-	✓	-	-	✓	✓	✓
LISFS	-	-	✓	✓	-	-	-	-	✓	-	✓
TagFS	✓	✓	✓	-	-	-	-	✓	✓	✓	✓
libferris	-	-	✓	-	-	-	-	✓	✓	✓	✓
LiFS	✓	-	✓	-	✓	-	✓	✓	✓	✓	✓

Table 2.2: Comparison of Semantic File Systems

The Semantic File System presented by Gifford [GJSJ91] extracts attribute/value pairs from file contents; these attributes are then represented in a virtual directory hierarchy. Conjunctive queries over attributes can be issued by navigating deeper into these hierarchy. Gifford's work is probably the first representant for a virtual file system based on metadata; similar approaches are followed by AttrFS [WGM95], which extends attribute-based file access with write operations, and LISFS [PSR06], where file paths are interpreted as logical formulas that may contain boolean operators. libferris [Mar06] focuses more on the integration of resources: it allows to mount a wide range of data sources (ranging from XML documents, over DOM trees extracted from running web browser instances, to remote data accessed via sockets) and describes them using extended attributes. An additional RDF store allows to add and retrieve custom metadata for files. TagFS [BGSV06] exposes keywords that are attached to files via virtual directory hierarchies; TagFS is built on top of a generic framework for semantic file systems. Presto [DELS99], although not primarily designed as a file system replacement, combines structural access as known from hierarchical file systems with attribute-based access. LiFS [ABG+06] additionally considers links between files, which are represented as contents of virtual directories; however it is a pure in-memory implementation and cannot be used for persistence of files.

Table 2.2 gives an overview on the features of these systems, and also compare their access mechanisms. This comparison shows that *virtual file hierarchies*, which represent the metadata attributes of files in the form of virtual directories and/or files, are supported by all approaches. Many of them provide access to file metadata via an *Application Programming Interface (API)* and/or a structured query language that allows to express more complex queries.

2.1.6 User Interfaces for File Manipulation and Browsing

In addition to technologies for storing and representing file metadata, we analyze the two main types of interfaces for file manipulation, *Command Line Interfaces* and the graphical *WIMP* paradigm. These two approaches are present in every desktop operating system in use today and can be considered as the *de-facto standard* for human-computer interaction. Finally, we discuss approaches that go beyond the state of the art in browsing and manipulation and describe extensions to the WIMP approach, as well as entirely novel approaches.

Command Line Interfaces (CLI)

The command line interface was the first metaphor for human-computer interaction that provided *direct response* to user input. Before, the use of batch-oriented *punch cards* caused delay times between user input and the machine's response. With a command line interface, a user is able to directly issue commands to the computer, which are immediately processed.

Despite their long history—the first command line interfaces were in place in the 1950s—the command line is still an important mechanism to interact with a computer and with file systems. This is also emphasized by the fact that the power of command line shells is still increasing, and new metaphors for command line shells are developed. For instance, Microsoft PowerShell [Wat07] provides, in addition to traditional command line tools, a sentence-like structure for commands in the form of *verb-noun* pairs, as well as an object oriented data model.

Considering this, command line interfaces are without doubt a powerful mechanism for human-computer interaction. However, as outlined in [GN96], seldom they do provide assistance or mnemonics for the user: although one can type arbitrary commands into a CLI, it is hard to find out in advance which commands are understood by the machine. Considering data management, CLIs usually do not provide assistance that goes beyond auto completion of file and directory names. Interestingly, in some operating systems the command line interface offers access mechanisms to file system metadata

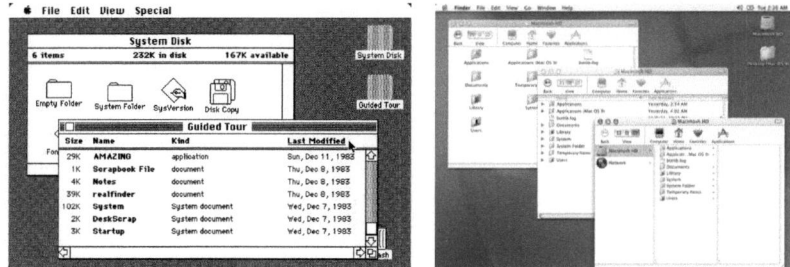

Figure 2.2: File management interface in Mac OS 1.1 and Mac OS X

that are not available through graphical interfaces: for instance, alternate data streams (cf. Section 2.1.2) can be accessed through the command line interface of Windows XP, but not through the graphical file browser.

Windows, Icons, Menus, Pointing (WIMP)

The WIMP paradigm [CW91, vD97] describes an interaction style that is mainly based on four elements: windows, icons, menus, and pointing devices. The paradigm was developed by Xerox PARC during the 1970s and has been made popular by the Apple Macintosh computer in 1984. It has been exerted by other operating systems and is still the standard interface for desktop operating systems and, consequently, for file management on the desktop.

Based on Douglas Engelbart's invention of the mouse [Eng70], the WIMP paradigm employs usually rectangular areas (*windows*) to visually indicate certain data contexts, e.g., the contents of one directory in the file system hierarchy. All windows share common elements like a title bar, a resizeable border, and buttons to minimize and maximize the window.

Graphic symbols (*icons*) are used to represent entities and information objects like files and directories. The impact of icon design on human search performance has been subject to several studies [Byr93, EB04, FNB06], and it can be taken as proved that, when carefully designed, icons are a practical representation of files and help users to recognize and relocate them. In the context of file systems, icons often represent the file type or, if the file content can be interpreted, a preview thereof. Additionally, file icons may be enriched by **decorators** that display additional information about the file.

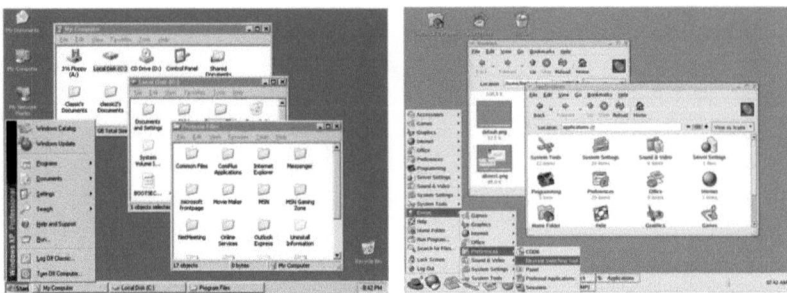

Figure 2.3: File management interface in Windows XP and Red Hat Linux

Actions that can be performed on files or directories are represented using *menus* (i.e., hierarchical collections of commands that can be selected and executed by clicking them with a pointing device), or by issuing keyboard commands. However, with increasing number of commands, menus can get overloaded, and desired commands become hard to find. This issue has been partially addressed by the usage of *split menus* [SS94], which have been in detail analyzed in [FM04]. Other approaches aim at improving menu usage by automatic movement of the mouse pointer [AAH06] or by dynamically adapting the screen estate that is used to select menu items [CG06]. However, file browsers found in standard operating systems usually do not offer numbers commands that would require deep menu structures; usually, there are five to seven menu items with at most one sub-level of commands.

Recent progress in the development of the WIMP paradigm was limited to graphical details like three-dimensional buttons, shadowed menus, and more realistic icons. There have been no major improvements in the basic interaction paradigms: consider Fig. 2.2, which shows a comparison of the file browser of *Apple Mac OS 1.1* from 1984 and *Mac OS X 10.1* (2001).

There is no major difference in representing user files in various operating systems, as can be seen in Fig. 2.3, which depicts file browsing utilities of *Windows XP* (with the "classic" skin applied), and *Red Hat Linux* with the *Nautilus* file manager.

We can observe that in the context of file systems the WIMP paradigm is used mainly for three tasks:

1. *Browsing.* Usually, one window is used to display the contents of one directory.

Figure 2.4: Folder icons in Windows XP, Windows Vista, Apple Mac OS X, and Linux/KDE

Files are depicted as icons, which indicate either the file type or show a thumbnail preview of the file contents. Directories are displayed using stylized folder icons, cf. Figure 2.4.

The user navigates through the directory structure by clicking (or double-clicking) on folder icons. Depending on the user settings and the implementation, this action either opens a new window displaying the contents of the opened directory (this behavior is sometimes referred to as *spatial* or *object oriented* metaphor), or displays the contents in the same window (*navigational* metaphor).

In the former case the navigation history is reflected by an increasing number of open windows, while in the latter case it is usually accessed through "back" and "forward" buttons, known from web browsers. In either case, directory windows normally provide a facility to navigate to the parent of the currently displayed directory. Some systems accomplish this by including the virtual parent directory in the icon list; other provide a designated "up" button for this task.

In both styles, the arrangement and order of displayed file icons can usually be configured by the user. Icons can either be freely arranged within the directory window, which allows for spatial organization of related files; however this information is often not persisted, and is not interpreted by search engines although the arrangement of icons on the desktop is a commonly used mechanism to express certain metadata [Mal83]. Alternatively, icons are automatically arranged by the browser in a grid or a list, and are sorted by user-selectable criteria, like file name, type, size, and modification date. The CoverFlow technique[4] uses preview images of file contents that are arranged similar to album covers in a shelf, which may probably be useful for visual content like pictures; however to the best of the author's knowledge there exist no studies that indicate whether this design actually improves the search and navigation experience.

---

[4]cf. http://www.apple.com/macosx/leopard/features/finder.html

In the WIMP paradigm, files are accessed (opened) by a double click on their icon. The application that is associated with this file type is opened, allowing to view or edit the file. The file's *context menu*[5] provides a list of alternative applications and viewers to use, as well as further operating system-specific actions.

The keyboard can be used to quickly access files by their name: most file browsers select a file after the user enters the first few letters of its file name. This may increase the speed of file and directory discovery if the directory list is long, and the exact beginning of the file's or directory's name is known to the user.

2. *Manipulation of files.* We can identify the following actions of manipulation on the file level: *create*, *delete*, *copy*, and *move*, although the latter can also be considered as manipulation on the metadata level since a file's path represents not only its physical location, but also a kind of user annotation. Files are manipulated either by selecting commands from a menu or by executing drag and drop gestures. In the first case, the command is selected either from the directory window's menu or from the file's context menu. In the second case, the pointing device is used to change the location of the file's representation on the screen, which is translated into a corresponding action.

The action that is carried out when the user executes a drag and drop action depends not only on the pointing device gesture and its source and destination objects, but also on modifiers like the selected mouse button or additionally pressed keys: for instance, dragging a file icon from one file browser window to another one causes the file to be moved, while a drag with a pressed *Alt* key may cause the file to be copied. Special icons can be used to execute certain actions using drag and drop, e.g., the *trash can* icon for deleting files.

3. *Manipulation of file metadata.* Only few file metadata fields can actually be directly changed by a user. The most prominent one, the file name, is normally editable by selecting a file and entering a new name. Most interestingly, the file extension, which is an essential part of the file name in all researched systems, is often hidden from the user. On the one hand, this avoids unintended changing of the file extension, but, on the other hand, may cause confusion since the displayed file name is not equal to the actual file name.

---

[5]The context menu is activated by clicking on the file with the secondary mouse button, or by pressing a special key while the file is selected.

Most other file metadata are either displayed in tabular form or, if this is not appropriate, in textual form near the file name. All common systems allow the user to open a window displaying more information using the file's context menu. Mac OS Finder (in the "column" view) and Windows Vista provide an area on screen where metadata for the currently selected file(s) are displayed without the need for a designated window. In Windows Vista, this pane can be used to manipulate metadata depending on the file type: for instance, tags and comments of Microsoft Office documents can be directly edited.

Other Approaches

The way user data is organized on the personal desktop, as described in the previous sections, has been subject to critics for a long time. Barreau and Nardi [BN95] have summarized the results of their independent studies on user behaviour and identified a preference of *location-based search* (i.e., navigational browsing through the directory structure) over *logical search* (i.e., text-based search using a search engine). Their studies also showed that users preferred to store their data into application-dependent locations instead of organizing them into their personal directory structure; a fact we attribute to the relatively low number of files under consideration (which might have changed since then because of the steadily increasing number of user data files). Additionally they have identified three types of information present on user desktops: *ephemeral*, which is subject to immediate action; *working*, that is frequently used; and *archived information*, which represents completed or historic work. Until today, file systems do not consider the different requirements for these information categories. In their critics to Barreau and Nardi's work, Fertig et al. however accredit the apparent preference for location-based search to the lack of proper search engines in the user study, and they point to more advanced alternatives [FFG96] that we will discuss in Section 2.3.

Gentner and Nielsen [GN96] have identified potential restrictions in functionality and usability that the WIMP interface puts on systems in their exemplary analysis of the Apple Macintosh user interface. They precisely criticize several aspects of the WIMP paradigm, including *direct manipulation*, the *see-and-point* principle, and the *WYSIWYG* (what you see is what you get) idea. Instead, they propose to investigate on interfaces that are driven by the powerfulness of human language, more expressive internal representation of information (a strategy that *semantic file systems* aim to utilize), and improvements of user interfaces—which are now, more than 10 years later, have become reality because of improved hardware.

Van Dam [vD97] has described various drawbacks and shortcomings of WIMP interfaces. As the most serious one, he identified the under-utilization of speech, hearing, and touch. While the usage of speech and hearing may be inappropriate in situations where noise is important (e.g., in open-plan offices), the usage of touch may actually improve the quality of data management, at least for certain application domains like digital audio libraries [LT07].

Under the assumption of the presence of a strictly hierarchical file system, several approaches that represent the contents of such a tree in ways different from those known from desktop systems have been presented. Most of them aim to cope with large numbers of files by not representing single files as information entities (as it is the case in the WIMP paradigm where each file is represented as an icon), but to *aggregate* the file system and allow the viewer to zoom in and out. *Ordered* and *Quantum Treemaps* [BSW02] are an extension to the treemap visualization paradigm originally presented in [Shn92]. Both approaches flatten the hierarchical tree of the file system to a plane; thus another proposed extension to treemaps, *beamtrees*, utilizes the third dimension to represent tree depth [vHvW02]. However, as the authors describe in their analysis of a user study, their approach does not always perform better than flat treemaps. Consequently the authors extended their approach using a pseudo-realistic rendering, where they represent the directory levels not as abstract rectangles or cylinders, but similar to botanical trees [vWvHvdW03]. Certainly, the full power of such a visualization method comes from interactions with the object, a question that has been investigated in numerous works (see below). Nguyen et al. [NH04] identify four categories of representation methods for hierarchies and give examples for each of them: *listings, outlines, connections,* and *enclosures*. In their work (which is preceded by work presented in [NH02]), they combine enclosure and connection to an interactive browsing metaphor.

Another presentation algorithm for tree structures has been presented in [BD04], where tree elements are represented using interconnected bubbles residing on a flat layer. Although the discussed target domain is the visual representation of software packages, this approach could be applied to hierarchical file systems as well. Similarily, Wang et al. [WWDW06] demonstrate how to apply a circle packing algorithm to the visualization of file system contents, which is also used in a slightly modified way by the Grokker search engine[6]. Robertson et al. [RCCR02] discuss an approach for representation of multiple overlapping hierarchies which could also be of benefit for the current desktop

---

[6]Grokker: http://www.grokker.com

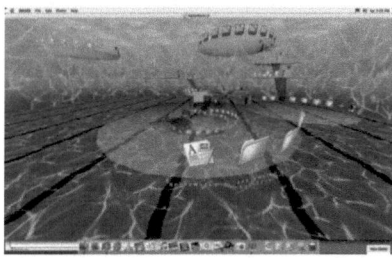 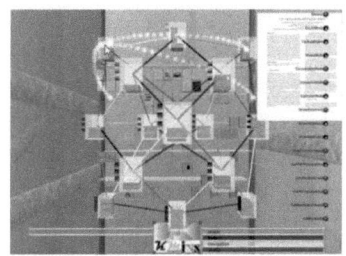

Figure 2.5: Three-dimensional user interfaces for file systems, from top left to bottom right: Bumptop [AB06], Bubbles [BD04], 3DOSX [Chi02], 3D document worlds [DAK+06]

situation (cf. Section 2.1.7). The work presented in [Wal05] targets to improve search and browsing experience by using scatter plots to display files in order to obtain an overview over a directory hierarchy based on multiple dimensions of metadata.

While all these approaches completely omit the WIMP (windows, icons, menus, pointing) interface paradigm, the work described in [Chi02] replaces the rectangular orientation of traditional file browsers with a 3D interface, where files and directories are arranged on interconnected circular layers. However, in all discussed interfaces *interactive navigation* is a key issue. Thus we expect that the role of more advanced interaction devices like multi-touch displays will increase; as shown, e.g., in [DH06].

Other approaches do not only represent the contents of the hierarchical file system, but add more organizational and navigational dimensions to files. The following works can be considered as predecessor of the *Semantic Desktop* (cf. Section 2.3) although they focus more on visualization and navigation than on semantic expressivity.

Presto [DELS99], in addition to its document-based data model, provides mechanisms to group documents using *collections* which are represented by ovals or piles, depending on their state (open or closed). Such collections can be grouped into *workspaces*, and *fluid collections* can be used to represent queries over the document space which are constantly populated—a concept that has been adopted in many software products (e.g., Mac OS X Finder[7] or Mozilla Thunderbird[8]). A similar user interface has been presented in [DES03] where files are organized and visualized using Venn diagrams, and colors are used to represent temporal file characteristics; e.g., the last accessed timestamp.

Agrawala et al. have studied the applicability of stacks (or piles) to the file system with the aim to develop a realistic feel for the digital counterpart of a real desktop, and to be operable by pen interaction in order to be used on Tablet PCs [Aga06, AB06]. However, they concentrate more on interaction required for manual organization and do not focus on semantic data organization. [DAK⁺06] describes interaction techniques for data gloves that can be used to manually annotate and relate files. Documents can be searched by issuing queries, and the resulting collections and associated metadata are displayed in 3D worlds which can be browsed and manipulated by gestures and postures issued through the data glove.

2.1.7 Challenges of Hierarchical File Systems

The file system serves as the backbone of all information that is processed by today's computers. Ultimately, every bit of information that is persisted is stored in files. However, applications make use of the file system in very different ways: we believe that the multiform utilization of the file system is rooted in the drawbacks and vulnerabilities that today's file systems exhibit [RSK04], some of which we describe in this section.

Multiple Scattered Hierarchies

Hierarchical trees are a commonplace way of organizing information items, even if they often are unsuitable to organize data according to the needs of various users and the demands of different situations. Trees do not allow for more sophisticated ways of organizing files: the tree of a file system may be considered as simplified *classification scheme*, and a file can be placed at exactly one node within this scheme.

---

[7]Mac OS X Finder Features: http://www.apple.com/macosx/features/finder
[8]Thunderbird Saved Search folders: http://alek.xspaces.org/2004/12/08/thunderbird-saved-search-folder

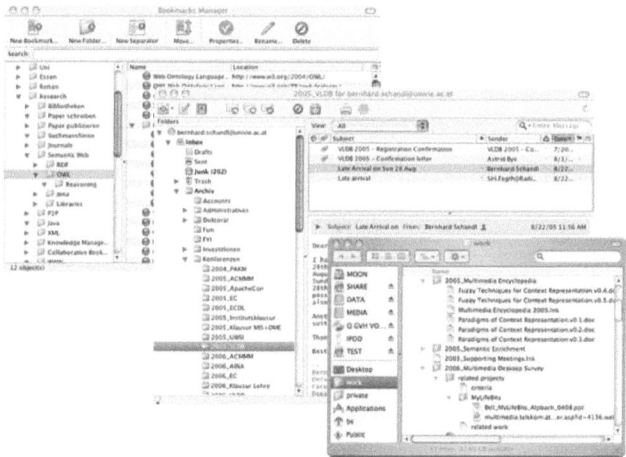

Figure 2.6: Multiple scattered hierarchies on a user's desktop computer

Computing environments allow us to use multiple hierarchies for different types of information items; however these different hierarchies (which can be seen as disjunct *information spaces*) are maintained in inconsistent ways, are often system- or application-dependent, and are user-customizable to variable degrees (see Figure 2.6). For instance, in a standard desktop environment we can observe disjunct hierarchies for files, web bookmarks, e-mail messages, contacts, and applications, as well as application-specific hierarchies (cf. Section 2.1.4).

Such scattered hierarchies have both advantages and drawbacks. One advantage is that users are given the option to organize the information objects according to different criteria in different hierarchies. For example, they may arrange files based on temporal aspects, while they arranges the start menu using alphabetical order, and e-mails based on project context. However, these different hierarchies impose the restriction that information objects of different data types may not be organized within one single structure [Boa01]. To overcome this, Boardman et al. [BSS03] suggest a method to synchronize the different hierarchies in the user space, and Bergman et al. [BBMN06] propose to build an integrated hierarchy over all existing user data.

Missing or Inconsistent Shortcuts

Modern file systems try to extend the tight tree structure concept by introducing *shortcuts* (often also referred to as *links* or *aliases*), which are virtual tree nodes that refer to other nodes in the tree. However, shortcuts are not universally accessible and are often handled differently by file browsers and applications. On some systems, shortcuts are realized as simple files that contain the name of the destination node, and are not transparently presented to the user.

Mixture of Identification and Description

In hierarchical file systems the functionalities of *identification* and *description* are inseparably mingled. The combination of a file's path, its file name, and its extension is used both as system-wide unique identifier, as well as user-entered, descriptive attribute, since the path and the filename can be interpreted as set of user-defined labels. Moreover, this descriptive string is admixed with technical attributes (e.g., a letter that indicates the physical medium where a file is stored, and the file type extension). As a consequence, changing any of these user attributes (e.g., renaming one directory), intended to modify the file's description, also breaks its technical identifier and causes links to this file to become invalid.

Emphasis on File Types

As described above, organization hierarchies on typical desktops are often separated according to data types: bookmarks for web pages, e-mail folders for e-mail messages, address books for contact information, the start menu for applications, and so forth. Additionally, the user interfaces of most file systems use only the file type (mostly indicated by the file extension) to determine a visual representation for the file (e.g., an icon or a preview); see Figure 2.7 for an example. In seldom cases, users have the possibility to adapt the displayed information to their needs, e.g., by replacing the file icon or by attaching a color label. However, in terms of user-oriented information retrieval, the file type is of secondarily importance.

Weak Support for Browsing and Searching

The file hierarchy imposes restrictions on the efficiency of searching and browsing: since the user is only allowed to navigate along edges in the tree it is only possible to walk

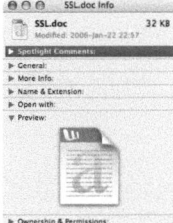

Figure 2.7: Typical file preview: no actual content

up and down in the hierarchy, except by using the shortcuts mentioned before. Additionally, most common file systems do not provide inherent indexing and searching capabilities that would improve search performance; such functionality must be provided by external components. Consequently, file systems do not provide the facilities to implement browsing and searching services that are based on semantic annotations or relationships between files.

Insufficient Support for File Metdata

Common hierarchical file systems provide means to store additional metadata to files, which have been described in Section 2.1.2. However, these possibilities are heavily under-utilized by applications. A typical metadata record for a simple spreadsheet file, as presented to the user, is depicted in Figure 2.8. Such metadata records are often not used because the interfaces for manipulating them are not integrated into the user's natural workflow, and the benefit of annotating files is not exposed by desktop systems; e.g., because they lack a facility to efficiently retrieve files based on these annotations.

Loss of Contextual Information

Closely related to metadata, a file's context is lost at the moment that it is saved to a storage medium. A file is treated by the file system as a *stand-alone object* without any relationships to other information units. This fact makes it difficult to localize files that are semantically related to each other, but stored at different locations in the directory hierarchy. File relationships can partially be modeled using the above-mentioned shortcuts, but shortcuts have no predefined, machine-understandable semantics and can therefore not be used for enhanced search or browsing mechanisms.

Figure 2.8: Typical file metadata: no information available

Many of the challenges and drawbacks discussed above are rooted in the missing support for descriptive data in file systems. A similar situation can be faced on the World Wide Web: the corpus of information in the Internet is mostly stored in the form of human readable documents, usually in the HTML format. The Semantic Web [BLHL01] is an approach to extend the WWW with machine-interpretable information in order to allow for the creation of more sophisticated services and applications. The technologies that have been developed in the context of this approach are potentially suitable to enhance information on the desktop, too. In the following, we introduce and discuss the Semantic Web technology family and its most important building blocks.

2.2 The Semantic Web: Expressing Knowledge about Resources

One of the basic goals of the Semantic Web [BLHL01] is to make knowledge about *resources* explicit, whereas the term "resource" stands for everything that can be described—physical objects, people, digital documents, or abstract concepts. Its intention is not to replace the traditional World Wide Web (or *web of documents*), which has been designed for content consumption by humans. Instead it aims to enrich it with a machine-processable data layer: on the Semantic Web, in addition to actual digital resources, descriptive metadata are published using a special language, RDF [DMM00, MM04, Bec04], and the vocabularies used therefore are defined by the means of ontology description languages (see below).

The Semantic Web today consists of a set of building blocks [SBLH06] that are inevitable for a global machine-oriented information system, and it is still subject to change, research and development. After a relatively long phase of being a purely scientific research topic, Semantic Web research is today heavily influenced by recent developments in the World Wide Web that are often subsumed under the label *Web 2.0* [Gre07]: the Web shifts from collections of static documents to rich, interactive applications that allow for easy user contribution and annotation of data.

- *Uniform Resource Identifiers.* URIs are used to identify resources on the Semantic Web. For a global information system it is crucial to provide a distributed way of *naming* that avoids conflicts and does not impose usage restrictions. All information represented on the Semantic Web must be mapped to URIs so that any authority can issue statements about them. While there is consent about the principal feasibility of the URI concept, it is still subject to debate [Cla02, PS03a, Boo03, PPS04, BL07] whether URIs should have intrinsic semantics and how to create meaningful or useful URIs.

- *Triples and triple stores.* As mentioned before, the Semantic Web uses RDF as format for the representation and the exchange of data. RDF represents all information in the form of triples, each of which consists of a *subject*, a *predicate*, and an *object*, and hence constitutes the atomic information unit on the Semantic Web. RDF documents consist of an arbitrary number of such triples (also called *statements*), of which each one is independent from the others.

    A number of *triple stores* (i.e., systems that persist RDF triples) have been developed; these differ greatly in their target domain and thus in their functionality and performance[9]. As with many database systems, there is no clear recommendation which is the best implementation, and which system will become a *de facto standard* for storage of RDF. Jena [CDD+04] and Sesame [BKvH02] have for long been the lead of development, but recently the OpenLink Virtuoso Server [EM07] has been getting more and more attention because of its good performance and its direct integration of Semantic Web and relational database technology.

- *Data conversion.* Shadbolt [SBLH06] indicates the extraction of RDF data from other data sources (e.g., XML and XHTML) as important since there are huge

---
[9]The World Wide Web Consortium maintains a list of such implementations at http://esw.w3.org/topic/SemanticWebTools.

amounts of data available in these formats on the World Wide Web. GRDDL [Con07] is a W3C Recommendation designed to provide such conversions. Efforts towards RDF-based representation of datasets stored in relational databases [BS04], LDAP directories [Die05, DA07], or many other data formats as done by the RDFizers project[10] show that the RDF model has the potential to be the common denominator for data exchange over the web.

- *Ontologies, rules, and inference.* The RDF semantics document states the following about the *meaning* of RDF graphs:

    "*RDF is an assertional language intended to be used to express propositions using precise formal vocabularies, particularly those specified using RDFS, for access and use over the World Wide Web, and is intended to provide a basic foundation for more advanced assertional languages with a similar purpose. The overall design goals emphasise generality and precision in expressing propositions about any topic, rather than conformity to any particular processing model [...].*
    Exactly what is considered to be the 'meaning' of an assertion in RDF or RDFS in some broad sense may depend on many factors, including social conventions, comments in natural language or links to other content-bearing documents. Much of this meaning will be inaccessible to machine processing and is mentioned here only to emphasize that the formal semantics described in this document is not intended to provide a full analysis of 'meaning' in this broad sense; that would be a large research topic. The semantics given here restricts itself to a formal notion of meaning which could be characterized as the part that is common to all other accounts of meaning, and can be captured in mechanical inference rules." [Hay04]

    Thus, it is intentionally necessary to extend the formal semantics of RDF with additional constructs; usually these are called *ontologies*. While there have been ontology languages developed to be used with RDF, OWL [DS04] has emerged as the *de-facto* standard for ontology modeling on the Semantic Web. It is likely that the existence of the three sub-languages of OWL (OWL Lite, OWL DL, and OWL Full) and the consequential freedom of choice between expressivity and simplicity

---

[10]http://simile.mit.edu/wiki/RDFizers

Figure 2.9: RDF graph example

helped to spread the usage of this language. Nevertheless, some problems and restrictions of OWL have been identified and addressed in a workshop series which started in 2005[11], which will lead to the development of OWL 2 [GHM+08].

2.2.1 Explicit Semantics

As mentioned above, RDF is the underlying meta model for data expressed on the Semantic Web. The minimum information unit in RDF is the *statement*, a triple of the form $< s, p, o >$ (*subject, predicate, object*) [MM04]. The basic intention behind this design is that RDF should enable to state *facts* about *things* (which are called *resources*), wheras—as in natural language—the subject identifies the thing the statement is about. The predicate identifies the characteristic or property that the statement refers to, and the object identifies one specific value of that property for the given subject.

A simple example of an RDF graph is given in Figure 2.9. Two resources are depicted (indicated by the ovals), each of which is identified by its URI. They are connected by a property with the name `pub:author` and are further described by two properties (`foaf:name` and `pub:title`, respectively). The three statements depicted in this figure can be written in *Turtle* notation [Bec07] as shown in Figure 2.10.

This design formalizes simple sentences from natural languages: RDF is capable to express *facts*. The Oxford Dictionary defines a fact as *"a thing that is indisputably the case"*. Thus, a RDF graph represents a piece of knowledge that is regarded as true by its author. The strong adhesion between the cited definition and the RDF model design is also reflected in the *Open World Assumption* (OWA): it is not possible to express *negated facts* in RDF, and everything that is not explicitly asserted to be true is considered to be unknown. Since in certain situations this functionality may

---

[11]http://www.webont.org/owled/

```
<http://www.cs.univie.ac.at/bernhard.schandl/foaf#me>
  pub:author <http://www.cs.univie.ac.at/bernhard.schandl/papers#survey> ;
  foaf:name "Bernhard Schandl" .

<http://www.cs.univie.ac.at/bernhard.schandl/papers#survey>
  pub:title "Information Management on the Desktop: A Survey" ;
```

Figure 2.10: RDF Turtle syntax example

be needed, [TPM07] describes an approach for identifying negated triples by a special type of reification. [PSH06] gives a comprehensive analysis of the implications that this design—the authors call it the *classical paradigm*—has for data modeling, and they give a number of examples where the classical approach allows for more realistic modeling in comparison to meta models used e.g., in object-oriented databases.

It is important to note that although the technology family around RDF is called *semantic* technology, RDF by itself does not make many assertions about the actual *meaning* of data expressed in RDF. As described in [PSH06] (Section 4.1), RDF does not even require that the same thing is identified by the same name (URI) in every context. Thus we can not really guess the meaning of an RDF graph without considering external knowledge. An RDF graph is connected to the *real world* only via the names (URIs) used in the graph; however, this connection is not made explicit within the RDF model. Cregan [Cre07] describes this as the problem of *symbol grounding* for the Semantic Web. Consequently the actual semantics of an RDF model must be defined outside the graph structure. *Ontologies* (cf. Section 2.2.2) are one means to express additional semantics albeit the core problems in matters of symbol grounding remain.

RDF by itself contains a minimum set of language constructs that have intrinsic semantics[12]. Most of these constructs deal with the description of containers (sequences, unordered lists, and lists of alternatives). Although RDF provides a straightforward and crisp vocabulary and relatively simple formal semantics for these elements (cf. [Hay04], Section 3.3), their meaning is not explicitly formalized:

---

[12] At this point it is important to notice that the inclusion of these constructs into the RDF core model obliterated the distinction between RDF as a meta model for data representation and RDF as minimal ontology language, although the question remains whether the core semantics of RDF statements, as described above, constitute an ontology as well.

> "It is important to understand that while these types of containers are described using predefined RDF types and properties, any special meanings associated with these containers, e.g., that the members of an Alt container are alternative values, are only intended meanings. These specific container types, and their definitions, are provided with the aim of establishing a shared convention among those who need to describe groups of things. All RDF does is provide the types and properties that can be used to construct the RDF graphs to describe each type of container. RDF has no more built-in understanding of what a resource of type `rdf:Bag` is than it has of what a resource of type `ex:Tent` is. In each case, applications must be written to behave according to the particular meaning involved for each type." [MM04]

The weak definition of container concepts in RDF may be a reason why they are used relatively infrequently. The concept of *reification* adds a level of *meta descriptions* to RDF graphs: using the reification vocabulary it is possible to assert *facts about facts* within the knowledge base. However, reification modeling is often not straightforward (cf. [Pow03] Section 4.3 where reification is called "the big ugly") and requires special consideration in the design of RDF storage systems [AR06].

As described before, the core element of the RDF data model is the *resource*. Interestingly, the family of RDF specification documents gives no clear definition of this crucial concept. The following statements about resources can be found in various parts of the RDF specification.

> "The Resource Description Framework (RDF) is a language for representing information about resources in the World Wide Web. [...] However, by generalizing the concept of a "Web resource", RDF can also be used to represent information about things that can be identified on the Web, even when they cannot be directly retrieved on the Web." [MM04]

> "To facilitate operation at Internet scale, RDF is an open-world framework that allows anyone to make statements about any resource." [KC04]

> "RDF properties may be thought of as attributes of resources and in this sense correspond to traditional attribute-value pairs. RDF properties also represent relationships between resources." [BG04]

> "All things described by RDF are called resources, and are instances of the class `rdfs:Resource`. This is the class of everything." [BG04]

> "*The things denoted are called 'resources', but no assumptions are made here about the nature of resources; 'resource' is treated here as synonymous with 'entity', i.e., as a generic term for anything in the universe of discourse.*"
> [Hay04]

The notion of "everything" being an RDF resource imposes a lot of choice to the designer of an information system. The structural indetermination of this term makes it hard for end users who are not familiar with RDF to find a common understanding on the foundations of RDF. The question of how to represent a resource (apart from displaying its URI) is also hard to answer, since a RDF resource is nothing without its properties. One could compare a RDF resource to a point in mathematics which has no dimension and can be made visible and tangible only by approximating it with a small filled circle on paper or a filled pixel on a computer screen. Nevertheless there exist generic browsers for RDF (mostly they present RDF using a textual interface as in Tabulator [BLCC+06] where resources are displayed using HTML hyperlinks, or a graph visualization [NL06] where resources are displayed as ovals connected by lines) and generic display frameworks that allow the definition of visualization rules based on ontologies, e.g., Fresnel [PBKL06] or RVL [MTCP04].

2.2.2 Ontologies and Conceptualization

As stated in the previous section, RDF does not specify the actual *meaning* of expressed statements. With RDF, any kind of statement can be asserted using arbitrary identifiers (URIs) for resources and predicates. Thus, one requires knowledge about the meaning of these identifiers (often referred to as *vocabulary*) in order to allow for meaningful interpretation of the data.

Ontologies are designed towards this problem, with *Web Ontology Language* (OWL) [MvH04] being the most prominent example of an ontology description language. The W3C OWL Specification document defines the term "ontology" as follows:

> "*OWL can be used to explicitly represent the meaning of terms in vocabularies and the relationships between those terms. This representation of terms and their interrelationships is called an ontology.*" [MvH04]

But what is "meaning" in the context of digital information systems? What are the characteristics that distinguish an ontology from a simple representation of facts? A good overview of what the term "ontology" denotes is given in [GG95], where also the most popular definition in computer science is discussed: Gruber [Gru93] defines an ontology as "a specification of a conceptualization"—this specification has been widely cited but leaves many questions open. One of these question is the missing definition of what a *conceptualization* constitutes: Guarino and Giaretta [GG95] propose to define conceptualization as "an intensional semantic structure which encodes the implicit rules constraining the structure of a piece of reality". A comprehensive overview on other definitions and interpretations of "conceptualization" is given in [LM99].

As described in [GG95], ontology as interpreted by the originators of the RDF family can be regarded as synonym to *vocabulary*. As stated in the previous section and described in [Cre07], the family of Semantic Web languages is a closed system of descriptions: resources and predicates are described using only resources and predicates. This understanding of meaning is reflected by the "RDF Semantics" part of the RDF specification:

> "*Exactly what is considered to be the 'meaning' of an assertion in RDF or RDFS in some broad sense may depend on many factors, including social conventions, comments in natural language or links to other content-bearing documents. Much of this meaning will be inaccessible to machine processing and is mentioned here only to emphasize that the formal semantics described in this document is not intended to provide a full analysis of 'meaning' in this broad sense; that would be a large research topic. The semantics given here restricts itself to a formal notion of meaning which could be characterized as the part that is common to all other accounts of meaning, and can be captured in mechanical inference rules.*" [Hay04]

This has serious consequences: to be understandable by humans, a formalized ontology must always be accompagnied by a human-understandable description (e.g., in textual or graphical form) of the intended meaning of the constructs used therein. To be processed by machines, the human knowledge about the ontology's meaning must be translated into processing instructions that are applied to the data. This may lead to an extended interpretation of the term "ontology": it can be viewed as a set of formalized rules that can be mapped to a combination of human interpretation and/or machine processing instructions.

Until now, the World Wide Web Consortium has defined two ontology languages in the course of their Semantic Web activities, RDF Schema (RDFS) [BG04] and Web Ontology Language (OWL) [MvH04]. The RDFS specification says:

> "*RDF [...] provides no mechanisms for describing [these] properties, nor does it provide any mechanisms for describing the relationships between these properties and other resources. That is the role of the RDF vocabulary description language, RDF Schema. RDF Schema defines classes and properties that may be used to describe classes, properties and other resources.*"
> [BG04]

Thus, RDFS is an application of RDF that simultaneously extends RDF so that specific vocabularies can be formalized. RDF Schema contains a small set of modeling primitives for *classes*, *literals* and *data types*, as well as predicate restrictions (*domain* and *range*) and a set of relations between these model elements (*sub-class* and *sub-property*). It also defines the RDF vocabulary for collections and reification as described in Section 2.2.1. However, it is of limited use if more complex issues are to be modelled (cf. an analysis of the availability of ontology constructs in various ontology languages [DKD+05]). As a consequence, OWL has been designed on top of RDF Schema. The OWL specification document starts with the following statement:

> "*OWL is intended to be used when the information contained in documents needs to be processed by applications, as opposed to situations where the content only needs to be presented to humans. [...] OWL has more facilities for expressing meaning and semantics than XML, RDF, and RDF-S, and thus OWL goes beyond these languages in its ability to represent machine interpretable content on the Web.*" [MvH04]

RDF and RDFS allow, in principle, for a certain level of syntactic freedom [Gra04] which makes it difficult to layer more advanced ontology languages on top of them. It had to be ensured that the model-theoretic semantics of OWL are retained when the ontology is expressed using RDF, which led to the design of three OWL dialects. *OWL Full* is the only true extension of RDF(S) and thus it is undecidable [Gra04], while *OWL DL* and *OWL Lite* allow only certain combinations of RDF(S) triples. The potentially negative implications of these decisions for the further development of Semantic Web technologies are discussed in [Gra04], where the author also proposes to reorganize the stack of Semantic Web languages using a novel RDF Schema language based on RDFS(A) [PH03].

Besides of complexity issues of the various ontology languages (an analysis on the complexity of various ontology operations is given in [Gra06]), *visualization* and *user interfaces* for ontology browsing and manipulation are still major open research issues. In principle, ontologies building upon RDF (including the OWL family [PSH07], DAML+OIL [HHPS01], and SKOS [MB05]) can be visualized using the same techniques as for RDF since they can actually be represented as RDF graphs. However, while methods for visualization of RDF instance data sets often do not scale to large graph sizes, the visualization of ontology graphs is additionally difficult because of the inherent complexity of ontology languages [TH06]. A comprehensive comparative study of ontology visualization techniques is given in [KHL$^+$07], and in [ABM04] an analysis of related tool implementations is given.

Several works have studied which ontologies are most frequently used on the Semantic Web. One of the first such studies is [DKD$^+$05], where the authors counted the results returned by the Swoogle Semantic Web search engine [DFJ$^+$04] and identified *Dublin Core*, *RSS*, *MetaVocab*, and *FOAF* as the most popular ontologies. Recently, statistics obtained from the Sindice search engine index [ODC$^+$08] and from *Ping The Semantic Web*[13] show that *FOAF*, the W3C *WGS84* vocabulary[14], and *SIOC*[15] are amongst the most popular ontologies and vocabularies. We can observe that all these ontologies are designed in a lightweight, easy-to-use style.

The question of which ontologies to use is an important one especially in the personal desktop environment. Ontologies tend to become complex, and it is critical that end users are able to work with such complex ontologies. Jones [Jon04] proposes the definition of *Personal Unifying Taxonomies* (PUT) for an ontological organization of personal information, and this formalized model of a person's information space can be enriched with semi-automated categorization or highlighting and summarization techniques. A similar proposal is described in [XC05] where ontologies are treated as plug-ins that can be dynamically used in a layered semantic desktop architecture. The authors use ontologies in the three layers *application*, *domain*, and *resource*, and queries issued by applications (and expressed using application ontology vocabulary) are mapped and translated to the corresponding domain and resource ontology vocabularies. PIMO [FGSSB06, SDvE$^+$06] is an ontology proposal for personal information management based on research experience from a number of preceding projects [Roh05]. It combines constructs from various ontology languages and extends them with constructs not present in current ontology standards (e.g., a *part-of* relation) as well as Web 2.0

---

[13]Ping the Semantic Web: http://www.pingthesemanticweb.com
[14]W3C Basic Geo Vocabulary: http://www.w3.org/2003/01/geo/
[15]Semantically-Interlinked Online Communities: http://sioc-project.org

concepts like tagging, wikis, and blogs.

2.2.3 Query Languages

To actually make use of data expressed in RDF, data sets have to be queried. Similar as in relational databases, queries express *which data is needed*, and leave the details of processing the data and collecting results to a query engine. The requirements for RDF query languages are similar to those for RDBMS query languages like SQL and are described in a document by the W3C RDF Data Access Working Group [Cla05]. Many query languages for RDF have been proposed; a good overview on them is given in [HBEV04]. However, efforts of the World Wide Web Consortium have lead to the design of a query language that is not represented in said study, SPARQL [PS08], which is a successor of the RDQL language [Sea04]. SPARQL is now supported by most RDF storage and querying systems (including Jena, Sesame, Virtuoso, and Joseki), and an exchange protocol for transmitting SPARQL queries and results via HTTP and SOAP is part of the SPARQL specification [Cla06]. However, currently SPARQL has no commonly accepted, well-defined formal semantics: [PAG06a] describes works towards a formal specification of the semantics of core fragments of SPARQL. Similar works are presented in [GHM04] where the authors define a notion of formal semantics for RDF graphs and a RDF query language. *Update* functionality is still missing in SPARQL; thus [SM07a] proposes such an extension which also considers Named Graphs [CBHS05b]. Finally, [AMS07] proposes extensions to SPARQL that provide functionality to query for arbitrary path structures, e.g., to find paths that connect resources within a graph.

2.3 Semantic Technologies for the Desktop

2.3.1 Introduction

The term *Semantic Desktop* [SBD05] describes a system that extends the personal computing environment of end users (the desktop) with Semantic Web technology in order to *(a)* strengthen the expressive power of desktop data management facilities to improve information search and retrieval, and *(b)* to connect the separate information spheres of the *web* and the *desktop* by a unified data model and common interfaces. One of the main motivations for research in this field is to improve *personal information management* [TJB06]; i.e., the ways users cope with the set of digital information they need in their professional and private contexts. Depending on the user's current context, data from various sources can become relevant for personal information management: a phone call from one's child, a photo sent to a work colleague, a meeting appointment in the customer's office, a letter written to the local tax authority, and last month's telephone bill are examples of items in the space of personal information.

Vannevar Bush described an universal device for personal information management in a broader sense, called the *Memex* [Bus45]. In principle, the Semantic Desktop follows the same objectives as the Memex: to relate and annotate items so that they can, if needed, be found more easily, or be found at all. The Memex uses *associative trails* to interconnect and relate information units, which is a simplified imitation of how we think the brain works. Consequently, one of the main characteristics of a semantic desktop is the ability to interrelate information objects in order to constitute a *personal data web*.

Although Bush's idea of the Memex is impressive, he could not foresee the substantial implications that the emergence of a global information network has imposed on personal information management. Today we can observe that more and more personal information is spread across multiple devices, making it even harder to interlink, find, and remember relevant information bits. The World Wide Web is an example of a distributed system where heterogeneous devices interoperate and constitute a global information space: data and services are connected by *hyperlinks* which allow the user (and, in a limited manner, machines) to navigate from node to node in this network. The Semantic Web continues this metaphor by enriching the traditional Web with machine-processable vocabularies used to describe resources (cf. Section 2.2.1). Applying this metaphor to the personal desktop could be one path to a unified view on information, for instance by seamlessly enriching personal desktop data with information from the web, or by improving the usage of web resources with context information derived from the user's desktop.

A semantic desktop most likely will follow certain design paradigms that—in the author's opinion—made the World Wide Web and, to a certain extent, the Semantic Web successful, and that most desktop systems in place today lack:

- *Shared information infrastructures.* URLs, HTTP, XML and (X)HTML form the basic technology corpus for information that is available on the World Wide Web. In the Semantic Web, URIs, RDF, and ontology languages (cf. Section 2.2.2) complete this infrastructure. These building blocks are understood by a wide range of software and tools, and web applications adhere to them, e.g., by accepting

HTTP requests as input (or *commands*) and by returning results formatted as XML or XHTML. Desktop systems currently lack such a rich structural basis, which hardens exchange and interoperability of data and creates barriers between applications (cf. Section 2.1.7).

- *Distributed unified naming.* The Web uses URLs and URIs to identify resources of all kinds. Alongside the most prominent URI types, `http` and `mailto`, there exist URI schemes for a magnitude of resource types, and the Domain Name System ensures that, in practice, every entity that registers for a name can use it without having to fear conflicts. Additionally it enables the creation of persistent names since it hides the physical location of a resource (e.g., an IP address) behind the logical location (its URI or URL). On the desktop, the `file` URI scheme can be used to identify file resources. However, a file URI is only valid within the context of the local system, and there exist no authority that avoids naming conflicts across systems.

- *Unified view on information.* Besides applications for special types of information (e.g., E-Mail or Instant Messaging), the Web browser has become the default user interface for humans to the World Wide Web. In contrast, the Semantic Web is still searching for *its* standard interface, as the activity in the research community indicates[16]. Although there exists a de-facto standard interface for file systems on the desktop (cf. Section 2.1.6), interfaces for the usage of concrete information objects are heterogeneous and differ greatly, even on the same platform.

The Semantic Desktop aims to bring characteristics of the Semantic Web onto personal devices (i.e., desktop computers, notebooks, mobile devices, etc.). In the following, we will describe criteria and dimensions by which we can analyze and classify approaches towards this direction.

2.3.2 Dimensions of the Semantic Desktop

A desktop system is a complex system in terms of both hardware and software: modern operating systems consist of hundreds of components, and the degree and quality of their cooperation has significant impact on the user's experience. The diversity and versatility of desktop systems is one of the success factors of personal computers, and many of our daily tasks, especially in personal information management both in the

---

[16]Semantic Web User Interaction workshop series: `http://swui.semanticweb.org`

private and in the business domain, have now become unimaginable to be performed without computer support.

However this versatility made it harder to understand the dimensions that influence the design of desktop systems, and the way users use and interact with them. A desktop system can be regarded as a highly connected mesh of components, where one component's characteristics influence many other parts, with possibly a number of intermediate steps. For instance, the input devices present on a laptop influence the usability of applications running on this machine, and the presence (or absence) of a certain communication protocol may have effects on the way information is shared between collaborators. In this section, we define dimensions of semantic desktop systems that may influence the way users work with them.

Data Model

The data model of an information system determines the conditions under which data can be processed and interpreted by the system. There exists no precise definition of what a *data model* constitutes [PS03b]; however it can be regarded as the *language* of a system, as it defines the constructs with which data can be expressed, and the rules that determine which constructs are correct; i.e., which data can be interpreted by the system. Together with its *meta data model* (i.e., the data model that is used to describe the system data model) the data model has direct and indirect implications on the capabilities that a system exposes and the operations one can perform on a given data instance.

Tightly coupled with the selection of a data model is the question of storage. For different data models, different storage mechanisms exist which differ in performance and scalability. Since storage capacity and computing power are potentially limited on personal computing devices, the designer of a Semantic Desktop system must find a tradeoff between functionality and performance, and mutual effects between them should be considered.

External Data Source Support

In a highly connected world, a personal information system cannot be considered without enabling relationships to other systems, especially sources of data that are relevant for personal information management. Integration of external data sources (both read-only and read-write) is possible only if the participating systems' data models are structurally and semantically compatible, i.e., data sets can be converted according to a system's needs. Especially the level on which data is integrated must be considered, since this influences the necessary conversion steps to establish interoperability [HK08].

Application Integration

The majority of personal information and descriptive data are created and consumed during work with specific applications. These applications make use of various aspects of a desktop system, including read and write operations on stored data and metadata. The characteristics of the data model and the underlying storage infrastructure influence the design and implementation of applications (cf. Section 2.1.4): any logic and expressivity that is provided by the storage system needs not to be re-implemented within specific applications. On the other hand, the right balance of expressivity must be found since from expressivity comes rigidity, and the more elements and constraints a data model defines, the higher is the probability that the data model required by an application is incompatible with the one provided by the Semantic Desktop system.

As described before, one goal of Semantic Desktop systems is to provide a unified view on semantically enriched information across applications. Usually such a view is implemented through an *Application Programming Interface (API)* or through *services* that can be used by applications. However, the large number of applications in place today makes it necessary to provide background-compatible transition paths so that information stored on a Semantic Desktop can also be accessed with legacy, "non-semantic" applications.

Operating System Integration

It is inevitable for a Semantic Desktop system to tightly cooperate with the operating system. Even more, a Semantic Desktop system may replace certain components of the operating system, or may render some of them unecessary. As Semantic Desktop systems mostly deal with the management of personal data, the primarily relevant components of the operating system include file systems and communication infrastructure. As described in Section 2.1.6, this may require to enrich or even replace the operating systems's user interface in order to make its features accessible to the user.

A major question is whether a Semantic Desktop system is able to deal with the diverging characteristics of different operating systems and their special components; especially the wide variety of options found in different file systems (cf. Section 2.1.2) may cause considerable adaption overhead.

User Interface

The user interface, as the communication point between a Semantic Desktop system and the end user, is a determining factor for the design of such an information system. Naturally, the user interface design must strongly consider the intended target audience of the system to be successful. Rohmer [Roh05] states that "*Semantic Desktop Computing is about people, more than about machines, architecture and protocols*" and emphasises the necessity of careful user interface and interaction design. Gentner and Nielsen [GN96] have identified shortcomings of the traditional WIMP (*windows, icons, mouse, pointer*) desktop interface (cf. Section 2.1.6) and discuss possible alternatives that aim to enhance system usability. Users vary in their experience, their expectations and their requirements, and these variables must be reflected when considering a user interface for a user-centric system.

Multi-User and Collaboration Support

In a highly networked world, collaboration between users is a crucial factor. People are collaborating on different levels of institutionalization, starting from preassigned project teams to ad-hoc collaboration across continents. Collaboration implies communication; however current desktop systems do only insufficiently support users with integrating communication tasks into their workflow. Instead, specialized utilities for communication are provided that cover certain communication *technologies* (e.g., e-mail or instant messaging) instead of communication *goals* (e.g., reaching a consensus decision, or collaborative meeting agenda planning). Semantic desktop systems should consider the infrastructural needs that emerge from collaboration, and enable such by adjusting their interfaces and workflows.

2.3.3 Light-Weight Extensions of Existing Infrastructure

As described in Section 2.1.7, common desktop systems and their file system do often not provide sufficient means to express semantically rich annotations and relationships. An approach to overcome this is the implementation of light-weight components that target specific functionality without abandoning the basic principles and paradigms already in place. Such a light-weight solution does not force the user to adopt completely new management paradigms and thus has significant advantages in terms of user acceptance.

Files

There exist lots of tools that attempt to overcome the limitations of hierarchical file systems. Files can be annotated with *tags*, which—if applied systematically—can also be semantically interpreted and queried. Tagging is supported by a variety of commercial products that are available for different platforms (e.g., Punakea[17] or Ultrafolder[18]). Some of these tools use infrastructure provided by the operating system or the file system (e.g., Spotlight comments[19] on Mac OS X), others employ application-specific databases or directories to store annotations. While the former allows for a certain level of interoperability at least on the specific platform, information stored by the latter class of tools seldomly can be used by any other tool. To the best of the author's knowledge, none of such tools uses a widely accepted, standardized format to represent their metadata.

A collection of such tools has been presented in [MH07]; these tools store links between files, expressed using RDF, by a combination of spotlight importers (cf. Section 2.1.2) and extended attributes (cf. Section 2.1.2) using simple user interfaces. Web ontologies can be imported, and selected concepts are represented as files, making them available for spotlight search.

More specialized approaches exist that deal only with certain file types, e.g., office documents: [IAD06] gives an overview on systems for integrating semantic annotations into word processor documents. As an example, Semantic Word [Tal03] employs a combination of manual annotation and content-based information extraction to store DAML+OIL annotations to text areas within a Microsoft Word document.

E-Mail

E-Mail has become one of the main applications of desktop computers during the last years, and thus it is clear that annotation mechanisms for e-mail messages and related information (e.g., contacts) have emerged. Many e-mail applications store e-mail messages as files, hence tools as described above could be used also with mail messages. However e-mail messages follow a certain inner structure and carry partially structured information (like sender or subject) that can be utilized by annotation tools.

Mail messages additionally possess inherent structured relationships to other entities: each mail message carries a globally unique id, issued by the mail server used for

---

[17]Punakea: `http://nudgenudge.eu/punakea`
[18]UltraFolder: `http://www.ultrafolder.com`
[19]Spotlight: `http://developer.apple.com/macosx/spotlight.html`

sending the message. The message's sender and recipient are referenced by their mail addresses, and preceding mail conversation can be tracked by message references. For these data, designated mail header fields are defined by the Internet Message Format Specification [Res01], and to the best of the author's knowledge these metadata can be regarded as the most frequently used on desktops.

Mail headers can also be used to store user annotations for messages. Although there are three defined header fields—`Subject:`, `Keywords:`, and `Comments:` [Res01]—, only `Subject:` is frequently used. Instead, non-standardized headers like, for example, `X-Keywords` or `X-Mailtags`, can often be seen, causing incompatibilities between systems when mail messages are stored on shared infrastructure, e.g., an IMAP server [Cri03], and are accessed via different machines running different software; e.g., MailTags[20], a plugin for Apple Mail. To a certain extent, tagging of mail messages is possible in other products like Mozilla Thunderbird or Microsoft Outlook.

Another approach is taken by online mail services like *Google Mail*[21]: instead of a folder hierarchy this service purely relies on tags and annotations that are attached to mail messages, and the relationships of messages and their replies (*conversions*). Such tags can be generated either manually or automatically by analyzing the textual content of mail messages.

Web Resources

On the web it is more commonplace to annotate resources than on the desktop. Collaborative tagging services for different media like web pages (e.g., del.icio.us[22]), images (e.g., Flickr[23]), or videos (e.g., YouTube[24]) have emerged together with their underlying core task: storage and distribution of user-generated content. Because of their large user numbers these services increasingly become a significant knowledge corpus, and many approaches and technologies how to semantically enrich the mostly unstructured annotations found in these systems have been presented [SM07b]. However it is unclear whether these technologies can be applied also to desktops since the large numbers of users and media objects that can be found on web services are not given in desktop environments.

---

[20] http://www.indev.ca/MailTags.html
[21] http://mail.google.com
[22] http://del.icio.us
[23] http://flickr.com
[24] http://www.youtube.com

2.3.4 Comparison of Semantic Desktop Approaches

Based on the criteria described in the previous section, we analyze a number of projects carrying out work toward a Semantic Desktop. When selecting projects we focused on such ones that aim to develop comprehensive infrastructures, instead of such ones that focus on specific functionalities and aspects of desktop data management, as described in Section 2.3.3.

Table 2.3 gives an overview on the projects and the applied criteria. Our selection includes pure research projects of various sizes as well as community-driven projects. In the following, we give a short introduction to the eight selected projects.

- *Nepomuk*[25] is a project that integrates the efforts of approximately fifteen european partners, including research institutes as well as industrial representatives. The main goal of the project is to develop standards and reference architectures for semantic desktop systems, and to integrate effort carried out by individual partners on an European level. A Java-based reference implementation of the Nepomuk framework is available for download; moreover, some core components of Nepomuk have been integrated into the K Desktop Environment (KDE[26]).

- *Haystack*[27] subsumes research work carried out by the MIT Computer Science and Artificial Intelligence Laboratory and can be regarded as one of the first projects that aimed to improve data management on the user desktop with semantic technologies. A number of different sub-projects are subsumed under the label "Haystack"; in this analysis we focus on the *Haystack Universal Information Client*[28] which is a universal management tool for personal data and can be downloaded from the project web site.

- *Chandler*[29]. The *Open Source Applications Foundation* is a non-profit organization working on the Chandler project. Chandler focuses on supporting tasks that people carry out in their daily work, especially in team constellations. The Chandler system consists of a server (*Chandler Hub*) and a client application, both of which are released under an open source license.

---

[25] http://nepomuk.semanticdesktop.org
[26] K Desktop Environment: http://www.kde.org
[27] http://freshmeat.net/projects/haystack/
[28] http://groups.csail.mit.edu/haystack/home.html
[29] http://chandlerproject.org/

- *Semex*[30]. The main focus of the Semex project is to create a platform for personal information management by integrating data from various sources and overlaying them with a personalized schema that can be modified by the user according to her needs. A prototype of Semex is available for download from the project web site.

- *DeepaMehta*[31]. In the DeepaMehta project the user desktop is entirely modelled as topic map, and the user is able to directly manipulate this map through a graph-based interface, instead of having to deal with different applications and file directories. It is the goal of the project to reflect the user's mental model in a visual adaequate style. DeepaMehta can be downloaded from the project web site or used online via the web browser.

- *OpenIRIS*[32] is a framework for the creation of personal knowledge maps and applications, developed and maintained by SRI International. It is part of the CALO research project[33] and bundles a set of standard PIM applications, including mail, calendar, and web and file browsers. Similar to the projects mentioned before, OpenIRIS is available for download under a LGPL license.

- *DBin*[34]. The main focus of DBin is peer-to-peer based exchange of knowledge and collaboration between multiple desktop within so-called *Semantic Web Communities*. Thus it can be seen as a complement to other approaches that concentrate mainly on the extraction and organization of data on single desktops. DBin is developed by the Universita' Politecnica delle Marche, and several prototypes are available for download from the project web site.

- *iMeMex*[35], developed at ETH Zurich, provides a unified data model and search and query mechanisms for personal information. It follows the goal of ad-hoc integration (or *pay-as-you-go* integration [FHM05]) in order to derive an integrated view on all data present on the desktop. Started in 2005, the project is still under development; yet, components of the framework are available for download via the project web site.

	Nepomuk	Haystack	Chandler	Semex	DeepaMehta	OpenIRIS	DBin	IMeMex
Data Model								
Meta Model	RDF / NRL (1)	RDF (7)	Items, Collections	RDF	Topic Maps (+ extensions), RDF	RDF	RDF	iDM (graph-based) (23)
Storage Layer	RDF2Go / Sesame2	In-memory DB	BerkeleyDB, Lucene	Jena in-memory DB (10)	MySQL, HSQL	Jena DB (16)	Sesame2	Apache Derby (RDBMS)
Metadata Model								
Ontologies	Four level model (2) with predefined core ontologies	Predefined specific ontologies	Predefined ontology	Predefined domain model	Predefined high-level concepts (13)	Predefined high-level concepts (subset of CLIB) (14, 15)	Predefined ontology	No predefined schema
Extensibility	Based on NIE (3)	Adenine (9)	Python data structures (21, 22)	Malleable Schemas (12)	Base Java class	OWL Ontologies	Brainlets (27)	iDM Resource View Classes (23)
Integration / Interoperability								
External Data Sources	Data wrapper/ crawler framework	Data Extractors (defined by demonstration) (26)	IMAP, iCal	File System	SQL, IMAP, SMTP, IMAP	Harvester for file system, e-mail	RDF import and export	File system, XML, IMAP, RDBMS, RSS
Data Mapping	Alignment engine with user feedback (5)	-	-	Reference reconciliation (11)	-	Bayesian classifier	Resource matching	Incremental integration (planned) (24)
Application Programming Interface	Access via SOAP/REST, application plugins	-	CalDAV, WebDAV, HTTP	-	SOAP, EJB	XML-RPC	-	HTTP, WebDAV (25)
Operating System	Integration in KDE Core	-	-	-	-	-	-	File events (planned)
User Interface								
Interface Metaphor	Knowledge Workbench	View Prescriptions, Lenses (7,8)	Tree- and list-based item browser	Tree-based search and navigation	Graph-based resource browser	Tree-based item browser	Tree-based topic browser	Tree-based resource browser
Implementation	Standalone (RCP)	Standalone (RCP)	Standalone (Python) + Web interface	Standalone (Java)	Standalone (Java) + Web interface	Standalone (Java)	Standalone (RCP)	AJAX Web interface
UI Extensibility	RCP plugins (GnoGno framework)	Declarative (Adenine) (9)	Python classes (21)	-	Java classes + Java Server Pages	Application plugin framework (Java Beans)	Brainlets (RCP Plugins)	-
Collaboration								
Data Sharing	P2P Infrastructure (GridVine) (4)	-	Client/Server Publish/ Subscribe Mechanism	-	Shared workspaces (13)	(planned)	RDFGrowth (17) / Semantic Web Pipes (19)	(planned)
Access Control	RMU-Cube (6)	-	Item-based	-	Type-based	-	Restricted P2P Groups (20)	-
Synchronization	P2P-based replication (2)	-	Via dedicated server	-	-	Jabber-based Sync Protocol	P2P-based resource exchange (18)	(planned)

(1) Sintek et al, 2007
(2) Reif et al, 2007
(3) http://www.semanticdesktop.org/ontologies/nie
(4) Aberer et al, 2004
(5) http://dev.nepomuk.semanticdesktop.org/wiki/LocalDataAlignment
(6) Ioannou et al, 2007
(7) Karger et al, 2005
(8) Quan and Karger, 2004
(9) http://groups.csail.mit.edu/haystack/developers/adenine.html
(10) http://data.cs.washington.edu/semex/download/download.htm
(11) Dong et al, 2005
(12) Dong and Halevy, 2005
(13) Richter andPoelchau, 2008
(14) Cheyer et al, 2005
(15) http://www.cs.utexas.edu/users/mfkb/RKF/tree
(16) http://www.openiris.org/downloads/IRIS-nightly-doc-current/doc/dev/pdf/iris-developer-guide.pdf
(17) Tummarello et al, 2006
(18) Tummarello et al, 2004
(19) Morbidoni, 2008
(20) Tummarello et al, 2007b
(21) http://chandlerproject.org/Projects/PluginsTutorial
(22) http://chandler.osafoundation.org/docs/0.7/parcel-schema-guide.html
(23) Dittrich and Salles, 2006
(24) Blunschi et al, 2007
(25) Dittrich et al, 2005
(26) Hogue and Karger, 2005
(27) Tummarello et al, 2006a

Table 2.3: Comparison of Semantic Desktop projects

In the following we discuss the dimensions of semantic desktop systems, as outlined in Section 2.3.2, and describe how these are addressed by the presented approaches. The purpose of this analysis is not to give a benchmark, but to give a reference overview and to give starting points for the interested reader.

Data Model Most of the analyzed projects and approaches use *graphs* as meta model for data. With the exception of Chandler, DeepaMehta, and iMeMex, all projects use RDF (cf. Section 2.2.1) as graph representation format; thus we can consider RDF as a *de-facto* standard for the Semantic Desktop. DeepaMehta is based on a subset of Topic Maps[36]—which are conceptually similar to RDF [Gar03]—and extend them with an system-specific typing system [RVH05]. Chandler uses an object based data structure with a defined set of object types, while iMeMex defines an abstract data model that is sufficiently expressive to represent directed graphs [DS06] and uses an RDBMS to store its data instances.

It is important to note that all of these systems use a *graph-based* data model instead of the hierarchical data model common on desktop systems today. There seems to exist a common understanding that a graph structure is better suited to represent data on the desktop than strict hierarchies, and we expect graph storage structures to be present in the core of different operating systems during the next years, as is already demonstrated by the Nepomuk-KDE project[37].

Although most of the presented approaches have been developed and tested against specific storage layers, *storage abstraction layers* often hide the details of physical storage from the system logic. This seems reasonable in terms of portability and distribution, and the performance of such systems is approaching the requirements of desktop environments [SH09].

Meta Data Model Analogically, the meta data models of approaches under examination also follow a typical model: all systems—with the exception of iMeMex—define a *core ontology* that models the basic information units of the system. In most cases

---
[30]http://data.cs.washington.edu/semex/semex.html
[31]http://www.deepamehta.de/
[32]http://www.openiris.org
[33]http://www.ai.sri.com/project/CALO
[34]http://dbin.org
[35]http://imemex.ethz.ch/
[36]http://www.topicmaps.org/
[37]http://nepomuk-kde.semanticdesktop.org

this core ontology, or *domain model*, contains generic classes like *Person*, *Document*, or *Message*, and corresponding properties or relationship types, like *author of* or *recipient*. iMeMex does not predefine such types but allows data to conform to arbitrary schemas, where a schema consists of a set of attributes that can be applied to resources. Nepomuk defines its meta data model as a four-level ontology, where a representational layer and a set of core ontologies establish the foundation for the definition of application- and user-specific specialized models [RGH+07].

From the author's point of view, the similarity of the core ontologies in use may eventually lead to an agreement on a *desktop standard ontology*. Such agreement has already been reached on the web, where certain models enjoy great popularity (e.g., FOAF [GEP04]). If such a consensus could be reached, semantic interoperability between desktops could increase and thus the effort for manual information management could be significantly reduced.

However the uses of desktop data are manifold, which requires the possibility to extend the meta data model one uses. The analyzed projects differ significantly in the approaches they provide for this requirement. While some approaches focus on the *static modelling* of user ontologies (e.g., NIE[38] in Nepomuk, Brainlets [TMNP06] in DBin), the *process* of modelling an user ontology is only actually addressed by the concept of *malleable schemas* [DH05], which are used in Semex. We consider this an important contribution, since end users are often neither willing nor able to model complex, expressive schemas for their information space, and thus mechanisms which allow for semi-automatic, simplified creation and representation of such models are required.

Integration and Interoperability The issues of data integration and interoperability with other systems and applications are addressed differently by the analyzed approaches. Most of the presented approaches employ extensible *crawling and harvesting frameworks* which are populated by exemplary implementations, mostly in order to import file system contents, mail messages, and calendar information. However, harvesting mechanisms cannot provide live updates: modifications to data sources are reflected in the desktop data model only after the next crawling iteration. *Live integration*, i.e., translation of queries and result sets on-the-fly during query time is possible in some implementations (e.g., in the Nepomuk platform), but can cause performance problems when large data amounts have to be handled. While most approaches concentrate on

---

[38]http://www.semanticdesktop.org/ontologies/nie

the *static definition* of extractors and crawlers, Haystack presents a methodology where extractors for web data can be created *by demonstration*, without requiring programming skills from the user [HK04].

The alignment of such imported data towards the predefined meta data model or already existing user-defined models is done using a variety of mechanisms in addition to manual annotation. Nepomuk proposes the usage of an alignment engine with a user feedback mechanism[39], similar to a recommendation engine. In Semex, a *reference reconciliation* algorithm is used to detect references that differ in expression, but refer to the same entity [DHM05]. OpenIRIS uses bayesian classifiers to assign ontology classes to imported resources, and in iMeMex a framework for incremental integration similar to the algorithms described in [FHM05] is currently under development [BDG+07].

Vice versa, many systems provide interfaces through which external applications can address the system and use its services and data sets. Different technologies are employed for this, including SOAP/REST, HTTP, and XML-RPC. However all these interfaces require the client application to be specifically designed; only Chandler and iMeMex [DSKB05] expose their data structures via WebDAV [GWF+99], for which certain support is integrated into every desktop operating system and many applications. By doing so these systems allow a desktop user to browse through the data inventory as if she was browsing a hierarchical file system. We believe that it is neccessary for any semantic desktop system to provide such transition paths from existing systems and metaphors, both for applications and users.

A similar question is the one how a semantic desktop system can be integrated with an operating system already in place. The considered systems do, in general, not integrate with the operating system core; in contrast, most of them are implemented in programming languages that abstract from the details of operating systems, like Java. However, as long as the operating system (or their data storage sub-systems) do not provide sufficiently expressive metaphors for data management (which was only recently done by the Nepomuk-KDE project), the instantiation of such bridges will be neccessary in order to increase the feasibility of the Semantic Desktop approach.

User Interface Although their data model is graph-based, most considered systems rely on traditional metaphors (trees and lists) for their graphical user interface (cf. Figure 2.11). In some systems an additional graph browser can be opened if demanded. Mostly this view can be focused on the items of interest, e.g., the relationship a selected

---
[39]http://dev.nepomuk.semanticdesktop.org/wiki/LocalDataAlignment

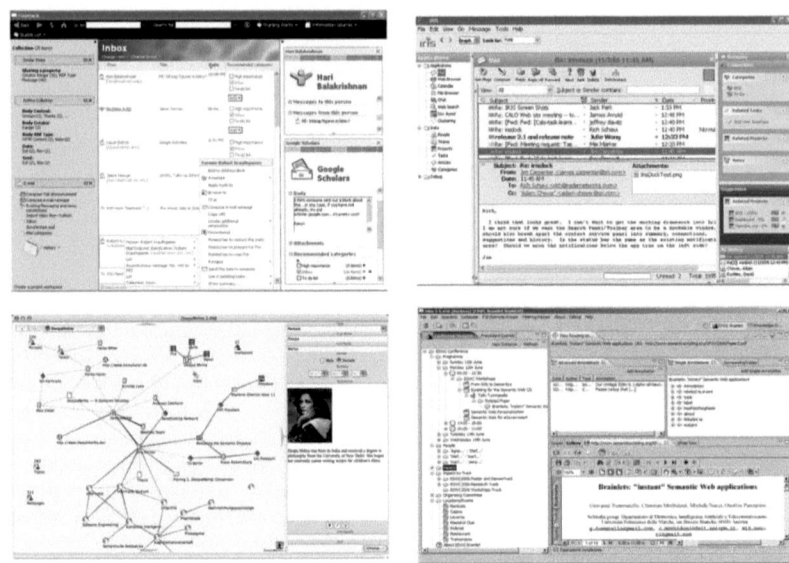

Figure 2.11: Semantic Desktop user interfaces (from top left to bottom right): Haystack [KBH+03], OpenIRIS [CPG05], DeepaMehta [RP08], DBin [TMN06]

resource participates in. In these systems, the tree view gives an overview on the available information items, and details for selected resources (including attributes and relationships to other items) are displayed in a designated screen area.

Only DeepaMehta chooses a graphic representation of its data set as main navigational concept. Topics are depicted as icons and are connected by colored edges; detailed information for selected topics is displayed in a designated screen area. The need to browse large graph structures is avoided by representing queries as topic icons that can be opened (i.e., executed) or refined by adding further criteria [RP08].

An interesting approach is taken in Haystack, where user interface elements (including actions that can be executed from the views) are defined using a combination of RDF and Python; the actually displayed interface is hierarchically composed from renderings of then visible information items [QHSK02, Kar07]. One great strength of this approach is that the rendering code can be reused in different contexts, e.g., an e-mail address can be displayed equally in different contexts without the need to re-define the interface description.

Most of the presented projects' user interfaces are implemented as standalone applications (mostly in Java), some of them using the Eclipse Rich Client Platform (RCP)[40]. In the author's opinion, the latter causes user interfaces to become more technology oriented than user oriented, since the core UI elements of the RCP (perspectives and views) are derived from the needs of software development but their usability for non-expert end users is questionable.

Extensibility in terms of data model and meta data model (see above) most often entails extensibility of the user interface. Here, different approaches can be observed: in many cases, a developer can extend the user interface by extending and implementing base classes provided by the system. In Haystack, user interface extensions can be defined using Adenine [QHSK02], a language combining elements from RDF and Python. DBin Brainlets [TMNP06] integrate the description of user ontologies and UI elements, which are actually implemented as RCP plugins; however both Haystack and DBin lack a simple user interface editor thus editing of source code is required.

Collaboration Support for collaboration tasks, including communication and information sharing, is addressed variably. The implementations range from simple integration of standard communication facilities like e-mail or instant messaging to dedicated infrastructures that allow fine-grained control of shared information and access.

Nepomuk employs a combination of a network event system and a peer-to-peer infrastructure [ACMHP04] to publish information relevant for other users and thus interconnecting desktop systems [GHM$^+$07]. This infrastructure is used to replicate information across the network; whereas access restrictions are defined by a 3-dimensional resource/metadata/user cube [ICK$^+$07].

In Chandler, a client/server based publish/subscribe infrastructure is established, where users can publish information items to a server, and other clients can register themselves for notification upon data changes. Access control rules are defined on a per-item basis and can be restricted to *read only* or *read+write* access for certain user groups.

DeepaMehta currently does not provide dedicated collaboration features, although such ones are envisioned for future versions [RP08]. Currently DeepaMehta workspaces can be shared between users who are notified by e-mail whenever a workspace is changed,

---

[40]http://wiki.eclipse.org/index.php/Rich_Client_Platform

and access control is currently limited to resource type-level.

DBin's main focus is exchange of information items within collaborative *groups of interest*. DBin used the concept of *P2P Information Groups* [TMN06] in previous versions, and is now experimenting with *Semantic Web Pipes* [TPM07, TM07]. The former is a peer-to-peer based infrastructure for exchange of RDF data where data is selectively replicated within user groups, while the latter is a modelling approach for the combination of RDF-based data sources that can be integrated using a set of operators. DBin provides access control to published databased on its group principle: data published to a group of interest is available to all members of this group.

In some projects (e.g., Haystack and Semex), collaboration is not considered at all since it is not in their research focus. However, the importance of collaboration is acknowledged and it is a common understanding that one cannot treat data management on the desktop without developing strategies how such data can be collaboratively used, either on a small scale (like a university department) or on a large (web) scale.

Conclusions

The projects analyzed in this section have different backgrounds, aims, and objectives, and are therefore comparable only in a restricted manner. However, results from these projects are partly complementary, and we can derive the following *lessons learned* from their consolidated analysis.

1. *The graph data model has established as de-facto standard for semantic desktop systems.* With the exception of one system, all presented approaches make use of graphs to represent personal information. From these, all but one use RDF to exchange and internally represent information graphs. In the future, compatibility with web technology will become even more important as the boundaries between the local desktop and the web increasingly disappear.

2. *External data sources need to be considered.* All presented architectures provide mechanisms to semi-automatically integrate data from external data sources; mostly such ones that are related to personal information, like e-mail or calendar data. Many systems are in place that are well designed for such specific kinds of data, and we conclude that data management on the desktop cannot be considered without building bridges to these.

3. *Adaequate user interfaces are still to be developed.* Although graphs are the pre-

dominant data model, user interfaces for browsing, searching, navigating, and manipulating graph data sets often map graph data to "traditional" interface metahpors, like trees and lists. While the backend components of the analyzed approaches often follow a radical approach and aim to entirely replace structures in place today, this claim does not hold for user interfaces.

4. *Consensus and cooperation between operating system developers is required.* Desktop computers are driven by operating systems, and their underlying storage structures, like hierarchical file systems, constitute an integral part of the them. In order to foster new, semantically enriched storage structures, operating system developers must agree on a core set of models, algorithms, and formats, to allow information interchange between different systems, as it is the case today with files and hierarchical folder structures.

5. *Collaboration and social interaction must be supported.* Exchange of information and communication consume a large share of knowledge workers' time. Although the desktop is continuing to be considered as a personal space, connections to other instances can increase productivity and work quality. A majority of analyzed approaches incorporate collaborative mechanisms; the ones that do not, nevertheless, agree on their necessity.

Part II

Concepts

Chapter 3

Siles: An Abstract Model for Semantic Representation of Data Assets on the Desktop

It is a very sad thing that nowadays there is so little useless information. — Oscar Wilde

In the previous section we have discussed the current state of the art in desktop data management, ranging from the analysis of capacities of hierarchical file systems that are in place today, over approaches that extend file systems in a lightweight fashion, to full semantic desktop projects. In the following section, we discuss our novel data model to represent personal data by describing a number of design considerations and requirements. We introduce, in an informal way, the basic concepts that we include in the model, and give a formal specification of the model elements.

3.1 Design Considerations

Typically, hierarchical file systems provide relatively weak organizational metaphors. More sophisticated information processing middleware can either be implemented as layers that entirely hide the file system structures from the outside (i.e., applications or end users); an example for this class are relational databases. Alternatively, they can establish data structures (for instance, triple stores) that coexist with file systems; we denote the latter as *hybrid approaches*. There, applications or end users simultaneously operate directly on both the file system and the additional structures. Such approaches for semantic enrichment of files are widely found, either providing very specific functionality (cf. Kante [MH07] or Punakea [Cor]), or constitute an all-embracing generic semantic layer that presents an integrated view on all user data (cf. NEPOMUK [GHM$^+$07] or Haystack [KBH$^+$03]). Without doubt such extended semantic desktop systems increase the data quality and experience for end users [SH08], they suffer from a number of fundamental problems:

- *Identiscription problem.* Hierarchical file systems intermingle the functions of *identification* and *description* of files [OG92]. In the context of a physical device, a file is uniquely identified by the combination of its *path* and its *file name*. However, the path and file name are also used to *describe* the file, and to relate it to other files (by putting them into a common directory). Consequently, when the description of a file is changed (e.g., when a directory is renamed), references to the file become invalid. As a further consequence, it is not possible to attach multiple descriptions to a file, since this would require storing it into multiple directories. This problem is only partially solved by using symbolic links or similar techniques.

- *Mapping problem.* File systems provide a minimal level of descriptive metadata in the form of file names and directories. If a semantic component is established in addition to a file system, it is desirable to include or reflect this information within the semantic layer; e.g., by mapping directory names to ontology classes. Often, such a mapping is not straightforward: since file names and directories usually have no formal semantics [DB99], their meaning cannot directly be captured and mapped to formal constructs.

- *Update problem.* Even if a mapping for a meaningful translation between a hierarchical file system and a semantic layer can be established, there remains the danger of inconsistencies that result from changes in one layer that are not propagated to the other one. To solve this, propagation mechanisms have to be integrated into file system implementations. This constitutes potential performance and security flaws because it requires hooking or modifying code on the operating system level.

- *Portability problem.* Nearly all native file systems support the storage of some form of metadata, e.g., extended attributes, alternate data streams, or resource forks. Since there exists no widely accepted standard for file metadata, this information is often lost when files are transfered across platforms. This may be one reason why such extended metadata facilities are rarely used by applications. A hybrid semantic system operating in parallel to a file system can either ignore platform-specific metadata management facilities (and thus loose the benefit of a tighter integration into the operating system), or use them and provide mappings to the semantic layer, which again raises the Mapping and Update problems.

Any hybrid approach that coexists with hierarchical file system must deal with these issues, which potentially leads to increased complexity and error proneness. Many of these problems could be solved if hierarchical file systems could be disbanded in favor of a commonly accepted semantic file system that allows one to store, annotate, and retrieve arbitrary data objects. Such a system could serve as the common infrastructure for a semantic desktop and its applications.

In the following we discuss requirements and design considerations for a data model of an integrated semantic file system. We emphasize the term *integrated* since many of the problems outlined in the previous section can be avoided by tightly coupling data with descriptive metadata. We outline the different aspects that we considered during the development of the abstract model and the definition of a concrete digital manifestation.

3.1.1 Identification

To overcome the identiscription problem described above, each file must have an unique, immutable identifier. Such a global unique id can serve as the reference for annotation and linkage of files. In order to support interoperability across sytems the identifier must be unique not only in the context of a single system, but on a global level. URIs [BLFM05] provide a powerful generic mechanism to globally identify resources, and they are designed to be minted without a central authority. As the generic specification for URIs also defines hierarchical URIs it is additionally straightforward to convert directory and file names to URIs.

3.1.2 Level of Abstraction

One major strength of file systems is their high level of abstraction: files can be used to store any kind of data and allow for arbitrary formats. It is important for a semantic file system that users and applications are not forced to fit their data into heavily constrained structures. On the other hand, semantics can only be derived from structure, therefore any semantic storage must impose a certain level of rigidness. From observing a variety of applications and systems both in the desktop and the Web domain, we can infer a need for the following structure elements:

- *Concrete and abstract resources.* Current file systems are based on the assumption that every thing has a digital representation (although files can have a content with zero length). This assumption is valid in file system-based environments since the representation of non-digital objects would make sense only if they can be further described, or if they can be brought into relationship with other (digital) objects—both features are, however, not offered by current hierarchical file systems. To facilitate the expression of information about non-digital real-world objects a personal information management system should also be able to represent e.g., persons, events, locations, etc. A semantic file system that supports digital and non-digital objects as well as relationships between them could significantly increase the potential expressivity of desktop applications. Additionally, sharing of data between applications could be improved if common classes of user data (e.g., contacts or appointments) were represented in an application-independent manner.

- *Ontological knowledge.* Semantic annotations, or annotations based on description logic, help to improve the automated processing and retrieval of information. Classes (or *concepts*) are regarded the basic structure element in many knowledge organization systems and ontology languages. To apply them to file systems, and to derive conclusions about files with similar properties, a semantic file system should be able to represent files as class instances and allow to perform reasoning over these data structures. Moreover, ontology classes could be represented as files themselves and could therefore be directly managed by the user, if this functionality is desired in a concrete application scenario.

- *Attributes.* Attributes can be used to describe files in structured form. They allow applications to store information that is not inherent to a file's content. If the meaning of a file's attribute is defined in an ontology it can be used consistently across different applications. However, it would also be possible to attach user-defined attributes in an ad-hoc style; in this case the attributes cannot be automatically processed but still may help the user to organize and retrieve information.

- *Relationships.* Many types of information cannot be attributed to a single file, but are represented by relationships between them; a fact also observed by end users [RSK04]. The World Wide Web is the best example of a knowledge base that gains its power mainly from links between web resources. The way that files are related to each other can be described in more detail by typed relations or by attaching additional information (attributes, other relationships) to them. Therefore, a semantic file system should support (annotated) relationships.

- *Tags.* Tags have become enormously popular through their use in many so-called *Web 2.0* applications. Tags expose a different level of semantic expressivity than classes and attributes, since the relationship between an object and its associated tags, as well as the relationships between tags, are not formally defined. Nevertheless, the popularity of tags shows that they may support the organization of information in a user-centric way and should therefore be supported by a file system targeted towards a semantic desktop.

In addition to the possibility to store and manage these organizational mechanisms, a potential increase of semantic expressivity could be gained from allowing one to define *mappings* between them. Such a mapping could provide additional information hints to the user when searching, and ease the manual annotation process, which often is cumbersome. For instance, one could map a certain attribute value to a tag, and further only use the tag instead of the attribute's name/value pair. This would release users from the need to remember the exact name and value for this attribute and allow for a more intuitive, human-centric application of formal semantics.

3.1.3 Compatibility with File Systems

Although the amount and complexity of data on a user's desktop steadily increases, the organizational metaphors for files have remained unchanged for decades. Since hierarchical file systems are not sufficiently expressive to represent machine-processable annotations, application-dependent parallel structures have been established. For instance, many tools for management of multimedia data (e.g., audio files or photos) extend the file system with application-specific semantics and thus face the same problems as hybrid semantic desktop approaches (cf. Section 2.3.3). These systems often use a mix of the hierarchical file system (e.g., MP3 files in directories named after artists), metadata embedded into files (e.g., ID3 tags), and data in application-specific databases (e.g., e-mail archive files). Naturally, the latter remain hidden to the outside. For user data stored in hierarchical file systems it is important that there exist smooth migration paths that allow users to "glide" into the semantic desktop. When transferring a hierarchical directory structure into a semantically enriched organization paradigm, the following requirements must be considered:

- *Organizational preservation.* No information that was present in the hierarchical system should be lost during the transition. This includes information that is implicitly present in file names and directories.

- *Navigational preservation.* A hierarchical file system provides certain navigation alternatives, and users are presumably familiar with them. For semantic files it must be ensured that similar navigational behavior is still supported. The main goal is that users can actually find objects in locations where they expect them to be.

- *Backwards compatibility.* Although a certain level of backwards compatibility can be achieved by inverting mapping algorithms that ensure organizational preservation, not all information contained in a semantic file system can be translated to the tree model of the hierarchical file system because a tree is not sufficiently expressive to represent certain aspects, (e.g., relationships between files). Maximized backwards compatibility can increase the acceptance of semantic systems on the desktop, especially when users are using legacy software that is not aware of the file system's semantic features. Thus, it is reasonable to invest research effort into the question of representing semantic networks by the means of hierarchical file systems.

3.1.4 Compatibility with the Web

A large amount of relevant information is available on the World Wide Web and, increasingly, the Semantic Web. Currently we can observe an *information gap* between data stored on a user's local machine on the one hand, and online resources on the other hand. An information architecture that uses a unified mechanism to identify information objects and makes them accessible regardless of their physical location could help to bridge this gap. This bridging could take place in two directions; first, it should allow users to semantically interconnect (and, consequently, retrieve and use) local and web resources, and second, it should be possible to selectively share local resources if needed without much effort, and thus make local information resources a part of the web.

3.1.5 Why not Plain RDF?

The RDF data model [KC04] is sufficiently generic to represent different organizational elements (including the ones described in Section 3.1.2), and many of them are already used in web applications. Many tools and libraries for manipulating RDF are available, and the performance of triple stores is steadily increasing (cf., e.g., [AMMH07]), hence RDF seems to be a natural choice for the representation of metadata in file systems.

RDF does not restrict the usage of relationship types; instead, ontology languages are used to do this. This freedom fosters the publication of data on the World Wide Web (as demonstrated, e.g., by the Linked Data initiative[1]) but, on the other hand, imposes restrictions on the applicability of RDF as information exchange format: when different applications access a shared data set they must agree on a common vocabulary, or define potentially complex schema mappings.

Moreover, the RDF data model does not contain the concept of *self-contained information units*. Instead, RDF data can be seen as a continuous stream of relationships between arbitrary resources. This paradigm is fundamentally different from what we can observe in file systems, where information is stored in discrete units, and is also different to the object-oriented modeling paradigm, in which a large share of applications are implemented, and with which many developers are familiar. We also suspect that the flat graph model stands—to a certain extent—in contradiction to the way humans perceive the world: commonly, objects and their properties are mentally aggregated and treated as integral units. Thus we envision a data model that is as generic and interoperable as RDF but simplifies the representation of object-oriented model elements.

3.1.6 Conclusions and Design Decisions

The issues discussed in the previous sections have lead us to the specification of a data model for a semantic file system that incorporates aspects from Semantic Web

---

[1] http://linkeddata.org

technology (usage of URIs, graph-based metadata structures, usage of ontology elements like classes and properties), object-oriented modeling (integrated view on objects and their properties), Web 2.0 (tags), and file systems (discrete content units).

As an atomic information element we choose to extend the file with semantic annotations of different kinds, and call such objects *siles*. A sile is a discrete unit of information; the content of a sile is—similar to a file—self-contained and does neither depend on any other entity, nor does it make any statements on other entities. To guarantee a unique identity for these discrete information units, we choose to identify a sile by a URI. URIs can take the form of simple names that carry no further semantics (like, for example, a UUID), or can imply mechanisms and protocols for accessing the resource that is identified by a URI (in the case of, e.g., `http:` or `mailto:` URIs). For the sile model we do not establish any constraints on the format of URIs or require a specific URI scheme. Since from our perspective URIs are used as opaque identifiers, we can safely leave the choice of a suitable URI scheme and URI minting algorithm to the concrete implementation.

This design implies that, in contrast to file systems, no *intrinsic semantics* is imposed on sile identifiers. In file systems, the full path of a file is composed of a series of directory names, each of which is chosen by a user and carries implicit or explicit meaning. We unhinge all kinds of contextual meaning from the sile identifier (the URI); instead we define a number of *annotation metaphors* that can be used to express the *extrinsic semantics* of a sile. We have chosen the following set of annotation metaphors to be included in the sile model:

- *Tags*. Tags are simple keywords that consist of a string of arbitrary length and arbitrary format. Tags are usually not chosen from a predefined formal vocabulary, hence the interpretation of a tag is entirely left to the end user. Certain problems arise in systems that use tags: for instance, it is not possible to resolve homonym or synonym conflicts without further analysis. Moreover, tags are always bound to a certain natural language which makes them unfeasible for end users not aware of this language. Nevertheless tags can help to classify and retrieve information in situations where end users follow a common understanding of tags. This is both the case when tags are applied in a single person's data space—we can assume that the person who issues a tag will be able to understand the meaning of this very tag later on—, or in cases where a user group shares a certain, informal vocabulary and has, to a certain extent, a common understanding of its meaning; as it is the case, for instance, in work groups or projects.

- *Categories.* The use of ontologies significantly extends the analysis possibilities that can be applied to documents in general and tags in special (e.g., full text search, string similarity metrics, natural language processing, and statistical methods). Ontologies establish frameworks of formal rules that can be used by reasoners to validate descriptions and to generate new, *implicit* knowledge out of existing information. *Classes* are a core concept in most ontology languages; however we can observe that non-expert users have difficulties in understanding the idea of classes and in perceiving the potentially high complexity of ontology instances. We suspect that one part of this problem is caused by naming: we can observe that the term "category" is often better understood by non-expert users than "class". For our data model we introduce categories as a way to annotate siles but we do not define rules on how categories are to be interpreted by a machine, or which reasoning rules can be applied to them.

- *Attributes.* Attributes are a basic modeling element in many information systems. An attribute describes a specific characteristic of an individual and usually consists of two parts: a *name* part that indicates which characteristic is described by an attribute, and a *value* part that represents the concrete occurrence of this characteristic with respect to the individual. Attributes are a highly generic mechanism for expressing information about individuals and can additionally be used in ontologies to indicate, for instance, class membership or to verify instance equality. As with categories, we do not impose such rules in our data model but leave the definition of such rules up to concrete implementations and applications.

- *Relationships.* Relationships can be considered as attributes whose value is an instance of similar characteristic as the described object. In our model we consider siles as first-class objects, and thus relationships are the subset of a sile's attributes whose value is a sile. By introducing relationships as a separate class of annotations, we emphasize the web-style character of our data model: using relationships, interdependencies between discrete information units are made explicit.

We do not predefine types or processing rules for categories, attributes, or relationships, but leave this to the concrete applications that make use of siles; an example of such such an application is described in [Sch06]. However we want to give our system the possibility to express interdependencies between different types of sile annotations, because we see the need of information management systems to maintain a certain level of data integrity. There exist a magnitude of mechanisms to express such information (e.g., ontologies, schema descriptions, or abstract modelling languages like UML). Similar to our vision of siles as generalized view on personal information, we use the term *spect*[2] to denote collections of interdependency rules between categories, attributes, and relationships.

We deliberately choose not to include a representation of any kind of *hierarchies* (like file system directories) in the model, since we are interested in the applicability and impact of the metaphors mentioned above *in the absence* of directories. Additionally, hierarchical structures can be simulated using relationships between objects, as shown e.g., in [SH09]. We are aware of the fact that this decision is contradictory to the requirement of compatibility with hierarchical file systems (cf. Section 3.1.3), thus hierarchical collections may be added to the data model at a later point in time.

By making information semantics extrinsic and representing them in a unified manner, a storage system for semantically annotated objects can act as a shared information infrastructure for different applications and services. Usually, applications will operate on a limited set of objects; e.g., ones that are available on a user's local machine, or ones that are stored on the working group's file server. In the following we use the term *repository* to denote a logically closed context of information interpretation. Such a context consists of a set of siles, including their associated content and annotations. The interpretation of the siles' annotations is only valid within the context of a given repository; a different repository may make completely different statements about siles and apply different rules on how annotations may be combined. The connections between such distinct repositories are established using *referenced siles*, i.e., pointers that refer to siles within an external repository. The identity of (and therefore, the connection to) a sile is established by a unique opaque identifier, the sile URI.

In terms of a physical unit, a repository can be regarded similar to the concept of a volume in a file system, or the concept of a host on the World Wide Web. In terms of a logical unit, it can be regarded as a collection of siles that share a logical context, e.g., the siles that have been created by a specific user, or the siles that are of relevance in the context of a research project. We do not define constraints on the inner structure of a repository; instead we define a set of operations that a repository must be able to execute and treat it in other respects as a black box.

---

[2]The name *"spect"* is derived from the term "spectacles", i.e., a means to provide the user with a clearer view on things.

3.2 Data Model

In the previous section we have informally introduced the concepts of a sile, its characteristics, and the various annotation classes that can be applied to siles. In the following we give a formal notion of siles and annotations by defining them in terms of sets. We start this by introducing a number of symbols that we use throughout this section.

Definition 1 [Symbols]

Let Σ denote the set of all siles in the university of discourse. Let $\mathbb{LIT}$ denote the set of all *string literals* which are finite sequences of characters from an *literal alphabet* α, and $\mathbb{B}$ the set of all *content literals* which are finite sequences of characters from an *content alphabet* β. Further, let $\mathbb{URI}$ denote the set of all *Uniform Resource Identifiers (URIs)*[3]. Let $\mathbb{T}$ denote the set of all *tags*, $\mathbb{T} \subseteq \mathbb{LIT}$, Let $\mathbb{C}$ denote the set of all *categories*, $\mathbb{C} \subseteq \mathbb{URI}$, and let $\mathbb{A}$ denote the set of all *attributes*, $\mathbb{A} = \mathbb{URI} \times \mathbb{LIT} \times \mathbb{URI}$. and let $\mathbb{L}$ denote the set of all *slinks*, $\mathbb{L} = \mathbb{URI} \times \mathbb{URI}$. Let $\mathbb{ANN}$ denote the set of *annotations*, $\mathbb{ANN} = \mathbb{T} \cup \mathbb{A} \cup \mathbb{C} \cup \mathbb{L}$, and let $\mathbb{SP}$ denote the set of all *spects*, as described in Section 3.1.6. Finally, let $\mathbb{ENT} = \Sigma \cup \mathbb{ANN} \cup \mathbb{SP}$ denote the set of all *entities*. Using this vocabulary, we can describe the data structures, constraints, and operations that constitute our data model.

Definition 2 [Siles]

A sile $s \in \Sigma$ is a six-tuple $s = (u_s, b_s, T_s, C_s, A_s, L_s)$. $u_s \in \mathbb{URI}$ denotes the *URI* (Uniform Resource Identifier) of sile s, $b_s \in \mathbb{B} \cup \bot$ denotes the sile's *binary content*, $T_s \subseteq \mathbb{T}$ is the set of the sile's associated *tags*, $C_s \subseteq \mathbb{C}$ is the set of the sile's associated *categories*, $A_s \subseteq \mathbb{A}$ the set of the sile's associated *attributes*, and $L_s \subseteq \mathbb{L}$ is the set of the sile's associated *slinks*. The set $ANN_s = T_s \cup A_s \cup C_s \cup L_s$ subsumes all annotations that are associated to s.

A sile $s \in \Sigma$ is uniquely identified by its URI u_s, hence the sile's URI u_s is a functional property of the sile:

$$\forall s_i, s_j \in \Sigma : u_{s_i} = u_{s_j} \longleftrightarrow s_i = s_j$$

This equality is the sole criterion that allows one to decide whether two given sile entities actually are *equal*. Especially does the sile model neither state that siles that share the same annotations (as described below) are considered equal, nor that siles are considered equal if they have equal content.

---
[3]URIs are treated as opaque identifiers and should be formatted according to [BLFM05].

Within the sile model, we do not impose constraints on the structure or the nature of a sile's binary content. Especially we do not define rules that state how the content is to be interpreted, or how one can deduce annotations from analyzing the content. Sile content may also be of arbitrary length, including zero.

Two examples of siles, an email message and a file, are depicted in Figure 3.1.

Definition 3 [Tags]

As annotations we denote the organizational metaphors of the sile data model that describe siles and bring them into context. As described above, annotations can be of four types: *tags, categories, attributes,* and *slinks*.

A tag is described and identified by a string literal and carries no further machine-processable semantics. Hence a tag associates a sile with a plain literal string, and it is sufficient to describe a tag $t \in \mathbb{T}$ by such a simple literal: $\mathbb{T} \subseteq \mathbb{LIT}$.

We consider two tags t_a and t_b as equal if their plain literal strings are equal, which in turn is the case if *(i)* they are of the same length, $length(t_a) = length(t_b)$, and *(ii)* each character on position i of tag t_a is equal to the character on position i of tag t_b, $char(t_a, i) = char(t_b, i), 1 \leq i \leq length(t_a)$.

Definition 4 [Categories]

As described before, a category annotation is a reference to an abstract concept entity that may carry machine-processable semantics, which in turn may be used to validate a data model or to enrich a set of annotations with implicit (derived) annotations. To ensure uniqueness, a category c is identified by a URI: $c \in \mathbb{C}, \mathbb{C} \subset \mathbb{URI}$.

It is obvious that categories are considered as equal if their URIs are equal[4]. We externalize any further details regarding the nature of categories, including semantic relationships to other categories, attributes and slinks, and annotation aspects, like e.g., human-readable labels or comments, from categories; instead, spects (see below) and domain-specific extensions can be employed for this purpose.

Definition 5 [Attributes]

In contrast to tags and categories, attributes are tuples of three elements: the *attribute name* identifies the characteristic that is described by the attribute. The *attribute value* represents the actual manifestation of the attribute with respect to the

---

[4]According to [BLFM05], URI equality is defined as string equality applied to the URIs' absolute forms

Example. A number of email messages on a personal desktop computer can be regarded as siles. By default, email messages carry unique *message-ids* which constitute the respective sile URIs. The bodies of the messages can be regarded as sile contents; the mail folder where the message is stored and its read/unread status can be attached to the message as tag. Metadata about the message (like the subject, sender and recipient, and the date of delivery) can be represented as attributes and slinks.

Such mail messages may be represented as follows[a]:

s_1 = (`msg:0BBF7468-7C34-4587-97E0-D8DB9E8CBDD9@univie.ac.at`,

"Sehr geehrte Damen und Herren, [...]",

{"INBOX","unread"}, {nmo:Email},

{(nmo:subject,"LV-Evaluierung SS 2009",xsd:string),

(nmo:receivedDate,"2009-04-05T16:54",xsd:dateTime)},

{(nmo:from,mailto:wolfgang.klas@univie.ac.at),

(nmo:to,mailto:bernhard.schandl@univie.ac.at)})

Similarly, a file in a file system may be represented using the sile model, whereas its URI is constructed using its absolute path[b]. In this example, no tags or slinks are attached, and the set of attributes is restricted to the file name and its creation date:

s_2 = (urn:uuid:c6b18466-eab4-4943-8699-62eb6dc229d9,

"\documentclass{report} [...]",{},{nfo:FileDataObject},

{(nfo:fileName,"file:///Users/bs/work/phd/phd.tex",xsd:string),

(nfo:fileCreated,"2008-11-07T12:41",xsd:dateTime)},{})

---

[a]For the examples we use prefixed QName notation ([BHLT06], Section 4) for URIs; annotation URIs refer to the NEPOMUK Semantic Desktop ontologies [MSSvE07].

[b]Note that we consider the usage of mutable file paths as URIs (which are meant to be immutable) as harmful practice [SH09].

Figure 3.1: Representation of mail messages and files using the sile model

sile, and the *attribute data type* identifies a rule set that describes the lexical value space (i.e., the set of literal strings that are valid for this attribute) as well as the intended interpretation of the value literal.

We use URIs to describe the attribute name and the attribute data type; hence the set of all possible attributes is $\mathbb{A} = \mathbb{URI} \times \mathbb{LIT} \times \mathbb{URI}$, and an attribute a can be written as 3-tuple: $a = (an_a, av_a, at_a)$, with $an_a \in \mathbb{URI}$, $av_a \in \mathbb{LIT}$, and $at_a \in \mathbb{URI}$.

Again, we do not associate to attributes formal rules regarding the interpretation and restriction of attribute names or attribute values and data types. For the former we outsource this description to spects and application-specific extensions of the data model; for the latter we follow the RDF semantics regarding data types which are defined in Section 5 of [Hay04].

Definition 6 [Slinks]

A slink $l \in \mathbb{L}$ relates a sile to another sile, whereas the nature of the slink is identified by the *slink name*. A slink can be regarded as a directed labeled edge in a graph, where siles form the graph nodes. Each slink leads from a *source sile* to a *target sile*, whereas the slink is attached to the source sile and carries a reference URI to the target sile. We use a URI for the name (the label) of the slink. Therefore, the set of all slinks $\mathbb{L}$ is the cartesian product of the set of all URIs and the set of all siles: $\mathbb{L} = \mathbb{URI} \times \mathbb{URI}$, and a slink l can be written as $l = (ln_l, ld_l)$, with $ln_l, ld_l \in \mathbb{URI}$.

As mentioned in the previous section, slinks and attributes share some common properties. Slinks can be seen as a special case of attributes whose value is a URI that references a sile. For this reason consider slinks first-class annotations, since they help to construct a *web* of siles and allow—in a metaphorical sense—to interconnect the otherwise separate data units.

Definition 7 [Spects]

Spects are used to define *applicability rules* for annotations. Applicability rules restrict the set of possible relationships between siles and annotations, and define when a given constellation can be regarded as consistent. Such consistency rules can be employed by a repository implementation *(1)* to ensure the internal consistency of its data model, *(2)* to infer new (implicit) annotations from existing ones, and by a client application in order *(3)* to restrict the set of possible annotation opportunities presented to the end user.

A spect $sp_i \in \mathbb{SP}$ defines four classes of applicability rules; *Category Hierarchy Rules*, *Attribute Applicability Rules*, *Slink Domain Applicability Rules*, and *Slink Range*

Applicability Rules.

Category Hierarchy Rules define subsumption rules between categories; in this sense, categories can be interpreted as classes from set theory. A category hierarchy rule $chr \in sp_i$ defines a relationship between two categories; thus it can be written as two-tuple $chr \in \mathbb{C} \times \mathbb{C}$. The semantic interpretation of a category hierarchy rules is as follows: if a sile s is annotated with category c_1, and the category hierarchy rule $chr_i = \{c_1, c_2\}$ exists in any known spect sp_i, sile s is also annotated with category c_2:

$$\forall s \in \Sigma, sp_i \in \mathbb{SP} : c_1 \in C_s \wedge \{c_1, c_2\} \in sp_i \longrightarrow c_2 \in C_s$$

Category hierarchy rules are *transitive*:

$$\forall sp_i \in \mathbb{SP} : \{c_1, c_2\}, \{c_2, c_3\} \in sp_i \longrightarrow \{c_1, c_3\} \in sp_i$$

Attribute Applicability Rules establish formal relationships between categories and attribute names: an Attribute Applicability Rule between an attribute name *an* and a category *c* states that a sile that is annotated with attribute *an* is also annotated with category *c*:

$$\forall s \in \Sigma, sp_i \in \mathbb{SP} : (an, av, at) \in A_s \wedge \{an, c\} \in sp_i \longrightarrow c \in C_s$$

A *Slink Domain Applicability Rule* between a slink name *ln* and a category *c* defines that a sile that is annotated with a slink with name *ln* it is also annotated with category *c*:

$$\forall s \in \Sigma, sp_i \in \mathbb{SP} : (ln, ld) \in L_s \wedge \{ln, c\} \in sp_i \longrightarrow c \in C_s$$

A *Slink Range Applicability Rule* between a slink name *ln* and a category *c* defines that a sile that is the destination of a slink with name *ln* is also annotated with category *c*:

$$\forall s, \overline{s} \in \Sigma, sp_i \in \mathbb{SP} : (ln, s) \in L_{\overline{s}} \wedge \{ln, c\} \in sp_i \longrightarrow c \in C_s$$

Examples for all classes of rules in the context of email messages are given in Figure 3.2.

Definition 8 [Repositories]

As described in Section 3.1.6, a repository is a closed context of interpretation, within which a set of entities (siles, annotations, spects) are considered to be valid. A repository indicates thus a set of entities that are considered as a separate, self-contained, and logically consistent knowledge corpus.

Example. A spect SP_{mail} describing the annotation vocabulary for e-mail communication may define the following rules. It defines a number of category hierarchy rules, amongst them the relationship between abstracts messages, email messages, and attachments:

$$\begin{aligned}CHR_{mail} = \{&(\texttt{nmo:Email}, \texttt{nmo:Message}),\\&(\texttt{nmo:Message}, \texttt{nie:InformationElement}),\\&(\texttt{nfo:Attachment}, \texttt{nie:InformationElement}), \ldots\}\end{aligned}$$

Using the following attribute applicability rules, attribute names are related to category names:

$$\begin{aligned}AAR_{mail} = \{&(\texttt{nmo:sentDate}, \texttt{nmo:Message}),\\&(\texttt{nmo:receivedDate}, \texttt{nmo:Message}),\\&(\texttt{nmo:messageSubject}, \texttt{nmo:Message}), \ldots\}\end{aligned}$$

Slink domain and range applicability rules define the relationship between category names and slink names:

$$\begin{aligned}SDAR_{mail} = \{&(\texttt{nmo:from}, \texttt{nmo:Message}),\\&(\texttt{nmo:to}, \texttt{nmo:Message}),\\&(\texttt{nmo:hasAttachment}, \texttt{nmo:Message}),\\&(\texttt{nmo:cc}, \texttt{nmo:Email}), \ldots\}\end{aligned}$$

$$\begin{aligned}SRAR_{mail} = \{&(\texttt{nmo:from}, \texttt{nco:Contact}),\\&(\texttt{nmo:to}, \texttt{nco:Contact}),\\&(\texttt{nmo:hasAttachment}, \texttt{nfo:Attachment}),\\&(\texttt{nmo:cc}, \texttt{nco:Contact}), \ldots\}\end{aligned}$$

Figure 3.2: A spect defining rules for the relationship between email categories and attributes

A repository $R \in \rho$ (where ρ denotes the set of all repositories) can be written as a 7-tuple $R = (\Sigma_{Rh}, \Sigma_{Rr}, \mathbb{T}_R, \mathbb{C}_R, \mathbb{A}_R, \mathbb{L}_R, \mathbb{SP}_R)$. It consists of a set of hosted siles Σ_{Rh} and a set of referenced siles Σ_{Rr}, which together form the set of the repository's known siles $\Sigma_R = \Sigma_{Rh} \cup \Sigma_{Rr}$. It further consists of sets of tags ($\mathbb{T}_R \subseteq \mathbb{T}$), categories ($\mathbb{C}_R \subseteq \mathbb{C}$), attributes ($\mathbb{A}_R \subseteq \mathbb{A}$), and slinks ($\mathbb{L}_R \subseteq \mathbb{L}$). Additionally, it consists of a set of spects $\mathbb{SP}_R \subseteq \mathbb{SP}$ that define the applicability rules that this repository applies to annotations, as described before.

A sile may be *hosted* in a given repository, or it may be *referenced* which means that it is interpreted as a pointer to a sile that is hosted in a different repository. We distinguish these two classes of siles based on the presence or absence of content: in the case of hosted siles, a content is present (although it may be of zero length); in the case of referenced siles, no content is present. Instead, the content may be retrieved by dereferencing the sile URI[5].

Thus, the set of all siles that exist within a given repository R (denoted by Σ_R, $\Sigma_R \in \Sigma$) can be separated into two subsets, the set of all siles that are hosted by this repository Σ_{Rh} and the set of all siles that represent references to siles hosted in other repositories Σ_{Rr}. Thus, the following rules hold for all siles stored within a repository:

$$\forall s \in \Sigma_R : b_s \neq \bot \longleftrightarrow s \in \Sigma_{Rh}, s \notin \Sigma_{Rr}$$

$$\forall s \in \Sigma_R : b_s = \bot \longleftrightarrow s \in \Sigma_{Rr}, s \notin \Sigma_{Rh}$$

The sets of hosted and referenced siles are disjunct,

$$\forall R \in \rho : \Sigma_{Rh} \cap \Sigma_{Rr} = \emptyset$$

and no siles other than hosted or referenced ones exist in a repository:

$$\forall R \in \rho : \Sigma_R \setminus (\Sigma_{Rh} \cup \Sigma_{Rr}) = \emptyset$$

We interpret the term "repository" in a broad manner: every system whose information can be represented within the sile model can be referred to as repository[6]. Since

---

[5]The procedure of dereferencing URIs is out of the scope of the abstract sile model, and depends on the format of the sile URI: for `http` URIs, dereferencing means to establish a connection to a remote HTTP server and to retrieve the content using e.g., a HTTP `GET` call. `imap` URIs may be dereferenced by establishing a connection to the respective IMAP server, and so forth. More details on the process of dereferencing in the context of the World Wide Web are given in [JW05], Section 3.1.

[6]In this context we refer to Chapter 7 where a number of such implementations are discussed.

siles are identified by URIs, every piece of information that can be identified by an URI can potentially become a sile, and its physical location can be regarded as sile repository.

The design of the sile model and the concept of repositories provide the possibility to make assertions about the same information on different places: while repository R_1 may hold the actual content of a sile, repository R_2 may hold annotations that have been extracted by analyzing the sile content, and repository R_3 may store user-defined annotations (e.g., tags) for the sile. While these data may share no common semantics, and their repositories may apply different storage technologies, these different pieces of information are still connected through the unique identifier of the sile, its URI.

3.3 A Query Framework for Siles

The definitions given in the previous section describe the *static data model* for siles. This model represents a framework that structures siles, their contents, and their annotations for further processing. In the following we describe generic abstract operators that use the elements from the sile data model. These operators are designed to be simple to understand and use, but can be combined and nested in order to formulate complex operations and queries.

In the following, we define three operator types:

- *Entity Extraction Operators* extract information parts out of entities; i.e., they provide access to the parts of entity tuples;

- *Entity Existence Operators* indicate whether a specific information entity exists; i.e., whether a tuple (or a combination of tuples) exists that represents a specific information constellation; and

- *Sile Selection Operators* select, from a set of siles, a subset that fulfils certain criteria.

The combination of these operators allows us to model complex expressions over the sile data model that can be used to retrieve information, decide whether siles fulfil certain required information constellations, and restrict sets of siles based on these decisions.

3.3.1 Prerequisites

Definition 9 [Basic Definitions]

Let $\mathbb{BOOL} = \{true, false\}$ denote the Boolean set, and let $\mathcal{P}(A) = \{x \mid x \subseteq A\}$ denote the powerset (i.e., the set of all subsets) of A.

3.3.2 Entity Extraction Operators

Entity extraction operators extract specific information from an entity. As each entity is described by several different characteristics, we need these extraction operators to be able to process these individual items.

Definition 10 [Sile Extraction Operators]

As described before, a sile s can be written as 6-tuple $s = (u_s, b_s, T_s, A_s, C_s, L_s)$. We define the following operators that extract the individual parts of these tuples as follows:

$$uri : \Sigma \mapsto \mathbb{URI}, uri(s) = u_s$$

$$content : \Sigma \mapsto \mathbb{B}, content(s) = b_s$$

$$tags : \Sigma \mapsto \mathcal{P}(\mathbb{T}), tags(s) = T_s$$

$$attributes : \Sigma \mapsto \mathcal{P}(\mathbb{A}), attributes(s) = A_s$$

$$categories : \Sigma \mapsto \mathcal{P}(\mathbb{C}), categories(s) = C_s$$

$$slinks : \Sigma \mapsto \mathcal{P}(\mathbb{L}), slinks(s) = L_s$$

We additionally introduce one extraction operator that returns all sile annotations, regardless of which type they are:

$$annotations : \Sigma \mapsto \mathcal{P}(\mathbb{ANN}), annotations(s) = T_s \cup A_s \cup C_s \cup L_s$$

Definition 11 [Annotation Extraction Operators]

For the atomic annotation types (tags and categories) we define two auxiliary operators that return the annotation's identifying characteristic (i.e., the tag label or the category URI, respectively). Since tags and categories only consist of one element, the definition of these extraction operators is straightforward:

$$text : \mathbb{T} \mapsto \mathbb{LIT}, text(t) = t$$

$$catname : \mathbb{C} \mapsto \mathbb{URI}, catname(c) = c$$

For the annotation types that are not atomic (attributes and slinks) we need operators to extract their parts. For attributes we define the following extraction operators:

$$attname : \mathbb{A} \mapsto \mathbb{URI}, attname(a) = an_a$$

$$attvalue : \mathbb{A} \mapsto \mathbb{LIT}, attvalue(a) = av_a$$

$$atttype : \mathbb{A} \mapsto \mathbb{URI}, atttype(a) = at_a$$

Similarily, for slinks we define:

$$slinkname : \mathbb{L} \mapsto \mathbb{URI}, slinkname(l) = ln_l$$

$$slinkdst : \mathbb{L} \mapsto \mathbb{URI}, slinkdst(l) = ld_l$$

Finally, we define a generic URI extraction operator $uri : \mathbb{ANN} \mapsto \mathbb{URI} \cup \{\bot\}$ that can be applied to all types of annotations:

$$uri(e) = \begin{cases} catname(e) & \text{if } e \in \mathbb{C} \\ attname(e) & \text{if } e \in \mathbb{A} \\ slinkname(e) & \text{if } e \in \mathbb{L} \\ \bot & \text{otherwise} \end{cases}$$

We can see that the *uri* operator returns a URI that can be used to identify the nature of the annotation for all types of annotations except tags. The result of this operator can, in general, *not* be used to compare annotations for equality, since for this all characteristics of an annotation must be considered.

To accomplish this, we introduce the annotation generic comparison operator $equals : \mathbb{ANN} \times \mathbb{ANN} \mapsto \mathbb{BOOL}$ that indicates whether two annotations are equal:

$$equals(e_1, e_2) := \begin{cases} true & \text{if } e_1, e_2 \in \mathbb{T} \wedge text(e_1) = text(e_2) \\ & \text{or } e_1, e_2 \in \mathbb{C} \wedge catname(e_1) = catname(e_2) \\ & \text{or } e_1, e_2 \in \mathbb{A} \wedge attname(e_1) = attname(e_2) \wedge \\ & \quad attvalue(e_1) = attvalue(e_2) \wedge atttype(e_1) = atttype(e_2) \\ & \text{or } e_1, e_2 \in \mathbb{L} \wedge slinkname(e_1) = slinkname(e_2) \wedge \\ & \quad slinkdst(e_1) = slinkdst(e_2) \\ false & \text{otherwise} \end{cases}$$

We also introduce a generic comparison operator $equalsIgnore : \text{ANN} \times \text{ANN} \mapsto \text{BOOL}$ that compares annotations without considering certain components, i.e., the value and data type in the case of attributes, and the destination sile in the case of slinks. For tags and categories, $equalsIgnore$ returns the same result as $equals$:

$$equalsIgnore(e_1, e_2) = \begin{cases} equals(e_1, e_2) & \text{if } e_1, e_2 \in \mathbb{T} \cup \mathbb{C} \\ true & \text{if } e_1, e_2 \in \mathbb{A} \wedge attname(e_1) = attname(e_2) \\ & \text{or } e_1, e_2 \in \mathbb{L} \wedge slinkname(e_1) = slinkname(e_2) \\ false & \text{otherwise} \end{cases}$$

3.3.3 Entity Existence Predicates

In comparison to the entity extraction operators which return specific parts of entities, i.e., siles or annotations, in the following we discuss *existence predicates*. These predicates indicate whether a specific data constellation is given in the context of interpretation, and correspondingly return a Boolean value (*true* or *false*). The context of interpretation Γ depends on the application: it may be a single repository R ($\Gamma = R$) or an arbitrary number of repositories $R_1, R_2, \ldots, R_n$, in which case the operators consider the union of all their annotations ($\Gamma = \bigcup_{i=1}^{n} R_i$). The context of interpretation can then be written as 7-tuple that subsumes all elements of the considered repositories $R_i, i = 1 \ldots n$:

$$\Gamma = (\Sigma_{\Gamma h}, \Sigma_{\Gamma r}, \mathbb{T}_\Gamma, \mathbb{C}_\Gamma, \mathbb{A}_\Gamma, \mathbb{L}_\Gamma, \mathbb{SP}_\Gamma)$$
$$= (\bigcup_{i=1}^{n} \Sigma_{R_i h}, \bigcup_{i=1}^{n} \Sigma_{R_i r}, \bigcup_{i=1}^{n} \mathbb{T}_{R_i}, \bigcup_{i=1}^{n} \mathbb{C}_{R_i}, \bigcup_{i=1}^{n} \mathbb{A}_{R_i}, \bigcup_{i=1}^{n} \mathbb{L}_{R_i}, \bigcup_{i=1}^{n} \mathbb{SP}_{R_i})$$

In the following, a $\cdot_\Gamma$ index indicates that all operators are defined with respect to a given context of interpretation Γ.

Definition 12 [Sile Existence Predicate]

We start with the very basic definition of a sile existence predicate, $exists_\Gamma : \Sigma \mapsto \text{BOOL}$ which returns whether a given sile exists in the context of interpretation, either in the form of a hosted or a referenced sile:

$$exists_\Gamma(s) = \begin{cases} true & \text{if } \exists R, R \in \Gamma \mid s \in \Sigma_R \\ false & \text{otherwise} \end{cases}$$

Definition 13 [Annotation Existence Predicates]

We can now define predicates that indicate whether a specific combination of entities (i.e., siles and annotations) is present in the context of interpretation. As the most generic predicate, $hasAnnotation_\Gamma : \Sigma \times \text{ANN} \mapsto \mathbb{BOOL}$ indicates whether a sile is annotated with a specific annotation by using the *annotations* operator:

$$hasAnnotation_\Gamma(s, a) = \begin{cases} true & \text{if } exists_\Gamma(s) \land a \in annotations(s) \\ false & \text{otherwise} \end{cases}$$

Also we define a predicate $existsAnnotation_\Gamma : \text{ANN} \mapsto \mathbb{BOOL}$ that indicates whether there exists any sile in the context of interpretation that is associated with a specific annotation:

$$existsAnnotation_\Gamma(a) = \begin{cases} true & \text{if } \exists s \mid exists_\Gamma(s) \land hasAnnotation_\Gamma(s, a) = true \\ false & \text{otherwise} \end{cases}$$

Additionally, we can define such annotation existence predicates for specific types of annotations. As tags and categories are atomic annotations, there is no need for type-specific definitions; instead we can directly reuse the already defined $hasAnnotation_\Gamma$ operator to define $hasTag_\Gamma$ and $hasCategory_\Gamma$,

$$hasTag_\Gamma : \Sigma \times \mathbb{T} \mapsto \mathbb{BOOL}, hasTag_\Gamma(s, t) = hasAnnotation_\Gamma(s, t)$$

$$hasCategory_\Gamma : \Sigma \times \mathbb{C} \mapsto \mathbb{BOOL}, hasCategory_\Gamma(s, c) = hasAnnotation_\Gamma(s, c)$$

as well as $existsTag_\Gamma$ and $existsCategory_\Gamma$:

$$existsTag_\Gamma : \mathbb{T} \mapsto \mathbb{BOOL}, existsTag_\Gamma(t) = existsAnnotation_\Gamma(t)$$

$$existsCategory_\Gamma : \mathbb{C} \mapsto \mathbb{BOOL}, existsCategory_\Gamma(c) = existsAnnotation_\Gamma(c)$$

For attributes and slinks, we must go into more detail since it should be possible to query for siles based on each individual part of an annotation. Hence, we define three variants of the $hasAttribute_\Gamma$ predicate:

- $hasAttributeName_\Gamma : \Sigma \times \mathbb{A} \mapsto \mathbb{BOOL}$ indicates whether a sile is annotated with an attribute that has given name, ignoring the attribute value and the attribute data type:

$$hasAttributeName_\Gamma(s, a) = \begin{cases} true & \text{if } \exists a' \mid exists_\Gamma(s) \land a' \in A_s \\ & \land\ attname(a) = attname(a') \\ false & \text{otherwise} \end{cases}$$

- $hasAttributeValue_\Gamma : \Sigma \times \mathbb{A} \mapsto \mathbb{BOOL}$ indicates whether a sile is annotated with an attribute that has a given value and data type, ignoring the attribute name:

$$hasAttributeValue_\Gamma(s, a) = \begin{cases} true & \text{if } \exists a' \mid exists_\Gamma(s) \wedge a' \in A_s \\ & \wedge\ attvalue(a) = attvalue(a') \\ & \wedge\ atttype(a) = atttype(a') \\ false & \text{otherwise} \end{cases}$$

- $hasAttributeNameValue_\Gamma : \Sigma \times \mathbb{A} \mapsto \mathbb{BOOL}$ indicates whether a sile is annotated with an attribute whose name, value, and data type are equal to the respective elements of the specified attribute. This operator is equal to the $hasAnnotation_\Gamma$ operator when applied to an attribute:

$$hasAttributeNameValue_\Gamma(s, a) = \begin{cases} hasAnnotation_\Gamma(s, a) & \text{if } a \in \mathbb{A} \\ false & \text{otherwise} \end{cases}$$

As an alias, we also define the predicate $hasAttribute_\Gamma : \Sigma \times \mathbb{A} \mapsto \mathbb{BOOL}$ as being equal to $hasAttributeNameValue_\Gamma$:

$$hasAttribute_\Gamma(s, a) = hasAttributeNameValue_\Gamma(s, a)$$

Correspondingly, we can define three variants of the $hasSlink_\Gamma$ predicate that consider the separate parts of slink annotations:

- $hasSlinkName_\Gamma : \Sigma \times \mathbb{L} \mapsto \mathbb{BOOL}$ indicates whether a sile is annotated with a slink that has a given name, ignoring the destination sile:

$$hasSlinkName_\Gamma(s, l) = \begin{cases} true & \text{if } \exists l' \mid exists_\Gamma(s) \wedge l' \in L_s \\ & \wedge slinkname(l) = slinkname(l') \\ false & \text{otherwise} \end{cases}$$

- $hasSlinkDestination_\Gamma : \Sigma \times \mathbb{L} \mapsto \mathbb{BOOL}$ indicates whether a sile is annotated with a slink with a given destination sile, ignoring the slink name:

$$hasSlinkDestination_\Gamma(s, l) = \begin{cases} true & \text{if } \exists l' \mid exists_\Gamma(s) \wedge l' \in L_s \\ & \wedge slinkdst(l) = slinkdst(l') \\ false & \text{otherwise} \end{cases}$$

- $hasSlinkNameDestination_\Gamma : \Sigma \times \mathbb{L} \mapsto \mathbb{BOOL}$ indicates whether a sile is annotated with a slink that has a given name and destination sile:

$$hasSlinkNameDestination_\Gamma(s,l) = \begin{cases} true & \text{if } \exists l' \mid exists_\Gamma(s) \wedge l' \in L_s \\ & \wedge\ slinkname(l) = slinkname(l') \\ & \wedge\ slinkdst(l) = slinkdst(l') \\ false & \text{otherwise} \end{cases}$$

In analogy to $hasAttribute_\Gamma$ we define the predicate $hasSlink_\Gamma : \Sigma \times \mathbb{S} \mapsto \mathbb{BOOL}$ which is an alias for $hasSlinkNameDestination_\Gamma$:

$$hasSlink_\Gamma(s,l) = hasSlinkNameDestination_\Gamma(s,l)$$

Based on the slink existence predicates $hasSlinkName_\Gamma$ and $hasSlink_\Gamma$, we can define two predicates that indicate whether siles are slinked to each other. We can define $areDirectedRelated_\Gamma : \Sigma \times \Sigma \mapsto \mathbb{BOOL}$ that indicates whether a sile s_s is annotated with a slink to another sile s_d, whereas u_{s_d} denotes the URI of sile s_d:

$$areDirectedRelated_\Gamma(s_s, s_d) = \begin{cases} true & \text{if } \exists l \mid exists_\Gamma(s_s) \wedge exists_\Gamma(s_d) \\ & \wedge\ l \in slinks(s_s) \wedge slinkdst(l) = u_{s_d} \\ false & \text{otherwise} \end{cases}$$

In addition to the *directed* variant we also define an *undirected* variant $areRelated_\Gamma : \Sigma \times \Sigma \mapsto \mathbb{BOOL}$ that indicates whether two siles are related, regardless of the direction of the slink:

$$areRelated_\Gamma(s_a, s_b) = \begin{cases} true & \text{if } areDirectedRelated_\Gamma(s_a, s_b) = true \\ & \vee\ areDirectedRelated_\Gamma(s_b, s_a) = true \\ false & \text{otherwise} \end{cases}$$

3.3.4 Sile Selection Operators

Based on the existence operators, we can define operators that *select* siles based on specific criteria. Selection operators are always applied to a base set of siles and return a subset of this set. This subset contains only siles that fulfill specific criteria.

The definition of the selection operators based on the existence predicate is straightforward; basically it is constituted by wrapping each annotation existence predicate by an operator that returns all siles $s_i \in \Sigma$ for which the respective existence predicate is *true*. Thus we give here only a list of all operators without further explanation.

$TagSiles : \mathcal{P}(\Sigma) \times \mathbb{T} \mapsto \mathcal{P}(\Sigma)$
$TagSiles(S, t) = \{s_i \in S \mid hasTag(s_i, t) = true\}$

$CategorySiles : \mathcal{P}(\Sigma) \times \mathbb{C} \mapsto \mathcal{P}(\Sigma)$
$CategorySiles(S, c) = \{s_i \in S \mid hasCategory(s_i, c) = true\}$

$AttributeNameSiles : \mathcal{P}(\Sigma) \times \mathbb{A} \mapsto \mathcal{P}(\Sigma)$
$AttributeNameSiles(S, a) = \{s_i \in S \mid hasAttributeName(s_i, a) = true\}$

$AttributeValueSiles : \mathcal{P}(\Sigma) \times \mathbb{A} \mapsto \mathcal{P}(\Sigma)$
$AttributeValueSiles(S, a) = \{s_i \in S \mid hasAttributeValue(s_i, a) = true\}$

$AttributeNameValueSiles : \mathcal{P}(\Sigma) \times \mathbb{A} \mapsto \mathcal{P}(\Sigma)$
$AttributeNameValueSiles(S, a) = \{s_i \in S \mid hasAttributeNameValue(s_i, a) = true\}$

$AttributeSiles : \mathcal{P}(\Sigma) \times \mathbb{A} \mapsto \mathcal{P}(\Sigma)$
$AttributeSiles(S, a) = AttributeNameValueSiles(S, a)$

$SlinkNameSiles : \mathcal{P}(\Sigma) \times \mathbb{L} \mapsto \mathcal{P}(\Sigma)$
$SlinkNameSiles(S, l) = \{s_i \in S \mid hasSlinkName(s_i, l) = true\}$

$SlinkDestinationSiles : \mathcal{P}(\Sigma) \times \mathbb{L} \mapsto \mathcal{P}(\Sigma)$
$SlinkDestinationSiles(S, l) = \{s_i \in S \mid hasSlinkDestination(s_i, l) = true\}$

$SlinkSiles : \mathcal{P}(\Sigma) \times \mathbb{L} \mapsto \mathcal{P}(\Sigma)$
$SlinkSiles(S, l) = \{s_i \in S \mid hasSlink(s_i, l) = true\}$

$$DirectedRelatedSiles : \mathcal{P}(\Sigma) \times \Sigma \mapsto \mathcal{P}(\Sigma)$$
$$DirectedRelatedSiles(S, src) = \{s_i \in S \mid areDirectedRelated(src, s_i) = true\}$$

$$RelatedSiles : \mathcal{P}(\Sigma) \times \Sigma \mapsto \mathcal{P}(\Sigma)$$
$$RelatedSiles(S, d) = \{s_i \in S \mid areRelated(s_i, d) = true\}$$

Each of these operators can be applied to a given base set of siles S and returns a result set of siles. This base set could, for instance, be derived from the given context of interpretation: based on the selection of the base set, either only hosted siles ($S = \Sigma_{\Gamma h}$), referenced siles ($S = \Sigma_{\Gamma r}$), or the full set of siles $S = \Sigma_\Gamma = \Sigma_{\Gamma h} \cup \Sigma_{\Gamma r}$ can be used as base set. Alternatively, the operators can be arbitrarily nested in order to form more expressive queries. The following set of boolean operators can be used to state combinations of selection operators:

$$and : \mathcal{P}(\Sigma) \times \mathcal{P}(\Sigma) \mapsto \mathcal{P}(\Sigma) \qquad and(S_1, S_2) = S_1 \cap S_2$$
$$or : \mathcal{P}(\Sigma) \times \mathcal{P}(\Sigma) \mapsto \mathcal{P}(\Sigma) \qquad or(S_1, S_2) = S_1 \cup S_2$$
$$not : \mathcal{P}(\Sigma) \mapsto \mathcal{P}(\Sigma) \qquad not(S) = \{s_i \mid s_i \in \Sigma \wedge s_i \notin S\}$$

3.4 Summary

In this section we have discussed the abstract sile model. Its basic constituents are *siles*, which are units of digital contents, and different types of *annotations* that can be attached to siles: *tags* are plain, unstructured keyword strings; *categories* are formally specified classes which are identified by a unique id; *attributes* are typed name/value pairs, and *slinks* are labelled connections between siles. Furthermore we have defined *spects* that are a lightweight notion for ontological knowledge, and our understanding of a *repository*; i.e., a logically closed unit that hosts a set of siles.

The presented query framework for sile data covers all static elements of the sile data model, which were introduced in the previous chapter. It allows one to formulate expressions that evaluate the state of siles and their annotations, i.e., tags, categories, attributes, and slinks. As such it is appropriate to model information needs that arise in concrete applications, and it is suitable to retrieve sile entities that fulfil certain criteria.

However, the model exposes the following limitations:

1. *Restricted Domain* — The query algebra can be only applied to siles, not to other elements of the sile model. It can not be used to query for annotations; e.g., it is not possible to retrieve a list of all tags, or to query which rules are defined within a spect.

2. *No Joins* — The query algebra defines no possibility to join objects; e.g., it is not possible to query for siles that share common, equal annotations.

3. *Unspecified Data Type Semantics* — Attribute annotations contain a URI that identifies the attribute's data type, i.e., the way its value has to be interpreted. Since the query algebra abstracts over concrete data types, it does not define semantics for this interpretation; for instance, it does not specify an ordering for data type values, or arithmetic operators.

4. *No Aggregate Functions* — The algebra does not specify aggregate functions, thus it is not possible to e.g., count the number of siles that fulfil a certain criterion.

We are aware of the fact that the lack of these features may cause problems for certain information needs, and plan to further extend the query language in the future in order to cover additional use cases. Nevertheless we do not want to abandon our goal of providing a model and a query algebra that are simple to understand and to use, and this goal must be considered when designing model extensions.

Chapter 4

An Application Programming Interface for Siles

> *If debugging is the art of removing bugs, then programming must be the art of inserting them.* —
> Unknown

In Chapter 3 we have presented an abstract data model for the representation of siles and their annotations. This data model allows for a comprehensive description of data assets, their annotations, and their relationships. We have also discussed an abstract algebra and a collection of operators and predicates that can be used to analyze and query these information entities. Together they form a found framework to represent semantically enriched information objects, and to retrieve such objects based on their semantic descriptions. However it is the goal of this thesis to provide an infrastructure that allows for interoperable information exchange for desktop applications, which may be both information producers and consumers. In this section, we describe an abstract Application Programming Interface (API) that translates the abstract model into an implementation-centric specification, which can be taken as a reference for implementations. Then, we show how the presented specification can be used in the context of the application scenarios discussed in Section 1.1.

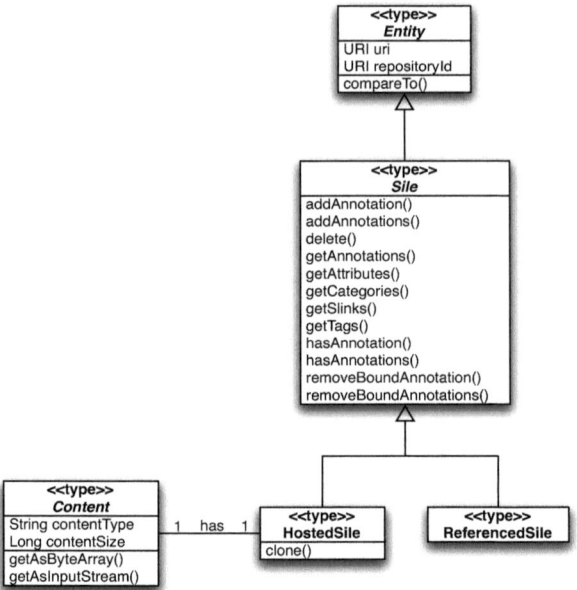

Figure 4.1: Sile type hierarchy

4.1 API Specification

We partition the specification of the Sile Application Programming Interface (API) into three parts. In the first part, *entities*, we describe the main types of the API, their properties, and their methods. In the second part, *filters*, we describe how the generic sile operators and predicates are represented by an object hierarchy. In the third part, *repository*, the methods that have to be implemented by a sile repository are listed and described.

4.1.1 Entities

Entities are the information units in the sile class hierarchy. An entity in the context of the sile model is any object that can be uniquely identified by a URI. No further restrictions are put on an entity's behavior or characteristics.

The `Entity` type is the root of the sile type hierarchy. An entity has two properties; one is a URI that identifies the entity itself; the second one is a reference URI to its *home repository*. Entities must be comparable to ensure safe handling and comparison; hence we include a *compareTo* method.

Siles

An abstract sile tuple $s = (u_s, b_s, T_s, A_s, C_s, L_s)$ (cf. Section 3.2) is mapped to an instance of the type `Sile` (cf. Figure 4.1). This type extends the `Entity` type by methods for adding, retrieving, and removing annotations. We will discuss the type hierarchy for annotations below; for now it is sufficient to say that because different types of annotations have specific characteristics, we introduce individual getter methods for each annotation type to retrieve annotations that fulfill certain criteria.

The `Sile` type allows access to a sile's associated annotations (i.e., the annotation sets contained within a sile tuple, namely T_s, A_s, C_s, and L_s) through the generic methods `addAnnotation()`, `addAnnotations()`, `getAnnotations()`, as well as `removeBoundAnnotation()` and `removeBoundAnnotations()`. Note the naming difference between the `add` methods and the `remove` methods; we will discuss the difference between an `Annotation` and a `BoundAnnotation` below. We also introduce special getter methods for the four different types of annotations, `getAttributes()`, `getCategories()`, `getSlinks()`, and `getTags()`, because these can be used to retrieve sile annotations based on type-specific characteristics. For instance, the `getTags()` method retrieves only those tags that match a defined pattern, specified as regular expression.

The sile URI u_s can be accessed by the inherited `uri` attribute of the `Entity` type. For accessing the content, we have to distinguish between *hosted* and *referenced* siles, for which we introduce sub-types of the `Sile` type, `HostedSile` and `ReferencedSile`. Each `HostedSile` instance holds exactly one reference to a `Content` instance, while instances of the `ReferencedSile` type do not.

Such a content object is characterized by a *contentType* and a *contentSize* property, and the actual content can be accessed as byte array or as input stream, depending on the aspired processing. Through this type, access to the content element b_s in a sile tuple is realized.

The content access mechanism for `ReferencedSile` instances is out of the scope of this specification and may depend on various factors, e.g., the URI scheme of the referenced sile: depending on this scheme, the actual sile content may be accessed by

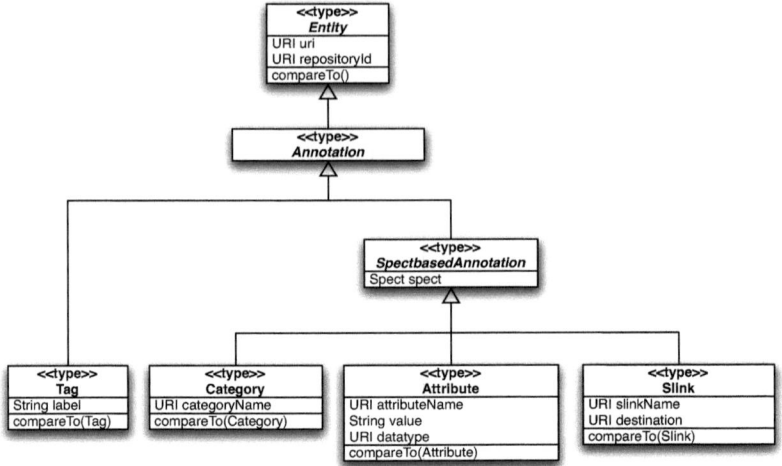

Figure 4.2: Annotation type hierarchy (abstract annotations)

connecting to a remote server, by reading a file from a local file system, or by directly interpreting the URI as content (cf. the `data:` URI scheme [Mas98]).

Furthermore, in contrast to a `ReferencedSile` a `HostedSile` can be cloned. The reason for the impossibility to clone referenced siles is that the URI is used to uniquely identify and distinguish siles. Simultaneously, the URI of referenced siles is the pointer to its hosted equivalent, which resides in another repository. However, if a referenced sile would be cloned, it would receive a new URI, and thus the reference to its hosted counterpart would be lost. In contrast, hosted siles can be cloned by assigning a new URI to the clone, and slinking them to their originals. Because of these restrictions, the `clone()` method is defined only for the class `HostedSile`.

Annotations

As described in Section 3.2, the sile data model describes four types of annotations, *tags, categories, attributes,* and *slinks*. To subsume these types, we model them within

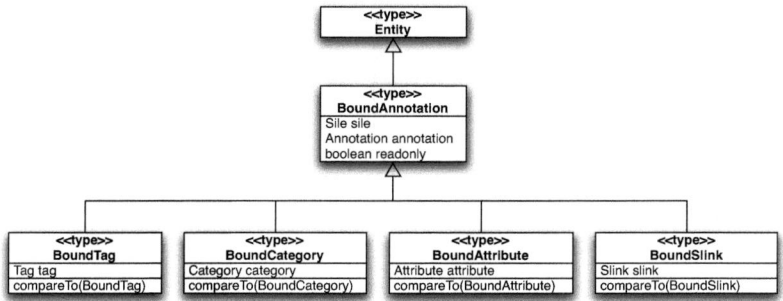

Figure 4.3: Bound annotation type hierarchy

a type hierarchy that is rooted by an abstract `Annotation` type. Additionally, every annotation constitutes an entity, thus `Annotation` is a sub-type of `Entity`[1]. Additionally we introduce the interface `SpectbasedAnnotation` that is used for all annotations that may be related to information defined in a Spect, i.e., for categories, attributes, and relationships (see below).

In addition to the properties and operations inherited from the base classes `Entity` and `Annotation`, the annotation classes provide members and methods for accessing the information that is specific to the respective annotation types. Moreover they provide specific `compareTo` methods to check annotations for equality.

It is important to note that the four annotation classes discussed here represent *generic annotations*, not concrete instances that are attached to a sile. To distinguish the former from the latter, we introduce the hierarchy of *bound annotations*. A bound annotation is an annotation that is attached to a sile. Any instance of `BoundAnnotation` holds a reference to the sile it is attached to (cf. Figure 4.3) as well as to the actual `Annotation` instance it represents (cf. Figure 4.4).

Bound annotations constitute the link between siles and annotations in the API: each instance of `BoundAnnotation` holds a reference to the sile it is attached to; and the annotation getter methods in the `Sile` type return instances of `BoundAnnotation` or its sub-types, respectively.

---

[1] The URI for tags should be minted based on the tag's label.

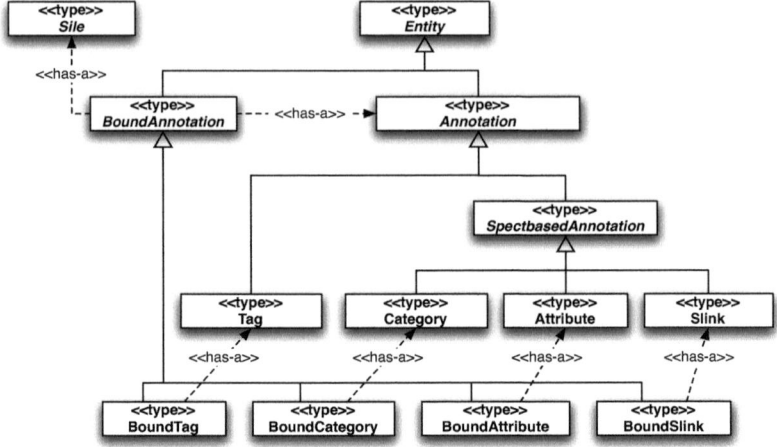

Figure 4.4: Annotation type hierarchy (complete)

4.1.2 Spects

The Sile Application Programming Interface introduces *Spects* as basic notion for a simplified set of semantic constructs. A spect describes a number of relationships between *categories*, *attributes*, and *slinks*, and its main purpose is to provide a (simplified) view on the rules defined in a formal model, e.g., using an ontological language, an entity-relationship model, or an object oriented model, in order to allow a user-friendly representation. These ontological constructs are abstracted and faceted by the Spect interface, and thus can be used to accordingly represent annotation concepts in a user interface, and to ease navigation within potentially large sets of annotation types.

A spect contains three groups of *consistency rules* that a repository may use to validate its set of siles and annotations. The types of rules are reflected by methods defined in the Spect interface as follows:

1. *Category Hierarchy Rules* — In addition to methods that return all categories defined in a spect (`getAllCategories()`) and that retrieve a category identified by a URI (`getCategory()`, the Spect interface defines three methods that can be used to traverse the asserted category hierarchy: `getRootCategories()` returns all

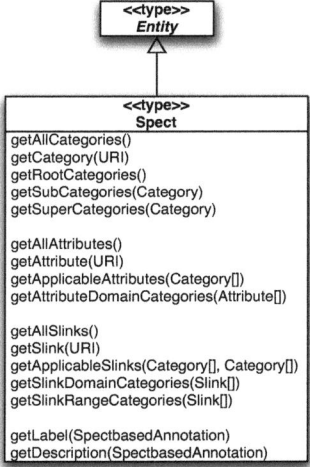

Figure 4.5: Spect type

categories that have no defined super-categories; `getSubCategories()` returns the sub-categories and `getSuperCategories()` returns the super-categories of a given category.

2. *Attribute Applicability Rules* — The spect type defines a method to retrieve all attributes defined by the spect (`getAllAttributes()`) as well as the methods `getApplicableAttributes()` and `getAttributeDomainCategories()`, that reflect the spect's attribute applicability rules.

3. *Slink Domain and Range Applicability Rules* — Spect defines the methods `getApplicableSlinks()`, `getSlinkDomainCategories()`, and `getSlinkRangeCategories()` for these purpose of returning the defined slink domain and range applicability rules, respectively. Additionally, `getAllSlinks()` enumerates all slinks that are defined within the spect.

In addition to these three types of rules, the Spect interface introduces two further rule sets that describe aspects of human-friendly rendering of spect-based annotations, *Entity Label Rules* and *Entity Description Rules*.

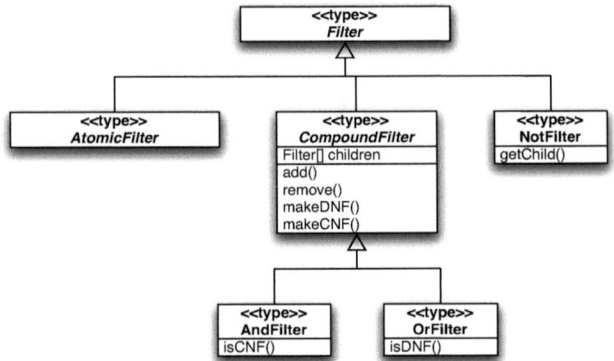

Figure 4.6: Filter type hierarchy (root types)

1. *Entity Label Rules* — A spect may define human-readable labels for all entities defined within the spect. These labels may be used by a user interface to render visual or aural representations of the entity. Note that although it is not formally required, it is recommended that within a spect labels are assigned uniquely to entities. However they should never be used to programmatically distinguish entities; the entity URI is designed for this purpose.

   A user interface may apply the entity URI or a fragment of this to represent an entity if no label is defined for this entity by the spect.

2. *Entity Description Rules* — A spect may define a textual description for all kinds of entities. Such a description text may explain the intention and meaning of entities in a human-readable and -understandable way.

4.1.3 Filters

Filter types are used to model the abstract query algebra described in Section 3.3. A filter is in fact an entity that *matches* siles, depending on certain annotations that are attached to it. In other words, a filter can be used to reduce a given set of siles so that the result set is a subset of the original set, and so that every member of the result set is a sile that matches the criteria specified by the filter.

The Filter API described in the following is designed to be highly generic. It only considers elements from the sile data model (cf. Section 3.2) and is not designed towards a specific implementation. Hence the way the filter API can be implemented depends on the underlying storage architecture; e.g., a given filter can be translated to a query language such as SQL or SPARQL.

The Filter API defines a root type `Filter` which has two sub-types; `AtomicFilter` and `CompoundFilter`. While an atomic filter represents a specific characteristic that can be matched against a sile, compound filters can be used to combine filters and form arbitrarily complex expressions. Currently the API contains two compound filters, `AndFilter` and `OrFilter`. In combination with `NotFilter` (which is modeled as atomic filter, see below), according to De Morgan's laws, every expression consisting of only these compound filter types (and atomic filters) can be transformed into *conjunctive normal form* (CNF) or *disjunctive normal form* (DNF), which is an essential prerequisite for the representation of sile filters in common query languages. Thus the `CompoundFilter` type defines two methods `makeDNF()` and `makeCNF()` that returns semantically equivalent representations of the filter in disjunctive or conjunctive normal form, respectively.

According to the different annotation types (tags, categories, attributes, and slinks), a set of atomic filters are defined and described in the following.

Tag Filters Tags are, in fact, plain string literals, thus the set of tag filters is very limited. In its generic form, a `TagpatternFilter` takes a pattern definition in the form of a regular expression, while the specialized `TagFilter` performs an exact match on the tag string. We choose regular expressions since they are capable of representing a wide area of string patterns, and are also well supported by many storage systems and can thus be translated to concrete query languages.

Category Filters A category is identified by a URI, and consequently this is the only criterion that can be used to restrict siles. The `CategoryFilter` represents such a restriction entity.

Attribute Filters Attribute filters can be used to filter siles by considering combinations of the attribute name and the attribute value (which is always represented as string literal, cf. Section 3.3.4). When filtering for an attribute a, one can con-

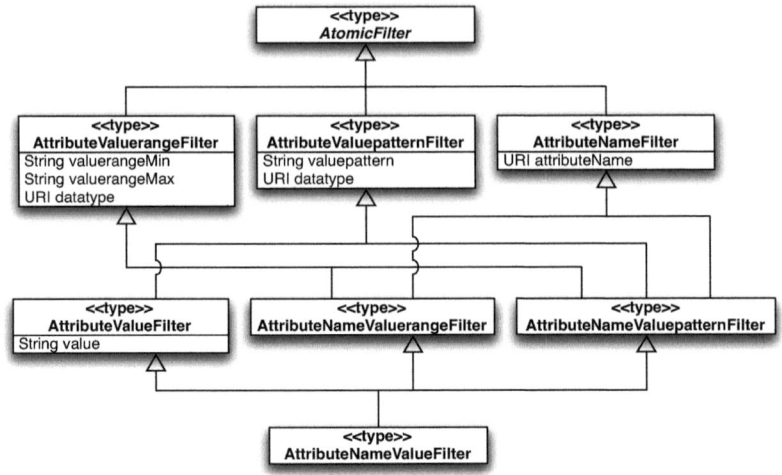

Figure 4.7: Attribute filter type hierarchy

sider the attribute name *attname(a)* or the attribute value and data type combination, *attvalue(a)* and *atttype(a)*. The three basic filters `AttributeValuerangeFilter`, `AttributeValuepatternFilter`, and `AttributeNameFilter` select siles based on their value (which can be represented either by a range or a regular expression pattern) and their name, respectively. By combining these variants, a set of additional attribute filters can be derived (Figure 4.7), with `AttributeNameValueFilter` being the most specialized one: it matches only siles that are annotated with an attribute that has exactly the given name, value and data type.

Slink Filters Sile entities can take two roles within slinks (relationships); either they can be the *source* of the slink (in which case we denote the slink an *outgoing slink*), or it can be the slink's *target* (then, the slink is called *incoming*). Consequently, one can perform searches for incoming and outgoing slinks, or a combination of both.

Slinks are described by their *name* which is expressed as a URI; however this URI can be considered or ignored when searching for slinked siles. We define two classes of filters, `SlinkFilters` and `SileFilters`. The former consider slinks with specific name, while the latter considers slinks with specific source or target siles. Both can be combined to

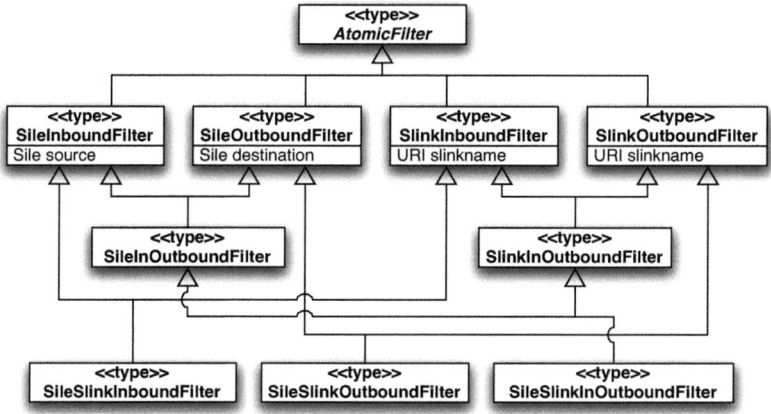

Figure 4.8: Sile and slink filter type hierarchy

a `SileSlinkFilter`, see Figure 4.8.

NotFilter Filter expressions can be *negated* by encapsulating them into a `NotFilter`. A `NotFilter` inverts the sile selection of its child; i.e., it selects all siles that are not selected by its child filter.

Compound Filters Compound filters are used to logically connect other filters, both atomic and compound filters. A compound filter contains a set of sub-filters (called *children*) that are combined by a boolean operator. The `CompoundFilter` type (cf. Figure 4.6) defines two methods, `add()` and `remove()`, that add and remove child filters to the compound filter. We have defined two compound filters, `AndFilter` and `OrFilter`. An `AndFilter` returns the intersection of its children's result sets, while an `OrFilter` returns their union set.

4.1.4 Repository

A *Repository* is an entity that manages instances of the sile data model, i.e., siles, annotations, and spects, and is able to execute queries represented using the filter type hierarchy. It is the central access point for operations on sile data. Thus, the repository interface hides the implementation details from the client application, similar to the file system API of an operating system which hides the details of file storage and physical access from an application that operates with files.

This design allows the repository to wrap different manifestations of siles and annotations. The most important tasks of a repository implementation will be the storage and management of siles and their annotations, as well as the execution of read (search) and update (creation, deletion, modification) operations. However the actual implementation can be freely chosen. A repository can be implemented using a relational database system (RDBMS), RDF triple stores, plain files, or any other technology that is suitable to implement the repository interface. To demonstrate the flexibility and wide applicability of the sile model and its API, three exemplary implementations of the repository interface are discussed in Chapter 7.

The repository interface can also be used to integrate external data sources into the sile model. By doing so, a *mediator-wrapper* architecture (cf. [Has08]) can be built which establishes a unified view on a heterogeneous information landscape. The sile model is designed so that it can capture many different types of information; initial considerations for specific information classes (namely, object-oriented languages and relational databases) are discussed in Section 5.4.

Within such an architecture, a repository can act as a *mediator* that subsumes informations stored in further repositories. Using a combination of mediators and wrappers, an *integrated view* on different, heterogeneous information sources could be established. Typically, personal information is stored not only on one physical device (e.g., the personal desktop computer), but is scattered across multiple systems and is represented in varying forms: in addition to personal siles stored on the local system, there may exist a shared file server for the project team, an IMAP mail server, and a blog service on the web. All these data silos could be wrapped by components that implement the repository interface, and hierarchical mediators can provide integrated views on these wrapped data sources. Such an scenario is depicted in Figure 4.9: here, two mediators are used to integrate different data sources which are related to *private* and *work* information contexts, respectively. These are again integrated by the top-level mediator that subsumes all *personal* information under one consistent view. All wrappers and mediators implement the repository interface and can thus be arbitrarily nested. An application can choose either to use the top-level *personal* mediator, or directly connect to the *private* or *work* mediators, depending on which data set the user intends to work

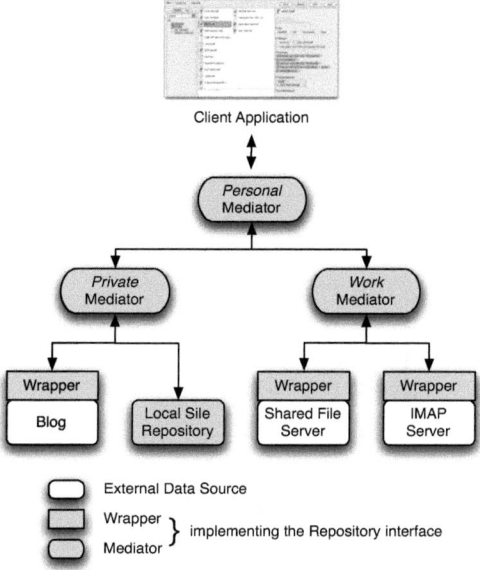

Figure 4.9: Mediator-wrapper architecture using the repository interface

with.

The repository interface itself defines several groups of operations, which are briefly described in the following.

1. *Sile Management.* Siles can be created either as *hosted siles* or as *referenced siles* (cf. Section 4.1.1). The URI of a hosted sile is defined (minted) by the repository where it is created, while the URI of a referenced sile must be specified by the application; consequently, the method createHostedSile() takes no parameter, while createReferencedSile() takes a URI as parameter. Another method to create a new sile is to clone a hosted sile through the cloneSile() method. The conditions under which a cloning can take place are described in Section 4.1.1.

   Siles can be deleted using the deleteSile() method. Deletion of a sile means that both the sile's content and its associated annotations (including its incoming

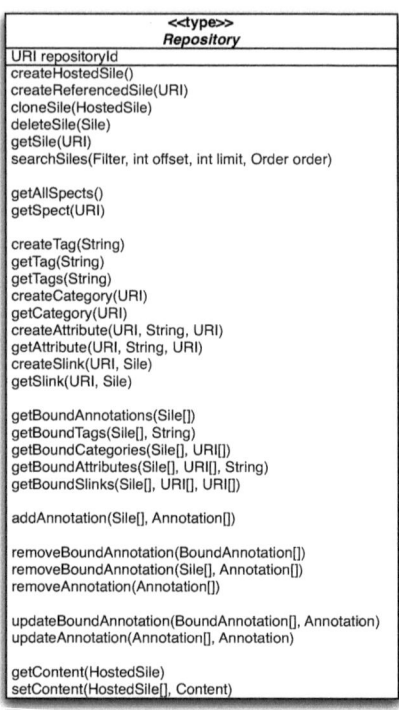

Figure 4.10: Repository type

slinks) are deleted. Note that the deletion of a sile may have effects of external repositories that hold references to the deleted sile: these references become invalid[2].

Siles can be retrieved either directly when their URI is known (via the `getSile()` method), or they can be searched based on filter expressions. As described above, a filter is a possibly nested collection of criteria, and the `searchSiles()` method takes a filter as input and returns a list of siles which meet the specified criteria. Using the `offset` and `limit` parameters, the number of results may be restricted,

---

[2] A synchronization mechanism for sile repositories is out of the scope of this work

similar to the OFFSET and LIMIT clauses of SQL or SPARQL. The order parameter specifies a rule that defines the ordering of the result list[3].

2. *Spects.* The spects registered by the repository can be retrieved by the two methods getAllSpects(), that returns all registered spect, and getSpect(), that returns a specific spect which is identified by a URI. We do not define the procedures to register or un-register spects; currently this is out of the scope of this API. Instead, an application may assume that the set of spects registered in one repository does not change during the repository's lifetime. However, it may be possible that such behavior is defined by later versions of this API, e.g., through the definition of methods that register and un-register spects or to modify spect elements (cf. Section 4.1.2).

3. *Annotation management.* The repository interface defines a create() and get() method for each type of annotation. A client application should use these calls to retrieve instances of annotations before they can be used, e.g., before a sile is annotated. The reason for this design is to ensure that the repository is aware of any annotation instances before they are actually used. Depending on the repository implementation, this helps to maintain internal structures like indices or annotation tables.

The methods createTag(), createCategory(), createAttribute(), and createSlink() are used to create instances of the respective annotations if they do not already exist in the repository. In this context, "exists" means that the annotation has been created before; it does not necessarily imply that the annotation is also *used* (i.e., it is bound to one or more siles). The methods getTag(), getCategory(), getAttribute(), and getSlink() return instances of already existing annotations. All get methods provide parameters that specify the characteristics of the annotation, e.g., the category URI or the attribute value. Additionally, getTags() retrieves multiple tags at once, whereas the tags are selected by a regular expression pattern.

One must distinguish the abovementioned get() methods that return generic annotation instances from the methods that return *bound annotations*, i.e., annotation instances that are attached to a sile. The repository interface provides a generic method getBoundAnnotations(Sile[]) that returns all annota-

---

[3] A number of ordering types are defined by the API; e.g., AttributeValueAscendingOrder. These are not discussed here in more detail

tions that are bound to a set of siles (whereas the set also can consist of only one sile), as well as specific methods `getBoundTags()`, `getBoundCategories()`, `getBoundAttributes()`, and `getBoundSlinks()` return only a subset of these which can be restricted using annotation type-specific parameters.

Annotations can be bound to, and unbound from siles using the `addAnnotation()` and `removeBoundAnnotation()` methods. `removeBoundAnnotation()` has two variants; one takes as parameter a set of `BoundAnnotation` instances which are removed from the repository's database; the other one takes two parameters of type `Sile[]` and `Annotation[]` and removes all passed annotations from the passed set of siles. Thus a client application can remove a certain set of bound annotations without first retrieving all the `BoundAnnotation` instances by which they are represented. Additionally, `removeAnnotation()` can be used to remove all occurrences of an annotation from the entire repository.

To modify annotations, two methods are provided: `updateBoundAnnotation()` updates a set of bound annotations with a new annotation, while `updateAnnotation()` updates all occurrences of an annotation with a new annotation. Note that by using these methods, not only annotation specifics (e.g., an attribute value) can be updated, but also the *annotation type* can be changed: for instance, it is possible to replace a tag annotation with a category annotation for all siles within a repository by using the `updateAnnotation()` call.

4. *Content Management.* Finally, the `Repository` interface defines two methods to retrieve and update the content of hosted siles; `getContent()` and `setContent()`. Note that it is not possible to retrieve or update the content of a referenced sile since per definition such siles do not have associated content within the repository. Instead, the retrieval mechanism for referenced siles is determined by the type of the sile's URI.

4.2 Usage Examples

In this section we outline the usage of the sile API by the means of pseudocode examples. These are meant to show the API calls that can be used by an application to retrieve information stored in a sile repository. In the following example, we use simplified URN identifiers for all names of categories, slinks, and annotations. For the sake of brevity, we treat URI parameters for method calls as normal strings in the examples.

In our scenario, an instant messaging client has been extended to store information about chat sessions, contacts, and transferred objects using a local sile repository. In our example, three persons discuss their research work within a chat session. During this session, they discuss a blog entry that was found by one of the participants, and they discuss a document that was written by one participant.

First, the application obtains a reference to a repository instance; the means of doing so remains unspecified by the API. When a new IM session is initiated, the application creates a new sile that represents this session:

```
Repository repo = ... ;
HostedSile session = repo.createHostedSile();
```

In order to retrieve the transcript at a later point in time, the application annotates all sessions with an appropriate category and attributes. To describe its vocabulary, the client uses a vocabulary of urn:im: URIs. For this purpose the application retrieves the corresponding annotation object—in this case, a category—from the repository,

```
Category cSession = repo.getCategory("urn:im:Session");
```

and attaches it to the sile that represents the session.

```
session.addAnnotation(cSession);
```

Note that the application does not decide to explicitly store the chat's start time; this is not necessary because the repository automatically annotates a sile with its creation date.

The application also adds slinks that connect the conversation to their participants; let us assume it is a chat between three people. The application uses numerical account ids to identify contacts; thus the corresponding siles can be retrieved via a query that considers a category and an attribute:

```
AndFilter filter = new AndFilter();
filter.add(new CategoryFilter("urn:im:Account"));
filter.add(new AttributeNameValueFilter("urn:im:account-id", "9182745",
    "xsd:string"));
Sile john = repo.searchSiles(filter, 0, 1, null)[0];
```

Similarly, the application searches for the siles that represent other participants; e.g., ann and me. Now, the application establishes slinks that connect the sile that represents the conversation to the siles that represent the participants. For this, we uses the slink types `urn:im:participant` and `urn:im:initiator`:

```
sile.addAnnotation(repo.getSlink("urn:im:initiator", ann));
sile.addAnnotation(repo.getSlink("urn:im:participant", john));
sile.addAnnotation(repo.getSlink("urn:im:participant", me));
```

Whenever a message is posted into the chat, the application creates a sile that represents this message (which is again automatically annotated with its creation time). It stores the message text as content, and attaches a category and sender annotation. Also it connects the message sile to the sile that represents the chat:

```
Sile message = repo.createHostedSile();
message.setContent(new StringContent("hi bernhard, nice thesis! :-)"));
message.addAnnotation(repo.getCategory("urn:im:Message"));
message.addAnnotation(repo.getSlink("urn:im:author", john));
session.addAnnotation(repo.getSlink("urn:im:message", message));
```

The discussion now is about a particular blog entry found by one of the participants. She posts the URL into the chat, which is recognized by the IM application. Thus, the application can add a reference to the blog entry (which the repository now treats as referenced sile) and slink it to the message, and (to simplify later retrieval) to the entire conversation:

```
ReferencedSile externalResource =
    repo.createReferencedSile("http://blog.beef.de/thesis/");
message.addAnnotation(repo.getSlink("urn:im:topic", externalResource));
session.addAnnotation(repo.getSlink("urn:im:topic", externalResource));
```

Later, the participants discuss a document that one of the participants has recently written. One of the participants posts the document into the chat, whereby it is downloaded by the IM client application and stored as a hosted sile. The application slinks the document to the sender, and slinks the conversation to the document:

```
HostedSile document = repo.createHostedSile();
document.setContent(new ByteContent([...]));
document.addAnnotation(repo.getAttribute
    ("sile:label", "semantic_web_report.pdf", "xsd:string"));
```

```
document.addAnnotation(repo.getSlink("urn:im:author", john));
session.addAnnotation(repo.getSlink("urn:im:topic", document));
```

Since the chat participants agree on the version sent by John, the user tags the received document with a note that it has been approved. This is accomplished by a component in the instant messaging application that allows the user to add comments or tags to items,

```
document.addAnnotation(repo.getTag("approved"));
```

and to the discussion as a whole:

```
session.addAnnotation(repo.getTag("phdthesis"));
```

When the discussion is finished, the client application stores the end time of the conversation:

```
session.addAnnotation(repo.getAttribute("urn:im:end-time", now(),
    "xsd:dateTime"));
```

Later on, our user wants to catch up items discussed in the chat session. She remembers that on this particular day there were several chat sessions, and that the particular document was discussed with John. Thus, using a sile browsing application, she looks for the sile that represents John and issues a query that looks for all documents that were discussed with John a couple of weeks ago. Since the filter API does not support sub-queries or joins, we need to implement this search by two distinct queries; the first one looks for John, the second one returns all chat sessions John attended that took place within one week.

```
// search for John
AndFilter filter = new AndFilter();
filter.add(new CategoryFilter("urn:im:Account"));
filter.add(new AttributeNameValueFilter("urn:im:nickname", "john",
    "xsd:string"));
Sile result = repo.searchSiles(filter, 0, 1, null)[0];

// search for chat sessions with John within a week
filter = new AndFilter();
```

```
filter.add(new CategoryFilter("urn:im:Session"));
filter.add(new SileInOutboundFilter(result));
filter.add(new AttributeNameValuerangeFilter("sile:creation-date",
    "2008-07-07T00:00:00", "2008-07-13T23:59:59", "xsd:dateTime"));
Sile[] results = repo.searchSiles(filter, 0, 0, null);
```

The generic sile browser allows her to scan the tags of all resulting sessions. After she has found the session that is tagged with "phdthesis", she issues a query so that she will be presented all items that were discussed during the session:

```
Sile session = ... ;
Sile[] result = repo.searchSiles(
    new SileSlinkInboundFilter(session, "urn:im:topic")), 0, 0, null);
```

In this case, two siles will be returned: one that represents the blog entry that was discussed during the meeting, and another one that represents the document that was approved during the chat session.

In these examples we have shown how applications can use a personal sile repository to store arbitrary kinds of information. Only a few API calls are needed to annotate siles with attributes, tags, or categories, or to put them into relationships by creating slink annotations. Applications can read and write sile contents, and can create references to external data sources; for instance, to web resources.

Although the sile model and its query framework have certain limitations (e.g., the lack of sub-queries), they are able to cover a wide range of information demands. The API does not require the programmer or the user to formulate complex hierarchical queries; instead searched information can be iteratively retrieved.

In practice, applications will employ a mixture of predefined and dynamically generated filter expressions to find information. For instance, the envisioned instant messaging application could, during startup, issue a query to retrieve all user contacts, while it also could provide an interface that allows the user to search for chat sessions that have been annotated with a specific tag.

4.3 Summary

In this section, we have introduced the Sile application programming interface, which is derived from the abstract sile model discussed in the previous section. The static part of the Sile API consists of a set of types that reflect all model elements of the sile model, i.e., different types of siles, annotations, and filters. The dynamic API, in the form of the Repository specification, represents operations on sile data sets. The API has been specified in a generic UML notation so that it can be easily transformed to any object-oriented language. Finally we have demonstrated how the API can be used in concrete exemplary application scenarios.

Part III

Implementation

Chapter 5

Digital Manifestation of Siles

The nicest thing about standards is that there are so many of them to choose from. — Ken Olsen

The abstract data model presented in Section 3.2 shares several characteristics with the well-known RDF meta model [KC04]: *(1)* both use graph-based data structures for representing annotations (in particular, relationships) of digital and non-digital resources, and *(2)* both are designed to be extended by user- or application-specific vocabularies through the usage of ontologies. RDF recently emerged as a global interchange format for descriptive data on the web [BHAR07] and thus many tools, parsers, and databases are available. Thus it is a reasonable choice for the physical representation of sile data, and in the following we define rules how the abstract model can be mapped to RDF graphs; however it would be perfectly valid to represent sile data in other formats like the relational model[1].

In this section, we introduce the building blocks that are required for such a mapping between the sile model and RDF. We introduce a basic core ontology in Section 5.1 that models the classes and properties which are used by the mapping rules between siles and RDF resources described in Section 5.2. Then, we describe how the elements of

---

[1]To prove this claim, we have also implemented a repository that maps sile annotations to IMAP mail message headers, cf. Section 7.3

the abstract query framework can be transformed to the SPARQL Query Language for RDF [PS08] in Section 5.3.

After this mapping to the Semantic Web technology family, we briefly discuss possible alternative representations by the means of object-oriented languages and relational database systems. These are not discussed in detail, but rather are meant to be directions for future work in this direction.

5.1 A Core Ontology for the Sile Model

We define a simple core ontology for the representation of sile data using RDF. This ontology defines a set of classes and attributes that formally represent the data elements of the RDF representation of siles. The ontology described here serves two main purposes; first, it defines a vocabulary that can be used for the exchange of sile data in the form of RDF, and second, it implies a minimal set of reasoning rules that can be applied when querying sile data.

Short Name	Full URI
sile:	http://www.semdav.org/2007/03/core#
rdf:	http://www.w3.org/1999/02/22-rdf-syntax-ns#
rdfs:	http://www.w3.org/2000/01/rdf-schema#
xsd:	http://www.w3.org/2001/XMLSchema#

Table 5.1: URI prefixes for the sile ontology

In this section we informally describe the elements of the ontology using the RDF Vocabulary Description Language (RDFS) [BG04]; we use the common abbreviated URI prefix notation with the name spaces enumerated in Table 5.1.

Classes

The root class for sile entities is the class `sile:Sile`. It indicates that a resource can be interpreted as sile. `sile:Sile` has two subclasses, `sile:HostedSile` and `ReferencedSile`, which indicate the type of sile within the repository. The two classes are marked as disjunct (cf. Figure 5.1).

The indication whether a sile is a `sile:HostedSile` or a `sile:ReferencedSile` is only valid w.r.t. a specific *data context*, i.e., usually within a repository instance. When sile data is exchanged between two contexts, the receiving entity must ensure that the sile data are accordingly transformed so that the data model remains in a consistent state. For instance, the receiving entity (repository) must check if any instance of `sile:ReferencedSile` in the received data set references to an already existing instance of `sile:HostedSile` by comparing the respective URIs. If this is the case, the sile data must be accordingly merged; i.e., the annotations contained in the received data set must be attached to the already existing instance of `sile:HostedSile`[2].

To model the rules that are manifested in a Spect (cf. Section 3.2), we define three classes that reflect the three annotation types that can be referred within a spect, `sile:AttributeName`, `sile:CategoryName`, and `sile:SlinkName`, These are subsumed by a class `sile:Annotation`. They are used to identify the names (URIs) of annotations within a spect definition, and they serve as domain and range for the properties that reflect the elements of a spect (see below).

The sile ontology defines a further class, `sile:Tagged`, which is the root class of all tag classes. Tags are, in principle, plain text strings attached to data objects; thus it would seem natural to represent them as RDF properties with a literal object, where the literal has a designated data type, and its value represents the tag literal. However, doing so would render them unusable for further semantic processing; e.g., connecting tags and ontologies, which would help to gain more information out of tags [HRS07]. Such processing can, by design, be applied only to RDF resources. Additionally, standard RDFS reasoning can be applied if we model siles that are tagged with a specific tag x as instances of a class, namely the class of x-tagged objects. Hence, we model tags as ontology classes that are subclass of a designated tag root class called `sile:Tagged`, and attach the tag's literal text as a label to the class.

Finally, the sile ontology defines the root class of all filters, `sile:Filter`, and its subclasses that basically reflect the filters defined in the sile filter API (see Section 4.1.3), i.e., `sile:CompoundFilter`, `sile:AtomicFilter`, and `sile:NotFilter`. For each compound and atomic filter, an appropriate class is defined. Each filter is further specified by properties that represent the criteria that this filter represents (see below).

---

[2]More details on the process of importing siles into a repository are discussed in Section 6.1

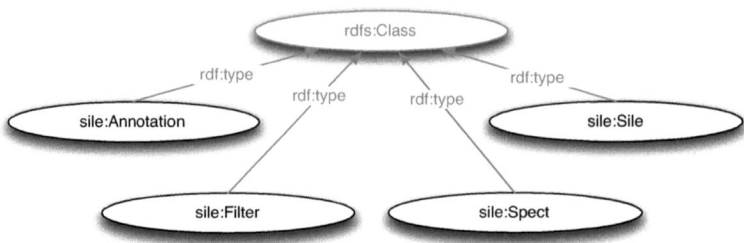

Figure 5.1: Sile ontology core classes

Properties

Annotation Properties To associate tag and category annotations to the sile resource, we use two specific properties: `sile:cat-type` and `sile:tag-type`. Both are modelled as sub-properties of `rdf:type` and thus can be generally interpreted as relationship between an instance (the sile) and a class (the category or the tag class). We further restrict the domain of `sile:tag-type` to subclasses of `sile:Tagged` since all classes that represent tags must be subclasses of this class.

Core Sile Attributes The sile core ontology defines a number of attributes that describe core properties of siles; these are depicted in Table 5.2. Each repository implementation should make sure these properties are always updated, and are always included when sile data are exchanged between systems. The date attributes are applicable to all siles, while the content-related description attributes are only applicable to hosted siles.

Additionally, the ontology defines two label attributes—`sile:sile-label` for siles, and `sile:tag-label` for tags—that define strings for human-readable representation of annotations. These are defined as subproperties of `rdfs:label` in order to allow generic RDF browsers to reuse the label information. For both, the ontology allows that an instance may have multiple labels; e.g., to support multi-language systems.

Core Slink Types In principle, all RDF properties that have an instance of `sile:Sile` as their domain and range can be considered as slinks. The Sile core ontology only defines two slink types that are sufficiently generic so that they can be used

Local Name	Domain	Range
creation-date	sile:Sile	xsd:dateTime
update-date	sile:Sile	xsd:dateTime
content-size	sile:HostedSile	xsd:long
content-type	sile:HostedSile	xsd:string
sile-label	sile:Sile	xsd:string
tag-label	sile:Tagged	xsd:string

Table 5.2: RDF properties for core attributes

as a starting point for the tailoring of sile ontologies (cf. Table 5.3). The top type, sile:related, indicates that two siles are somehow related. sile:cloned-from, which is a subproperty of sile:related, indicates that a sile was created by cloning another one. Thus the connection between a sile and its clones is retained.

Local Name	Domain	Range
related	sile:Sile	sile:Sile
cloned-from	sile:Sile	sile:Sile

Table 5.3: RDF properties for core slink names

Spect Properties A spect defines a number of relationships between different types of sile annotations. For each of these relationships, a property is defined in the sile core ontology. The properties sile:applicable-slink-domain and sile:applicable-slink-range indicate that a category (identified by its category name) can be used as domain or range for a slink (identified by its slink name). The property sile:applicable-attribute-domain indicates that a category can be used as an attribute's domain, and the properties sile:sub-category and sile:super-category are used to specific category hierarchies (see Table 5.4).

121

Local Name	Domain	Range
applicable-slink-domain	sile:SlinkName	sile:CategoryName
applicable-slink-range	sile:SlinkName	sile:CategoryName
applicable-attribute-domain	sile:AttributeName	sile:CategoryName
sub-category	sile:CategoryName	sile:CategoryName
super-category	sile:CategoryName	sile:CategoryName

Table 5.4: RDF properties for spects

Filter Properties The filter hierarchy has already been discussed in Section 4.1.3; the filter class hierarchy described above basically reflects this design in terms of an ontology. To represent the exact parameters of a concrete filter, a number of properties as indicated in Table 5.5 can be used. Filters may refer to annotation names and therefore the range of each filter property is also given in this overview table.

5.2 Representation of Sile Data as RDF

Siles

On the first sight it seems obvious to directly map siles to RDF resources and vice versa, as both can be considered as having their own identity and are, per se, independent from any other resource. While this approach is suitable in the one direction (representing siles as RDF), it may be impractical to transform every RDF resource as sile. As siles we consider only such objects that have a direct digital manifestation (similar to files), while in common RDF data there may exist abstract resources (so-called "non-information resources") or such ones that do not directly denote a specific concept (e.g., blank nodes). RDF resources may act as container for complex data structures (cf. Section 2.3 in [MM04]); artificial resources may be created to distinguish "real world objects" from their digital counterparts (cf. [ABK+07]), or blank nodes may be present. As a consequence, we require that each sile is represented as non-blank node and is explicitly typed as sile, as follows:

$$\exists s \in \Sigma \longleftrightarrow \{< u_s, \mathsf{rdf{:}type}, \mathsf{sile{:}Sile} >\}$$

We read this as follows: If a sile s_i exists, this sile is represented by a singleton RDF

Local Name	Domain	Range
attribute-name	sile:AttributeNameFilter	sile:AttributeName
valuerange-min	sile:AttributeValuerangeFilter	rdfs:Literal
valuerange-max	sile:AttributeValuerangeFilter	rdfs:Literal
valuepattern	sile:AttributeValuepatternFilter	rdfs:Literal
value	sile:AttributeValueFilter	rdfs:Literal
datatype	sile:AttributeValuerangeFilter sile:AttributeValuepatternFilter	rdfs:Datatype
source	sile:SileInboundFilter	sile:Sile
destination	sile:SileOutboundFilter	sile:Sile
slink-name	sile:SlinkInboundFilter sile:SlinkOutboundFilter	sile:SlinkName
category-name	sile:CategoryFilter	sile:CategoryName

Table 5.5: RDF properties for sile filters

triple set, and vice versa. This set (enclosed by braces) contains, in this case, only one triple (which is enclosed by angle brackets); this triple's subject is equal to the sile's URI u_i, its predicate is rdf:type, and its object is the URI sile:Sile.

Note that we do not require any other assertions to be made about a sile. In consequence, no further predicates can be derived from the fact that a resource is typed as sile:Sile, but, on the other hand, no further information is necessary to indicate that a resource can be interpreted as sile. This design allows one to selectively and easily enrich existing RDF data sets in order to obtain a representation that conforms to the sile model. Information that is available in the form of RDF data (e.g., as Linked Data [BHAR07] on the Semantic Web) can be interpreted as sile data by adding the typing triple to the resources of interest. All additional information about resources can be expressed via the mapping rules for annotations, as described in the following.

Annotations

Tags As described before, tags are represented by subclasses of the class `sile:Tagged`, and the tag label is attached to this class. Hence a tag is represented by a pair of RDF triples:

$$\exists t \mid t \in \mathbb{T} \longleftrightarrow \{<t', \texttt{sile:tag-label}, "t"\texttt{^^xsd:string}>,$$
$$<t', \texttt{rdfs:subClassOf}, \texttt{sile:Tagged}>\}$$

where t' is the URI of a tag class that is internally used to represent tag t. The first triple denotes the textual representation of the tag (using the common syntax for typed RDF literals), and the second one identifies the tag resource as subclass of the tag root class.

We then relate the sile to the tag class using the `sile:tag-type` property and thus are able to apply all reasoning operations for ontology classes also to tags.

$$\exists s \in \Sigma, t \in \mathbb{T} \mid t \in T_s \longleftrightarrow \{<u_s, \texttt{sile:tag-type}, t'>\}$$

Categories Categories roughly correspond to ontology classes and therefore can be directly mapped to RDF triples which express the type of the resource. This mapping does not consider class hierarchies and any entailment based on such, and the sile data model does not specify which mechanisms are used to infer implicit information: an implementation can choose to apply arbitrary mechanisms, like reasoners and rule-based systems, to categories, and by doing so generate additional category associations for siles and the corresponding RDF statements.

$$\exists s \in \Sigma, c_j \in \mathbb{C} \mid c \in C_s \longleftrightarrow \{<u_s, \texttt{sile:cat-type}, c>\}$$

Attributes Attributes can be mapped to RDF statements that have a *typed literal* as object. We define that the rules that are valid for typed literals in RDF (cf. Section 6.5 in [KC04]) hold also for sile attributes. Attributes are directly attached to sile resources using a simple RDF triple, whereas the attribute value literal and the attribute data type URI are encoded as typed literal:

$$\exists s \in \Sigma, a \in \mathbb{A} \mid a \in A_s \longleftrightarrow \{<u_s, an_a, "av_a"\texttt{^^}at_a>\}$$

Again, we use the RDF syntax for typed literals where the data type of the attribute value is attached to the literal representation of the attribute value using two hat signs.

For plain literals (i.e., literals that have no associated data type) we define that in the corresponding attribute annotation the `xsd:string` data type is used by default.

Note that we do not impose any constraints on the existence or cardinality of sile attributes. Both the sile model and the RDF model allow one to attach multiple attribute instances with the same name to one sile; however a sile cannot have two attributes that have identical name, value, and value type (as the sile data model is, like RDF, set-based).

Slinks — Slinks can be regarded similar to attributes: as slink we consider all statements whose object is a resource that is typed as sile. In other words, a slink is an attribute of the source sile whose value is the target sile. Slinks always *connect* two siles, so we model them as pairwise predicate on two siles. Slinks are always *directed*; correspondingly, we can define a mapping to an RDF triple that contains the URIs of the participating siles as subject and object, and the relationship name URI as predicate. The destination URI must be typed as `sile:Sile`:

$$\exists s \in \Sigma, l \in \mathbb{L} \mid l \in L_s \longleftrightarrow \{< u_s, ln_l, ld_l >, < ld_l, \text{rdf:type}, \text{sile:Sile} >\}$$

Content

In principle, it is possible to represent binary data in RDF using literals that are typed with the XML data types `xsd:base64Binary` or `xsd:hexBinary`. In several studies the average file sizes on personal computer systems has been analyzed [DB99, ABDL07]. These studies show that with the advent of multimedia data the number of large files—which are problematic to represent in RDF and XML—has increased. In 2004, while most files were smaller than 4 KB the mean file size by 2004 was 189 KB and increases by 12% p.a. Thus one could consider the representation of sile contents within the RDF format. However, representation of binary content as RDF data brings no additional benefit in our context: neither can it be queried using RDF query languages like SPARQL, nor can any RDF processor perform meaningful operations on such literals. Additionally, because of the necessary Base64-Encoding [Jos06] the data volume is significantly increased, and it becomes hard to perform search requests without prior decoding. Hence we avoid the representation of sile content in base64-encoded form; instead we leave the actual storage to the implementation.

However, we annotate a sile with attributes that describe the sile's content size and MIME type, for which we define the functions $size(\cdot)$ and $mime(\cdot)$. These functions return the corresponding values in the form of attribute values, which can be mapped to a RDF representation using the rules for attributes, as described above.

$$\exists s \in \Sigma, b \in \mathbb{B} \mid b = b_s \quad \longleftrightarrow \quad (\texttt{sile:content-size}, size(b), \texttt{xsd:nonNegativeInteger}) \in A_s,$$
$$(\texttt{sile:content-type}, mime(b), \texttt{xsd:string}) \in A_s$$

Examples

After having specified the mappings, we can now represent typical siles from our application scenarios. In Section 4.2 we have described how applications can make use of sile data to represent instant messaging chat session. In the following we describe how the representation of these sessions in RDF could look like.

The first sile that was created during this example was one that represents a chat session. It has been automatically assigned a URI by the repository, and it was annotated with a Session category by the instant messaging application. Thus its basic RDF representation looks as depicted in Listing 5.1, lines 1–15[3].

This example shows in the first line the sile URI that was automatically created by the repository when the sile was created. The second line indicates that the sile is a hosted sile, while the third line shows that it is annotated with a category called urn:im:Session. Lines 4 to 7 indicate the creation and update time stamps for the sile, which are automatically assigned by the repository on each update. Lines 8 and 9 contain information about the sile content, which is empty in this example. Lines 10 to 13 contain slinks to the single messages of this sile (some of them have been skipped in this example), and lines 14 and 15 represent the topic annotations that have been issued during the chat session; one refers to an external URI (i.e., a referenced sile); one refers to another hosted sile whose URI has been automatically assigned by the repository.

Listing 5.1, lines 17–24, shows the representation of one message entry that was part of this chat session. This message entry is slinked by the sile that represents the conversation (line 12), and in addition to the default attributes for siles and a category annotation (line 19) it contains a slink to the sile that represents the author of the message. The (abbreviated) RDF representation of the author is depicted in lines 26–31.

These examples demonstrated how siles are actually represented using RDF, a generic graph-based representation format for data. In the following section, we discuss how we translate filter queries, i.e., expressions that model information retrieval

---
[3] We use the Turtle notation for RDF [Bec07] in the following examples, and we assume the sile: and xsd: URI prefixes to be defined according to the respective specifications.

```
 1 <urn:uuid:57207370-6880-11dd-ad8b-0800200c9a66>
 2     a sile:HostedSile ;
 3     sile:cat-type <urn:im:Session> ;
 4     sile:creation-date "2008-07-11T16:21:14"^^xsd:dateTime ;
 5     sile:update-date "2008-07-11T17:14:21"^^xsd:dateTime ,
 6         "2008-07-11T17:19:12"^^xsd:dateTime ,
 7         "2008-07-11T17:32:02"^^xsd:dateTime ;
 8     sile:content-type "sile/empty"^^xsd:string ;
 9     sile:content-size "0"^^xsd:long ;
10     <urn:im:message> <urn:uuid:82d4a304-e50c-44f5-8040-bd1911341619> ,
11         <urn:uuid:1ee4afbb-d171-468b-9fb6-76bbebe732ef> ,
12         <urn:uuid:307f39e4-1c0a-4898-a8e2-7e2f3534a8a1> ,
13         [...] ;
14     <urn:im:topic> <http://blog.beef.de/thesis/> ,
15         <urn:uuid:9fb8f66f-6d17-429e-ab5d-d7dfe85f3308> .
16
17 <urn:uuid:307f39e4-1c0a-4898-a8e2-7e2f3534a8a1>
18     a sile:HostedSile ;
19     sile:cat-type <urn:im:Message> ;
20     sile:creation-date "2008-07-11T16:27:02"^^xsd:dateTime ;
21     sile:update-date "2008-07-11T16:27:05"^^xsd:dateTime ;
22     sile:content-type "text/plain"^^xsd:string ;
23     sile:content-size "30"^^xsd:long ;
24     <urn:im:author> <urn:uuid:8435222c-9675-473a-a989-e73af38a910b> .
25
26 <urn:uuid:8435222c-9675-473a-a989-e73af38a910b>
27     a sile:HostedSile ;
28     sile:cat-type <urn:im:Account> ;
29     [...]
30     <urn:im:account-id> "9182745"^^xsd:string ;
31     <urn:im:nickname> "john"^^xsd:string ;
```

Listing 5.1: Example RDF representation of siles

requests based on the sile model, to the SPARQL query language for RDF; these queries can then directly be issued to data that is represented according to the rules discussed in this section.

5.3 Transforming Sile Filters to SPARQL Queries

The *SPARQL Query Language for RDF* [PS08] has become the de-facto standard for querying RDF data sets. Together with the SPARQL protocol [CFT08] which defines how SPARQL queries and results are to be encoded and transported over a network connection, it has been a W3C Recommendation since January 2008.

SPARQL employs a *pattern matching approach* to query RDF data. A basic SPARQL query to retrieve the URIs of all siles that are defined in a repository is given in Listing 5.2[4]. In this example the SELECT query format is used, which returns a table of results, similar to SQL queries.

```
SELECT ?sile
WHERE { ?sile rdf:type sile:Sile . }
```

Listing 5.2: Simple SPARQL query

SPARQL provides another query form, CONSTRUCT, which can be used to create a new RDF graph that is filled with results from the WHERE clause. Listing 5.3 depicts a query that returns all hosted and referenced siles. The UNION statement is used to combine different graph patterns:

```
CONSTRUCT { ?sile rdf:type sile:Sile . }
WHERE
{
   { ?sile rdf:type sile:HostedSile . }
   UNION { ?sile rdf:type sile:ReferencedSile . }
}
```

Listing 5.3: SPARQL CONSTRUCT query

---

[4]The URI prefixes are omitted in the following examples.

Although there are a number of issues[5] that have been not addressed in the 2008 specification of SPARQL, the language is widely supported by a large fraction of RDF storage systems. It is also a core building block of many semantic desktop projects: as our analysis shows (cf. Section 2.3.4), most of them use RDF for data representation, and SPARQL to query these data.

Having the ability to map the Sile data model to RDF (cf. Section 5.1 and Section 5.2), it is natural to define a mapping of sile filters (cf. Section 3.3) to SPARQL. This allows us to formulate abstract sile queries over the sile model, and to execute such queries against sile data expressed in RDF. The transformation from the (abstract) filter model to SPARQL must consider the structure and semantics of SPARQL [PAG06a, PAG06b], as well as the absence of certain language constructs, e.g., negotiated patterns and subqueries.

Considering the proposed normal form for SPARQL queries [PAG06a] which eliminates certain situations in which the SPARQL semantics is ambiguous (cf. Sections 4.3 of [Cyg05]), we perform the translation of filters to SPARQL queries in two steps. First, we bring the filter into *disjunctive normal form*; second, we translate the elements of the normalized filter expression to SPARQL graph patterns. Note that this generic approach may produce redundant and non-optimal queries, thus one should apply query optimization algorithms to the resulting query. However this is out of the scope of this work; instead we refer to several approaches to SPARQL optimization that have been published (e.g., [SSB+08, HH07]).

Prerequisites

The filter API for Sile data is in detail described in Section 3.3. As we can see, filters are basically boolean expressions built of atomic filters and negated atomic filters, which are (recursively) grouped by compound filters (And and Or). Such an expression is said to be in *disjunctive normal form* if it consists of one or more disjuncts, each of which is a conjunction of one or more literals; and it is in *conjunctive normal form* if it consists of one or more conjuncts, each of which is a disjunction of one or more literals. In the case of the sile filter model, literals are atomic filters and negated atomic filters.

However, SPARQL does not provide direct means to query using such boolean expressions: it provides neither explicit AND, OR, or NOT operators. Thus we need to

---

[5]A comprehensive list of these is given at http://www.w3.org/2001/sw/DataAccess/issues; the features that the SPARQL working group is currently addressing are listed at http://www.w3.org/TR/sparql-features.

transform a filter expression into a suitable form before we can convert it into a SPARQL query. In the following we will discuss how the elements of disjunctive and conjunctive normal forms—i.e., conjunctions, disjunctions, and negations—can be translated to SPARQL in order to justify the selection of an appropriate normal form.

Representation of Conjunctions In SPARQL, the WHERE clause is used to specify *graph patterns*; i.e., sets of RDF triples in which each element (subject, predicate, or object) may be a variable [PS08]. *Group graph patterns* are the most primitive kind of grouping SPARQL graph patterns; the SPARQL semantics requires that *all* triple patterns within a group must match in order to constitute a valid result; i.e., the single elements of the graph pattern are AND-combined.

Representation of Disjunctions Results from different, independent graph patterns (i.e., *alternative solutions*) can be combined with the UNION statement. Two UNION-combined patterns P_1 and P_2 produce a solution if P_1, or P_2, or P_1 and P_2 match, whereas all matches are reproduced in the solution. Thus we can consider the SPARQL UNION statement as an equivalent to the logical OR.

Representation of Negations There is no basic negation operator in SPARQL since it is built on the Open World Assumption; i.e., one can only decide whether a fact is true, but not whether it is false. Instead, *negation as failure* [SS08] can be applied: the BOUND operator can be used to test whether a SPARQL variable has been assigned a value in the current evaluation context; i.e., whether it is bound to a solution. In combination with an OPTIONAL graph pattern one can test if a set of triples is asserted in the data set or not. OPTIONAL patterns are included in the evaluation solution if they are present, but do not cause the evaluation to fail if they are not present in the data. An example of negation as failure in SPARQL is given in Section 11.4.1 of [PS08].

Representation of Disjunctive Normal Forms Let P_1, P_2, ..., P_n denote *basic graph patterns*, i.e., sequences of triple patterns. AND-combined filters can be represented within a basic graph pattern, since all triples within the pattern must match in order to obtain a solution. As long as an atomic filter element can be matched to a basic graph pattern, we can represent the entire formula (in disjunctive normal form) as a UNION of the single basic graph patterns:

$$P_1 \vee P_2 \vee \ldots \vee P_n \mapsto \{\{P_1\} \text{ UNION } \{P_2\} \text{ UNION } \{\ldots\} \text{ UNION } \{P_n\}\}$$

Representation of Conjunctive Normal Forms Because SPARQL allows one to group UNION clauses, we can also represent a conjunctive normal form, which is an conjunction of alternatives (disjuncts). If $A_1, A_2, \ldots, A_m$ denote UNION-combined basic triple pattern (i.e., disjuncts as above), then we can transform a CNF formula as follows:

$$A_1 \wedge A_2 \wedge \ldots \wedge A_m \mapsto \{\{A_1\}.\{A_2\}.\{\ldots\}.\{A_m\}\}$$

In principle, DNF and CNF formulas can be converted into each other without information loss. However, for the purposes of an SPARQL-based implementation of the filter algebra, we choose disjunctive normal form because we assume that CNF formulas are mentally harder to formulate and will therefore less often be used by end users. The rationale behind this assumption is that conjunctions (of which DNF formulas consist) appear to be a more natural way to describe information demands than disjunctions[6]. In the following we briefly outline how we generically transform a filter expression into DNF, and how we convert such a DNF filter into a SPARQL WHERE clause.

Algorithm:makeDNF

Input: A filter F

Output: DNF representation of F

if F *is an* AtomicFilter **then**
| return F ;
end

if F *is an* AndFilter **then**
| **if** F *has only atomic children* **then**
| | return F ;
| **else**
| | return $makeAndDNF(F)$;
| **end**
end

if F *is an* OrFilter **then**
| return $makeOrDNF(F)$;
end

Algorithm 1: Conversion of filters to DNF

---

[6]This decision is mainly driven by user interface considerations; for a detailed discussion of these issues we refer the reader to [Tod08].

Step 1: Filter Normalization

Under the assumption that negation can be applied to atomic filters but not to compound filters (cf. Section 4.1.3), we can use the distributive law to reorganize the hierarchical nesting of filters so that the resulting filter is always in DNF. The function makeDNF(·) that returns a DNF representation of a filter is described in Algorithm 1. This algorithm recursively moves conjunctions upwards and redistributes disjunctions according to De Morgan's laws so that they are flat; i.e., they only contain conjunctions. Algorithm 2 and 3 describe the detailed procedures for `And` and `Or` filters.

The resulting filter is either *(1)* an atomic filter, *(2)* an `AndFilter` that contains only atomic filters as children, or *(3)* an `OrFilter` that contains either atomic filters or `AndFilters` that contain only atomic filters. In either case, the resulting filter is in DNF and can be directly converted to a SPARQL `WHERE` statement, as described in the following.

Step 2: Transformation to SPARQL

The conversion of a DNF filter into a SPARQL can be performed as follows, where we demonstrate the transformation by the example of a SPARQL `CONSTRUCT` query. As described before, `CONSTRUCT` query always creates an RDF graph (i.e., a set of triples) that is constructed by binding variables in the construct pattern to results from the query solutions. For each solution found, an instance of the triple pattern specified in the `CONSTRUCT` clause is added to the result graph, whereas all variables in the `CONSTRUCT` clause are bound to the corresponding nodes of the query solution.

Sile filters are used to search for siles, and siles are represented as RDF resources; thus we define one target variable `?t` that is used as *common variable* across all filters. This variable will hold the sile URI if a match is found in the data set. Besides this common variable, each filter mapping may use *internal variables*; i.e., variables that are used only within the filter's result pattern, and *anonymous variables*; i.e., placeholder variables that are bound but not further evaluated. In SPARQL, the scope of variables is always global (cf. Section 4.1.3 of [PS08]), thus we employ a random name generator to ensure uniqueness of internal variable's names across the entire query.

The `CONSTRUCT` triple pattern used for searching siles always at least contains the target variable `?t` as well as the sile's *type information*; i.e., a statement of the form

```
?t rdf:type ?type .
```

Algorithm: makeAndDNF

Input: An `AndFilter` F

Output: DNF representation of F

let $F' =$ an empty `AndFilter` ;

for *all children F_i of F* **do**
    if *F_i is an `CompoundFilter`* **then**
        | $F_{help} \longleftarrow$ makeDNF(F_i); add F_{help} to F' ;
    else
        | add F_i to F' ;
    end
end

let $F'' =$ an empty `AndFilter` ;

let $O[][] =$ a 2-dimensional array of `OrFilters` ;

for *all children F'_i of F'* **do**
    if *F'_i is an `AtomicFilter`* **then**
        | add F'_i to F'' ;
    end
    if *F'_i is an `AndFilter`* **then**
        | add all children of F'_i to F'' ;
    end
    if *F'_i is an `OrFilter`* **then**
        | add all children of F'_i into a new row of $O[][]$;
    end
end

if *$O[][]$ is empty* **then**
    | return F'' ;
else
    $F''' \longleftarrow$ an empty `OrFilter` ;
    fill F''' with deMorgan-distributed elements of $O[][]$;
    return F''' ;
end

Algorithm 2: Conversion of AND-filters to DNF

Algorithm: makeOrDNF

Input: An `OrFilter` F

Output: DNF representation of F

let $F' = $ an empty `OrFilter` ;

for all children F_i of F **do**
    if F_i is an `AtomicFilter` **then**
        | add F_i to F'' ;
    end
    if F_i is an `CompoundFilter` **then**
        $F_i^n \longleftarrow$ makeDNF(F_i) ;
        add all children of F_i^n to F' ;
    end
end

return F' ;

Algorithm 3: Conversion of OR-filters to DNF

where `?type` indicates the sile type within the queried repository, i.e., `sile:HostedSile` or `sile:ReferencedSile`. The sile type information is always included in the result graph since it is required by the mapping component to build corresponding objects based on the result graph.

Additionally, the query may be used to ask for additional information about the sile, including but not restricted to its core attributes (cf. Section 5.1). The SPARQL query transformation engine allows the client to specify a set of attribute names whose values are, if present, added to the return graph. Consequently, statements of the form

    `?t property ?v .`

are added to the query's `CONSTRUCT` and `WHERE` clause. In the latter they are encapsulated within an `OPTIONAL` block since siles that are not annotated with the property should nevertheless be included in the result set. The variable `?v` in the above statement is an internal variable, as described before, and `property` is a placeholder for the attribute name URI.

Each atomic filter defined in Section 4.1.3 can be mapped to a conjunction of triple patterns and filters; for instance, a `TagFilter` that searches siles that are annotated with the tag "important" can be mapped to the triple pattern depicted in Listing 5.4. This pattern consists of three triples which are connected through an internal variable as described above. Triple 1 connects the target variable (`?t`) using the `sile:tag-type` predicate to the resource that represents the tag (which is identified by the internal variable `?32d885`); triple 2 states that the tag resource must be a subclass of `sile:Tagged`, and triple 3 states that the `sile:tag-label` must be equal to the string "important".

```
1 {
2   ?t sile:tag-type ?32d885 .
3   ?32d885 rdfs:subClassOf sile:Tagged .
4   ?32d885 sile:tag-label "important"^^xsd:string .
5 }
```

Listing 5.4: SPARQL triple pattern for a `TagFilter`

Algorithm: negatePattern

Input: A set of clauses C

Output: A set of result clauses R and helper clauses H

for *all elements C_i of C* **do**
  if C_i *is a triple pattern* **then**
    create a new triple pattern P by substituting all non-variables C_{ij} in C_i with internal variables ;
    add P to R ;
    for *each internal variable P_j in P* **do**
      add `FILTER`(P_j = C_{ij}) to H ;
      add `FILTER`(!bound(P_j)) to R ;
    end
  end
  if C_i *is a* `UNION` *pattern* **then**
    apply negatePattern($\cdot$) to the left children of C_i ;
    apply negatePattern($\cdot$) to the right children of C_i ;
  end
end

Algorithm 4: Conversion of negated filters

The transformation of negations (`NotFilters`) requires additional effort because

SPARQL does not provide explicit negation of triple patterns; instead we must apply *negation as failure* as described before. We employ a generic two-step mechanism to convert negated atomic filters to graph patterns. First, we transform the negated filter into graph patterns as described before. Second, we negate the resulting graph patterns according to Algorithm 4 which takes as an input a set of clauses (i.e., elements of a graph pattern; currently, we support the transformation of basic triple patterns and UNION patterns[7]) and creates a set of result clauses and *helper clauses*. Both are added to the query's WHERE clauses, whereas the helper clauses are encapsulated in an OPTIONAL block. The idea behind this approach is to make sure that for every variable in the negated pattern there exists a filter expression that makes sure that the variable is not bound.

An example of the query that is created from a negated TagFilter is depicted in Listing 5.5. In this example, the three triples from Listing 5.4 have been wrapped by an OPTIONAL clause, and all resources and literals have been substituted by internal variables. For instance, the property sile:tag-type has been replaced by the internal variable ?642bc3 (line 8). To ensure a correct binding to results, each variable is bound to its actual value by a FILTER statement; e.g., for the sile:tag-type property this binding is depicted in line 9. Additionally, for each variable a FILTER(!bound()) is added in the WHERE clause which ensures that only results are returned for which *none* of the internal variables are bound.

```
1  CONSTRUCT
2  {
3    ?t rdf:type ?type .
4  }
5  WHERE
6  {
7    ?t rdf:type ?type .
8    ?type rdfs:subClassOf sile:Sile .
9    OPTIONAL
10   {
11     ?t ?642bc3 ?b10a64 .
```

---

[7]The conversion of FILTER expressions can be performed by inverting the inner filter expression according to the semantics defined in Section 11.3 of [PS08]. However it is currently not implemented because of the complexity caused by the diversity of possible FILTER clauses.

```
12      FILTER (?642bc3=sile:tag-type).
13      ?b10a64 ?87303d ?a9d2b2 .
14      FILTER (?87303d=rdfs:subClassOf) .
15      FILTER (?a9d2b2=sile:Tagged) .
16      ?b10a64 ?fb2633 ?68a96f .
17      FILTER (?fb2633=sile:tag-label) .
18      FILTER (?68a96f="important"^^xsd:string) .
19    } .
20    FILTER (!bound(?642bc3)) .
21    FILTER (!bound(?87303d)).
22    FILTER (!bound(?a9d2b2)).
23    FILTER (!bound(?fb2633)) .
24    FILTER (!bound(?68a96f)) .
25  }
```

Listing 5.5: SPARQL representation of a negated `TagFilter`

For the negation of **UNION** patterns we use one of De Morgan's laws, $\neg(A \vee B) \Leftrightarrow \neg A \wedge \neg B$, to *flatten* the **UNION** pattern, which results in a standard (**AND**-combined) graph pattern. For instance, a disjunction of two tag filters would be transformed as depicted in Listing 5.6, while the transformation result of the negation of said combination is depicted in Listing 5.7. There, the two tag patterns are now AND-combined (i.e., the **UNION** clause was flattened) and individually negated, as described before.

```
1  CONSTRUCT { ?t rdf:type ?type . }
2  WHERE
3  {
4    ?t rdf:type ?type .
5    ?type rdfs:subClassOf sile:Sile .
6    {
7      ?t sile:tag-type ?069f46 .
8      ?069f46 rdfs:subClassOf sile:Tagged .
9      ?069f46 sile:tag-label "new"^^xsd:string .
10   }
11   UNION
```

```
12    {
13      ?t sile:tag-type ?cac684 .
14      ?cac684 rdfs:subClassOf sile:Tagged .
15      ?cac684 sile:tag-label "important"^^xsd:string .
16    }
17  }
```

Listing 5.6: SPARQL representation of two OR-combined `TagFilters`

```
1   CONSTRUCT { ?t rdf:type ?type .
2   }
3   WHERE
4   {
5     ?t rdf:type ?type .
6     ?type rdfs:subClassOf sile:Sile .
7     OPTIONAL
8     {
9       ?t ?f16c81 ?2fbd42 .
10      FILTER (?f16c811=sile:tag-type) .
11      ?2fbd42 ?08c33f ?6ad79a .
12      FILTER (?08c33f=rdfs:subClassOf) .
13      FILTER (?6ad79a=sile:Tagged) .
14      ?2fbd42 ?0bed41 ?cc17fb .
15      FILTER (?0bed41=sile:tag-label) .
16      FILTER (?cc17fb="new"^^xsd:string) .
17    } .
18    OPTIONAL
19    {
20      ?t ?d3735a ?b3f7be .
21      FILTER (?d3735a=sile:tag-type) .
22      ?b3f7be ?18f315 ?0afc18 .
23      FILTER (?18f315=rdfs:subClassOf) .
24      FILTER (?0afc18=sile:Tagged) .
25      ?b3f7be ?30a2d0 ?2ace30 .
```

```
26      FILTER (?30a2d0=sile:tag-label) .
27      FILTER (?2ace30="important"^^xsd:string) .
28    } .
29    FILTER (!bound(?f16c81)) .
30    FILTER (!bound(?08c33f)) .
31    FILTER (!bound(?6ad79a)) .
32    FILTER (!bound(?0bed41)) .
33    FILTER (!bound(?cc17fb)) .
34
35    FILTER (!bound(?d3735a)) .
36    FILTER (!bound(?18f315)) .
37    FILTER (!bound(?0afc18)) .
38    FILTER (!bound(?30a2d0)) .
39    FILTER (!bound(?2ace30)) .
40 }
```

Listing 5.7: SPARQL representation of a negated AND-combination of two `TagFilters`

We can convert arbitrarily complex sile filter expressions to SPARQL using the presented algorithms. However we are aware of the fact that most current RDF implementations do not perform well if a query contains complex SPARQL `FILTER` patterns. The recent Berlin SPARQL Benchmark [BS09] underlines this: query Q5 of this benchmark, which of all queries contains the most complex `FILTER` patterns, exposes the weakest performance times on all tested systems, or even times out [BS08]. We consider this result as an important direction for research on triple stores, since it is obvious that more efficient solutions for this class of queries have to be found in order to make SPARQL more utilizable.

5.4 Discussion of Alternative Representations

RDF is a natural candidate for representing siles and their annotations, since its data model overlaps greatly with the characteristics of the sile model. However, it is not the only possible representation of siles. Although the more detailed discussion of alternative representation formats for siles is out of the scope of this work, we briefly indicate in the following two popular candidates: the Object Oriented model (OOM) and the Relational Model.

5.4.1 Object Oriented Model

The object-oriented model is probably the most widespread programming paradigm in use today. Thus, many applications use this paradigm to represent their data. Hence, objects are an interesting candidate to map to the sile model, since such a mapping would allow for direct integration of the sile model into applications; and it would reduce the effort required for adapting user applications towards a semantic desktop infrastructure. In the following we discuss aspects of a mapping between the sile model and the object oriented model; however, we do not define a formal mapping.

From Siles to Objects The object oriented model is sufficiently expressive to represent all aspects of siles; however, the open and flexible design of the sile model imposes a problem on a direct mapping. The natural way to map e.g., a sile attribute to an object would be to use the attribute URI as member name, and the attribute datatype as type of the member, and the actual attribute value as member value. However, sile annotations (especially attributes and slinks) are flexibly typed through their URIs, and there are no restrictions on which annotations can be attached to a sile: a sile may be annotated with arbitrary types and numbers of attributes and slinks. Consequently, a direct mapping to a static class description is not feasible.

This problem can be circumvented if the sets of applicable attributes and slinks are reduced through the usage of spects (cf. Section 3.2), which restrict the possible combinations of categories, attributes, and slinks that may occur. The rules defined in a spect can be converted into a number of class or interface specifications that reflect these valid combinations. Such converters have already been presented based on OWL ontologies (e.g., Jastor[8]). However, while the sile model permits the use of additional annotations that are not defined in a spect, these annotations cannot be represented in such a statically typed representation.

Still, a generic approach can be employed that only represents the generic sile model elements (i.e., siles, annotations, spects, and repositories) as objects. Such a generic object-oriented representation is part of the Sile API, which has been discussed in Section 4.1.

From Objects to Siles The most natural way for the mapping of an object's static aspects (i.e., their member fields and relationships to other objects) to the sile model is to represent the object itself as sile, and to represent the object's type information as

---

[8]Jastor: http://jastor.sourceforge.net

categories. For siles and categories, we have to find suitable URIs: these will depend on the characteristics of the used object-oriented language. Most modern object-oriented languages provide mechanisms to prevent naming conflicts, and these mechanisms can be used to mint URIs. However, while it may be straightforward to derive URIs for static aspects of objects (for instance, its type information), it depends on the programming language and the actual object's structure whether a persistent identifier can be derived for the object itself. For instance, Java defines for each object a `hashCode()` method. If such an identifier cannot be derived, one can always fall back to use (pseudo-)random UUID URIs [LMS05].

> **Example.** A Java object of type `String` could be represented by a sile with the URI `<urn:java:object:java.lang.String#969099747>` which may be generated using the `Object.hashCode()` method. To represent its type hierarchy membership, it could be annotated with a number of categories, including `<urn:java:type:java.lang.String>`, `<urn:java:type:java.lang.Object>`; to represent the interfaces it implements, the categories `<urn:java:type:java.io.Serializable>` and `<urn:java:type:java.lang.Comparable>` are added.

The instance variables of an object can be represented as a mixture of attributes and slinks. Primitive data types (like string, integer, a.s.f.) can be represented by attributes, while relationships to other objects (which are themselves represented as siles) can be mapped to slinks. The attribute and slink name URIs can be derived by extending the URI of the defining class with the field name, while the data type URI of an attribute representation can be derived from the programming language's primitive data types. As shown in the previous example, a plausible heuristics to derive URIs for types is to use a concatenation of the class' full-qualified class name (which includes the package name) and prefix it; e.g., with `uuid:java:type:`. For fields, the defining class' URI can be extended by the name of the field, which then can be used as attribute name (in the case of primitive data types) or slink name (in the case of objects).

> **Example.** In order to represent the member values of the sile from above example that represents a Java `String` object, it could be annotated with the attribute tuples (`<urn:java:field:java.lang.String.value>`, "Hello World!", `<urn:java:type:char[]>`), (`urn:java:field:java.lang.String.offset`, "0", `<urn:java:type:int>`), and (`<urn:java:field:java.lang.String.count>`, "12", `<urn:java:type:int>`), which represent the object's member fields.

The type and interface hierarchy can be mapped to a representation within a spect model. A type or interface hierarchy can be represented using class hierarchy rules, and applicability rules for attribute names and slink names can be used to reflect the static definition of types.

However, such a translation causes a certain information loss, and the re-conversion from the sile model to the object oriented model is not straightforward. Although one can reconstruct object field values from the sile representation, usually there exists no standard way to create objects. Many programming languages allow objects to have private constructors, or use factory methods. Static classes cannot be instantiated during runtime at all. It depends on the characteristics of the concrete object-oriented language which methods can be applied. While most object oriented languages provide mechanisms for reflective programming (e.g., Java's *Reflection API*[9]), customized code must be implemented that maps the generic representation in the sile model to the specifics of the target programming language. Our Java-based prototype implementation contains special handling for frequently-used data types, including `String`, `char[]`, `int`, and `long`.

5.4.2 Relational Model

The Relational Model [Cod70] is one of the most widely used meta models for information representation. It constitutes the theoretical and logical foundation of *Relational Database Management Systems* (RDBMS), which are used as part of a magnitude of applications and systems.

From siles to relations Similar as for a mapping of siles to the object-oriented model as described before, we face the problem that sile annotations are dynamically typed, while the relational model requires a fixed configuration of attributes, which must have

---
[9]http://java.sun.com/docs/books/tutorial/reflect/index.html

fixed names and types. Hence, the same approaches as described for the object-oriented model can also be applied when siles should be represented within a relational model.

In this respect the sile model is very similar to the RDF model, which can be (in its most simple form) represented by a single relation `triple ( subject, predicate, object )`. A number of works have described how the representation of RDF in relational data bases can be optimized (e.g., by considering additional knowledge about patterns occurring in RDF graphs [DWSK03], by using vertical partitioning [AMMH07], or by employing hypergraph structures to store RDF triples [WLHW08]).

From relations to siles The core element of the relational model, the *tuple*, can directly be mapped to a sile; however one must apply plausible heuristics to determine URIs for such tuples. The tuple's attributes can then be represented by sile attribute, whereas the attribute names can be generated by concatenating the tuple URI and the attribute name, and the attribute data type can be generated from the attribute's domain. The name of the tuple's relation can be used to mint a URI for a category annotation that can be attached to each tuple sile.

> **Example.** Let us assume that an instant messaging application uses an application-internal relational database to store data about the user's contacts. For each contact, the application stores the account id, a nickname, and the URL of the contact person's home page. Thus, the schema can be written as
> `contact ( account_id, nickname, url )`
> Assuming that we use virtual URN prefix `urn:im:` for all URIs, we can represent each tuple from this relation as a sile. We can create the data from this schema by using the `account_id` attribute to create the sile URI, and represent the nickname and the URL fields as attributes.

If present, we can utilize additional information from the relational schema: if an attribute is known to be a primary key, it can be used to mint the tuple's URI. If an attribute is known to be a foreign key, it can be modelled not as attribute, but as slink that refers to the sile that represents the foreign tuple.

The mapping between the sile model and the relational model becomes important in two use cases: first, by applying the relatively simple mapping rules that we have informally described above, we can represent data stored within an RDBMS as siles, and integrate them with data from other sources. Second, by inverting the mapping rules and using information from a spect (which can be regarded as a complexity-reduced version of an entity-relationship model), one can implement a specific sile repository for a subset of annotations (namely, the attribute and slink names that are defined in the spect). Such, performance optimization algorithms that are discussed in database literature can be applied. In the latter case, one would also need to map sile filter expressions to the appropriate database query language (e.g., SQL).

5.5 Summary

In this section, we have discussed how the elements of the abstract sile model can be represented using the Semantic Web technology family. We have defined a core ontology, expressed in RDFS, which represents the elements of the abstract model in terms of RDF classes and properties. Then we have discussed how sile instance data (i.e., siles and their annotations) can be translated into RDF triples, and vice versa. This mapping allows us to integrate sile data with the Semantic Web, and to interpret external RDF data sets as siles. Consequently, we have described algorithms that translate sile filter expressions into the SPARQL query language in order to execute such queries against RDF datasets. Finally, we have discussed directions towards alternative representations of sile data; namely, we have outlined mappings to the object-oriented model and the relational model.

Chapter 6

Serializing Sile Data

> *I write down everything I want to remember. That way, instead of spending a lot of time trying to remember what it is I wrote down, I spend the time looking for the paper I wrote it down on.* — Beryl Pfizer

Siles (and associated entities, like annotations, filters, and spects) are defined as abstract objects, and this characteristic leaves many degrees of freedom for repository implementations w.r.t. the details of digital representation of siles.

In Chapter 5 we have discussed in detail one possible representation of siles using the Semantic Web technology family. We have outlined how RDF can be used to represent siles and their associated annotations, and we have discussed how we can transform sile filters to SPARQL queries that can be executed against RDF models. In the following sections we build upon this representation in order to define mechanisms to transfer the elements of the sile model across repositories, between repositories and applications, and between applications. We introduce *silepacks*, a mechanism to represent collections of siles, annotations, spects, and filters as self-contained files, which can be used to transfer these data over established mechanisms. Moreover, we outline how sile data can be integrated with other data sources on the *Web of Data*.

As an alternative serialization mechanism for sile data we describe how the methods defined in the `Repository` interface (which is part of the Sile API, cf. Chapter 4) are implemented as an extension to the XML-RPC protocol [Win99]. Finally we indicate how the well-known WebDAV protocol can be used to transport siles and their annotations, which allows us to interconnect to a wide range of applications and systems already in place. These serialization mechanisms enable us to distribute sile-based systems across different systems and platforms, and to interconnect sile repositories within personal networks, intranets, or the World Wide Web.

6.1 Silepacks: Transportable Sile Containers

Dealing with personal information often includes *communication*: digital devices and data are used to convey information from a sender to a recipient. Files, being the prevalent means of information representation in the personal information domain, can be transported over a variety of channels. It is common to copy files from their source device onto transportable media, like optical disks, flash disks, or external hard disk, and transfer them to their target system. Files can also be easily attached to e-mail messages, and most instant messaging protocols include file transfer functionality. Finally, the World Wide Web itself is, in its basic nature, an infrastructure to transfer files between hosts, for which purpose the HTTP protocol was developed.

However, the weak features that a file system provides to organize data are even more reduced when files are transferred via one of these mechanisms. For instance, a file's path—which can be regarded as a sort of annotation—is usually lost when a file is transported from one system to another one; only the file name is retained because it is required by the transportation infrastructure (e.g., the HTTP layer) for identification purposes. File transportation infrastructures usually omit file annotation mechanisms provided by operating systems, like alternate data streams or extended attributes (cf. Section 2.1.2) because the syntax and semantics of these mechanisms are not standardized.

The sile model can be regarded as semantic extensions to files, and one of its design goals is to provide interoperability of file annotations between applications. However this applies not only to single instances (e.g., one repository that is installed on a personal computer) but also to distributed environments, which are commonplace today. Because of the infrastructure that is available today (see above), it is very easy for end users to transfer files. Thus it is natural to utilize these structures also for the transportation of siles. For this purpose we introduce *silepacks*, a mechanism to represent a set of siles, annotations, spects, and filters as a single, self-contained file which can be transferred using the mechanisms that are available today.

6.1.1 The Structure of a Silepack

We have defined the possibility to transfer silepacks using available file transfer infrastructure as a central requirement for silepacks. Therefore it must be possible to represent a silepack as a single file. As a silepack includes different kinds of information, including binary content and structured semantic annotations, we need a container format that wraps these data into a single file. The ZIP file format [Kat07] is a popular file format that is widely used for different applications (e.g., Java JAR files or OpenDocument files). The ZIP file format is suitable for encapsulating files since single files can be extracted without the need to read through the entire file. In addition single entries can be identified using a directory-like naming convention.

We have shown in Section 5.2 how we can represent siles and annotations in RDF. In the following we use RDF to encode all aspects of siles as described in this mapping. A number of serialization formats for RDF exist (e.g., RDF/XML [Bec04], N3 [BL06b], and Turtle [Bec07]) which have different advantages and verbosity. The Turtle syntax represents a reasonable tradeoff between efficiency in terms of machine processing and human readability, and is furthermore, to a large extent, compatible to the SPARQL triple pattern syntax. Therefore we choose the Turtle syntax whenever RDF data is encoded within a silepack.

The basic structure of a silepack is depicted in Figure 6.1. It contains four entries on the root level, `meta.ttl`, `siles.ttl`, `annotations.ttl`, and `filters.ttl`, as well as a subdirectory that contains all binary content objects, and a subdirectory that holds spect serializations. The metadata about the silepack at hand (i.e., its URI, creation date, and the id of its origin repository) are stored in the `meta.ttl` file; an example is given in Listing 6.1.

The entry `siles.ttl` contains a model that holds the URIs of all siles that are represented in the silepack, together with their type information (`sile:HostedSile` or `sile:ReferencedSile`). This index file can be used to quickly scan the silepack for the URIs of the siles that are stored within. The file `annotations.ttl` contains all annotations that are attached to the siles contained in the silepack. Within this file,

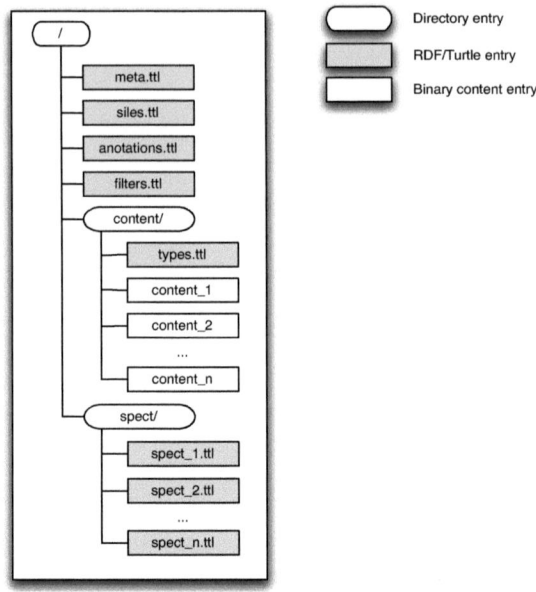

Figure 6.1: Structure of a silepack

annotations are represented in RDF according to the mapping rules described in Section 5.2. If loaded into a triple store, this model can be directly queried with SPARQL queries. Finally, the `filters.ttl` entry contains RDF representations of filters. All three files correspond to the model specified by the sile core ontology (cf. Section 5.1).

The siles' binary content streams are represented by the entries in the `content` subdirectory. There, for each sile an entry is created, whereas the entry name is the sile URI which is encoded according to the *URL encoding* algorithm [BLFM05]. This ensures that no characters that may appear in URIs but are usually not allowed in file names (e.g., : or /) are used in the entry name. Finally, the `content/types.ttl` entry contains an RDF model that holds the `sile:content-type` properties for all siles in the silepack. This file provides the means for direct interpretation of sile contents without the need to parse the entire annotation model, which is contained in the `annotations.ttl` file.

To distinguish spects within a silepack, each spect is stored in a separate entry

```
1  <urn:uuid:e4e1150e-8939-44d3-9d82-953b643aa6ba>
2      a <http://www.semdav.org/2008/07/silepack> ;
3      sile:creation-date "2008-08-12T16:02:31.188Z"^^xsd:dateTime .
```

Listing 6.1: Silepack `meta.ttl` file example

within the spect sub-directory. As with content entries, the entry name is derived by encoding the spect URI.

6.1.2 Exporting and Importing Silepacks

The process of exporting silepacks from, and importing them into a repository requires several steps to be performed in order to ensure the integrity of the sile model. In the following we briefly outline these procedures.

Export We denote as *export* the process of selecting entities from a repository and assembling them into a silepack. We do not specify the exact procedure for creating a silepack: a repository implementation may provide additional services that a client can use to obtain a complete silepack, or a client application may assemble a silepack by combining entities that it reads from a repository. In any case the following guidelines need to be considered.

If entities are to be exported from a repository, the silepack creator should populate the silepack with self-describing metadata: it should mint a permanent, unique silepack URI, it should indicate the silepack's creation date, and it should include a URI that references the repository where the silepack contents have been exported from. All these data are written into the `meta.ttl` entry in the silepack's root directory.

A repository may decide to include siles either as hosted siles or as referenced siles. In the former case, the sile URI is retained as it is stored by the repository, and the sile content is included as an entry under the content directory. In the latter case, the repository must mint a new URI for the referenced sile. This URI can be used by a recipient of the silepack to reference to the hosted version of the sile, which remains within the exporting repository.

A repository also needs to decide which spects should be included in a silepack. In principle, the silepack structure provides the flexibility to include an arbitrary number of spects, and the spects are independent from the sile annotations that they are packed with. The question of whether a spect should be included when a silepack is created depends on the application scenario: if data is frequently exchanged between two parties, they will be aware of the spects they are using and thus the spects need not to be included in every silepack that is transferred between them. On the other hand, if one decides to publish a silepack on the World Wide Web for public download, it will make sense to include all relevant spects in order to allow clients to interpret the information stored in the silepack.

Import Siles are imported into a repository by loading the contents of the silepack and integrating it into the existing data set. The specification of the `Repository` interface (cf. Section 4.1.4) does not define methods that allow a client to load spects or filters into the repository, and it does not provide methods to store or retrieve filter expressions. Hence, a repository implementation may choose to either support only the import of siles (which can be accomplished through calls defined in the `Repository` interface), or it may provide additional methods and interfaces to upload silepacks (for instance, it may accept silepacks to be uploaded via the `setContent()` method and interpret the uploaded content accordingly). Therefore the procedures for integrating spects and filters into a repository are out of the scope of this work and remain unspecified.

When siles are loaded from a silepack into a repository, the repository implementation must interpret the imported hosted siles as *copies* of the original siles. This implies that the repository must mint new URIs for the siles, and it may refer to the originals of the imported siles (which will likely still reside in the silepack's origin repository) as referenced siles. This reference can be implemented by creating a codesile:cloned-from slink (cf. Section 5.1) from the clone to the original. This procedure is not required for referenced siles within the silepack, since the sile model allows the instantiation of multiple referenced siles with the same URI.

6.2 Sile Systems as Part of the Web of Data

More and more data is exposed on the web using RDF as common data interchange format. The *Linking Open Data* (LOD) initiative [BHAR07] encourages people and institutions to publish data using the World Wide Web and Semantic Web infrastructures, and propose to apply four basic principles that enable a unified view on the *Web of Data* [BL06a]:

1. Use URIs as names for things.

2. Use HTTP URIs so that people can look up those names.

3. When someone looks up a URI, provide useful information.

4. Include links to other URIs. so that they can discover more things

Data sources of impressive size have been made public recently (an overview is given in Figure 6.2), including DBpedia (RDF representation of Wikipedia) with 91 million triples, Geonames (60 millions), DBLP bibliographic data (15 millions) and 2000 US census data (700 million triples). The publication of RDF data from existing data sources is facilitated by tools like D2RQ [BS04], and transformation languages like GRDDL [Con07] which map data sources (like relational databases or XML documents) to RDF.

The RDF representation of siles as described in the previous section is the basis for a sile systems to participate in this Web of Data. For a conformant repository implementation, the four principles described above can be implemented as follows.

1. Siles are per definition identified by URIs; thus the first rule requires no further adaption.

2. A repository implementation is free to choose arbitrary URIs for siles; the identifiers for hosted siles are always minted by the repository. Thus an implementation should ensure that "correct" (in the sense of LOD) URIs are created. For instance, instead of using UUID URIs, like

    ```
    <urn:uuid:0e323733-11d5-4aa2-a772-000277d3bf03>
    ```

    the repository could mint a corresponding HTTP URI of the form

    ```
    <http://siles.mydomain.org/sile/0e323733-11d5-4aa2-a772-000277d3bf03>
    ```

    which carries an equal amount of information as the previous form, but additionally can be directly resolved by a client.

3. The term *useful information* depends on the context of the request. LOD encourages service providers to use *content negotiation* ([FGM+99], Section 12), which

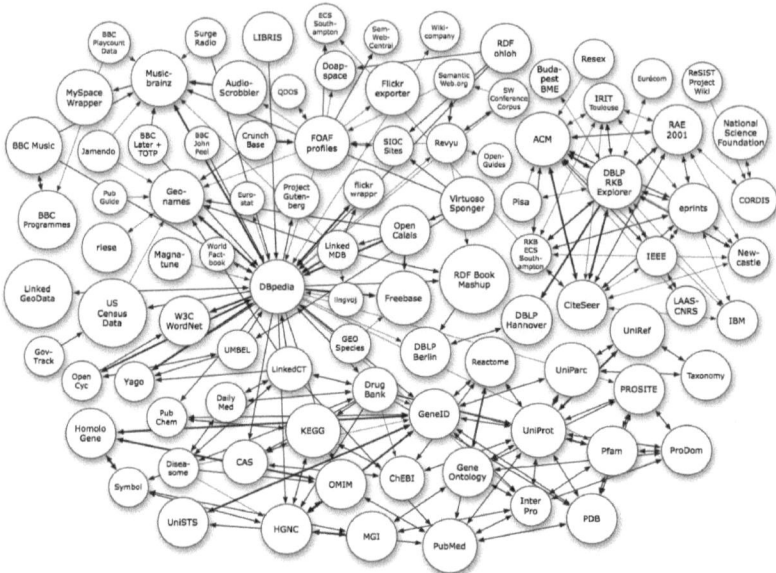

Figure 6.2: The Linked Open Data cloud as of March 2009 [CJ09]

allows the client to specify the type of information it is interested in. HTTP redirects can be used to point the client to either human-readable information (e.g., in the form of (X)HTML) or machine-interpretable data (in the form of RDF). In the context of siles, a repository implementation could mint four URIs per sile, each of which refers to an individual type of data. For instance, for the sile described above, requests to the four URIs

```
<http://siles.mydomain.org/content/0e323733-11d5-4aa2-a772-000277d3bf03>
<http://siles.mydomain.org/ann/0e323733-11d5-4aa2-a772-000277d3bf03>
<http://siles.mydomain.org/page/0e323733-11d5-4aa2-a772-000277d3bf03>
```

```
<http://siles.mydomain.org/sile/0e323733-11d5-4aa2-a772-000277d3bf03>
```

return the content, the annotations (as RDF), or a HTML page that describes the sile, respectively. The fourth URI serves as generic URI which, depending on the request the client has sent, redirects to one of the three special URIs.

With the exception of a human-readable (X)HTML representation through the `/page` URI, requests to these URIs can be directly mapped to sile API calls. For delivering the sile content, data received via `Repository.getContent()` can be used. The RDF model to be returned for the `/annotations` URI can be created by executing a `Repository.getAnnotations()` call for the respective sile, and then applying the RDF conversion rules (as discussed in Section 5.2) to the resulting set of annotations. The API does not provide a direct human-readable representation of siles (which would be returned for the `/page`) URI; however such a page can easily be created by either iterating over the set of annotations for a sile, or by rendering its RDF representation in a human-friendly way.

4. Siles can be annotated with *slinks* which are basically typed links to other siles. As arbitrary digital resources (as long as they are identifiable by URIs) can be interpreted as siles, RDF properties between such resources can be interpreted as slinks. It is out of the scope of this work to define methods how to automatically establish links between resources. Nevertheless, the sile model provides a basis for algorithms like content-based feature extraction or analysis of interaction logs [Oko08].

This discussion shows that siles are predestined to participate in the Web of Data, which can be the basis for a large number of applications that combine data from various sources. However, currently the Web of Data is a *read-only* infrastructure, since it does not specify how published data can be updated or manipulated in a uniform way. Therefore it is not possible to map the entire set of sile operators (as manifested in the Sile API, cf. Section 4.1) to the LOD architecture. To accomplish a full distribution of sile systems, we have to apply other techniques, of which we discuss one example in the next section.

6.3 Distributing Sile Systems via XML-RPC

Often, the scope of tasks involved with personal information management cannot be restricted to a single machine or data repository, but have to be considered in the context of distributed system. Even in situations where data is *personal* in the narrower sense (i.e., it is private to one person and not relevant for others) the need to distribute functionalities and data sets across different systems may arise. In collaborative envi-

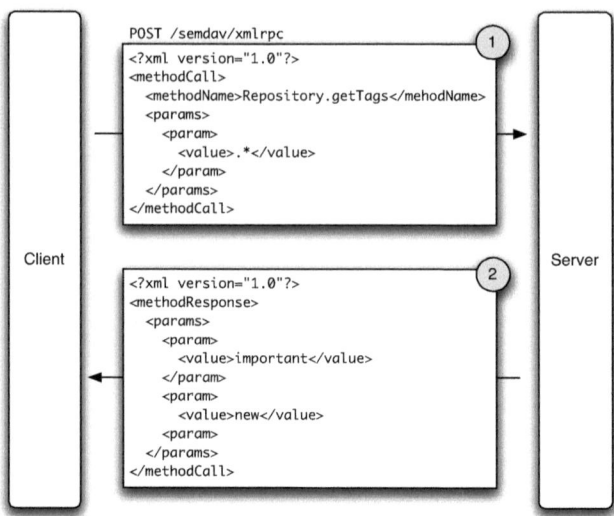

Figure 6.3: Example XML-RPC communication: request (1) and response (2)

ronments (for instance, distributed project teams) the necessity to instantiate shared repositories that can be accessed by all eligible parties occurs frequently.

The sile model and the sile API presented in the previous sections are a data model for the representation and annotation of personal information objects. The given definitions do not restrict the application of this model to a single system; rather, the presented representation of sile data as RDF and the possibility to encapsulate sile data into self-contained units (silepacks) indicate that we desire to make the sile model suitable for distributed and collaborative application scenarios.

In the following we outline an implementation of the sile API based on the XML-RPC protocol [Win99]. XML-RPC is a set of specifications that define how procedure calls can be executed remotely by representing call requests and responses as XML and transporting this XML data via HTTP POST methods. A typical XML-RPC procedure call, as well as an outline of the transported XML data, is depicted in Figure 6.3.

XML-RPC has significant advantages over other remote procedure call protocols (e.g., CORBA, Java-RMI, or SOAP) because

1. it has an open, documented specification;

2. its structure is easy to understand and simple to use;

3. it uses XML as data representation, for which many tools (editors, parsers, validators, schema languages, etc.) exist;

4. it uses HTTP as transport infrastructure and can therefore be distributed on the World Wide Web, and other HTTP features like user authentication can be applied.

However, XML-RPC has some serious limitations, the most important of which is its restriction to a set of basic data types. With the exception of `<struct>` and `<array>` (which are not suitable for polymorphic data types), it provides no mechanism to encode and transport complex types or appication-specific data structures. Although the building blocks of the sile model elements can be represented by primitive XML-RPC data types, the `Repository` interface requires polymorphism since many operations return collections of abstract supertypes[1]. Thus we face the decision whether to stay fully compliant to the original XML-RPC specification, but accept limitations or modifications to our original sile API, or to define our own extension to the XML-RPC protocol that is able to transport the information required by our model.

We do not see additional benefit by strictly conforming to the original XML-RPC specification: any client or server that will operate on sile objects will have to implement specific serialization and deserialization algorithms, regardless of which approach has been taken. It makes no sense for a "generic" XML-RPC client, i.e., one that has no knowledge about the sile data model, to access the sile repository interface, because it will not be able to process the returned data in a meaningful way. Therefore we see the justification for our decision to define extensions to the XML-RPC protocol (which we call *SemDAV/XMLRPC*); namely, we define specific data types that represent the data objects used in the sile API, including siles, annotations, spects, and filters.

6.3.1 Data Types

We introduce a dedicated XML namespace[2] for the definition of our data type extensions; this is required to separate the XML-RPC elements within a method request from

---

[1] For instance, the `getBoundAnnotations(Sile[])` method returns a collection of `BoundAnnotation` objects, which in fact contains specialized instances for the various annotation types; i.e., `BoundTag`, `BoundAttribute`, and so forth.

[2] http://www.semdav.org/2008/07/xmlrpc/datatype

```
1  <semdav:ReferencedSile
2    xmlns:semdav="http://www.semdav.org/2008/07/xmlrpc/datatype">
3    <semdav:repositoryId>
4       http://schandl@semdav-imap.univie.ac.at/
5    </semdav:repositoryId>
6    <semdav:sileUri>
7       message:466ADA28-40B3-4F26-AE6D-CB002A9DCF18@univie.ac.at
8    </semdav:sileUri>
9  </semdav:ReferencedSile>
```

Listing 6.2: Sile serialization example

the sile-specific data types. We introduce sile data types for all elements of the sile data model and the sile API. The following basic serialization rules apply[3]:

- *Entities* are serialized by an XML element whose local name corresponds to the name of the entity class as defined in the sile API. The entities' members are represented as sub-elements of the entity element.

- *Entity members* are serialized by an XML element whose local name is equal to the name of the member field as defined in the sile API.

- *Literal values* like strings and URIs are serialized as plain character strings.

An example for these serialization rules, applied to a hosted sile, is given in Listing 6.2. We see that a sile holds two URIs; one that identifies the sile's home repository; the second is the sile's own URI (in this case, the URI refers to an e-mail message), according to the class diagram depicted in Figure 4.1 (page 94). The xmlns namespace declaration applies to the ReferencedSile element as well as to its sub-elements.

As an example for a serialization of an annotation, Listing 6.3 shows a serialized Tag instance. This annotation consists of two elements, a URI (repositoryId) and a plain string (label).

---

[3]We give here only an informal description; a formal specification of the rules has been defined by the means of a RELAX NG schema.

```
 1  <semdav:Tag
 2    xmlns:semdav="http://www.semdav.org/2008/07/xmlrpc/datatype">
 3    <semdav:repositoryId>
 4      http://schandl@semdav-imap.univie.ac.at/
 5    </semdav:repositoryId>
 6    <semdav:label>
 7      new
 8    </semdav:label>
 9  </semdav:ReferencedSile>
```

Listing 6.3: Tag serialization example

Note that this serialization does not distinguish basic data types for literals. We choose this design since the sile data model uses only two basic data types, *string* and *URI*. All URIs can be directly represented as strings, and the sile API defines for each entity member field which data type is used.

Several methods of the Repository interface use array parameters and return values. We use the XML-RPC standard method to transport object arrays, which is to encapsulate the elements into a nested <array><data>...</data></array> element structure. Per definition, XML-RPC permits to mix types within an array, hence we can represent sub-types of the array's base type in the serialization. Listing 6.4 shows an example of such a serialization, where three tags are represented in a list form.

Sile content, which may be represented in arbitrary binary form and thus potentially problematic to include in XML, is encoded using the Base64 algorithm [Jos06]. In this encoded format, it can be safely treated as XML plain text, and it can be used as parameter or return value for method calls and responses. Together with the content itself, the content type is always passed to allow any agent to correctly interpret the content stream. Listing 6.5 shows an abbreviated example of a serialized content object.

Filters are serialized using the same basic serialization rules as outlined above. For all atomic filters, the API specification defines the names of member fields that characterize the filter criteria. For compound filters, the list of their children filters is encoded within an element <children>...</children> according to the serialization rules for arrays (see

```
<array>
   <data>
      <value>
         <semdav:Tag>
            <semdav:repositoryId>
               http://schandl@semdav-imap.univie.ac.at/
            </semdav:repositoryId>
            <semdav:label>
               new
            </semdav:label>
         </semdav:Tag>
      </value>
      <value>
         <semdav:Tag>
            <semdav:repositoryId>
               http://schandl@semdav-imap.univie.ac.at/
            </semdav:repositoryId>
            <semdav:label>
               important
            </semdav:label>
         </semdav:Tag>
      </value>
      <value>
         <semdav:Tag>
            <semdav:repositoryId>
               http://schandl@semdav-imap.univie.ac.at/
            </semdav:repositoryId>
            <semdav:label>
               junk
            </semdav:label>
         </semdav:Tag>
      </value>
   </data>
</array>
```

Listing 6.4: Tag array collection example

```
1  <semdav:Content
2    xmlns:semdav="http://www.semdav.org/2008/07/xmlrpc/datatype">
3    <semdav:content>
4      PD94bWwgdmVyc2lvbj0iMS4wIiBlbmNvZGluZz0iVVRGLTgiPz4K
5      [...]
6      dCI+CgkJPHRleHQvPgoJPC9kZWZpbmU+CgkKPC9ncmFtbWFyPgo=
7    </semdav:content>
8    <semdav:contentType>
9      text/plain
10   </semdav:contentType>
11 </semdav:Content>
```

Listing 6.5: Content serialization example

above). An example filter is depicted in Listing 6.6; this `AndFilter` consists of a tag filter and a category filter.

Spects, in their generic form, are serialized in the form of lists, each of which represents a group of rules specified in the spect. Thus, a spect element has a structure as indicated in Listing 6.7; as an example for the contents of each sub element an attribute applicability rule is depicted.

The elements `<uri>` and `<label>` describe the spect itself: they contain the spect URI and a human-readable label of the spect. The elements `<allAttributes>`, `<allCategories>`, and `<allSlinks>` enumerate all annotations that are defined by this spect. The following elements describe the semantic relationships between the spect elements: applicability rules for attributes and slinks, and sub/super category relationships (cf. Setion 3.2). The `<labels>` and `<descriptions>` elements enumerate human-readable labels and description texts for spect elements.

A spect can basically be interpreted as a set of maps that reflects the associations between spect elements. Spects contain two classes of maps: *1:1-maps* map one element to another one, and *1:n-maps* map one element to a set of elements. For instance, a *sub-category* rule defined in a spect can be interpreted as a mapping from a category (*key*) to a list of categories (*values*); i.e., a 1:n mapping relationship. To reflect this

```xml
<semdav:AndFilter
   xmlns:semdav="http://www.semdav.org/2008/07/xmlrpc/datatype">
   <semdav:children>
      <semdav:CategoryFilter>
         <semdav:categoryURI>
            http://www.semdav.org/2007/03/contenttype#PlainText
         </semdav:categoryURI>
      </semdav:CategoryFilter>
      <semdav:TagFilter>
         <semdav:tagText>
            new
         </semdav:tagText>
      </semdav:TagFilter>
   </semdav:children>
</semdav:AndFilter>
```

Listing 6.6: Filter serialization example

```xml
<semdav:Spect
    xmlns:semdav="http://www.semdav.org/2008/07/xmlrpc/datatype">
    <semdav:uri>http://www.semdav.org/2007/03/contenttype#</semdav:uri>
    <semdav:label>Sile Content Type</semdav:label>
    <semdav:allAttributes> ... </semdav:allAttributes>
    <semdav:allCategories> ... </semdav:allCategories>
    <semdav:allSlinks> ... </semdav:allSlinks>
    <semdav:applicableAttributesForCategories>
        <semdav:entry>
            http://www.semdav.org/2007/03/contenttype#RichText
        </semdav:entry>
        <semdav:list>
            <semdav:Attribute>
                <semdav:attributeName>
                    http://www.semdav.org/2007/03/contenttype#length
                </semdav:attributeName>
                <semdav:value>
                </semdav:value>
                <semdav:datatype>
                    http://www.w3.org/2001/XMLSchema#int
                </semdav:datatype>
            </semdav:Attribute>
            [...]
        </semdav:list>
    </semdav:applicableAttributesForCategories>
    ...
    <semdav:superCategories> ... </semdav:superCategories>
    <semdav:labels> ... </semdav:labels>
    <semdav:descriptions> ... </semdav:descriptions>
</semdav:Spect>
```

Listing 6.7: Spect serialization example

Local Element Name	Mapping	Key	Value(s)
applicableAttributesForCategories	1 : n	Category	Attribute[]
applicableSlinksForDomainCategories	1 : n	Category	Slink[]
applicableSlinksForRangeCategories	1 : n	Category	Slink[]
superCategories	1 : n	Category	Category[]

Table 6.1: Serialization of spect applicability rules

structure in XML-RPC, we introduce the elements `<entry>` and `<list>`: each map entry is encapsulated by an `<entry>` element. Each `<entry>` element has two sub-elements: one element which is interpreted as the entry's key, and a `<list>` element which contains the values for this key. For each element indicated in Table 6.1, a category URI is the key, and the appropriate serialization elements indicate relationships to other entities. For instance, the `<applicableSlinksForDomainCategories>` element contains a category as key, and a list of slinks as elements, which means that the category is a valid domain for the slink.

6.3.2 Calls and Responses

XML-RPC defines the basic structure of communication between a client and a server as follows. A client sends an XML document with a root element `<methodCall>`, and the server replies with a document that is rooted by a `<methodResponse>` element. As stated by the XML-RPC specification, the `<methodCall>` element must contain one `<methodName>` sub-element, which contains the name of the method to be called. The method names of the sile API calls are given in Figure 4.10. To allow a repository to offer additional services using the same port, a `Repository` prefix is added to each method's name.

To encode input parameters for the method call, a `<params>` element must be added to the `<methodCall>` element, and each parameter specified therein must be encapsulated in a `<param><value>...</value></param>` element structure. It is important to distinguish between calls that require multiple parameters (e.g., `Repository.createTag(String)`) and calls that require collections (arrays) as parameters (e.g., `Repository.getAnnotations (Sile[])`). In the former case, one `<param>` ele-

```xml
<?xml version="1.0" encoding="UTF-8"?>
<methodCall xmlns:ex="http://ws.apache.org/xmlrpc/namespaces/extensions">
    <methodName>Repository.createReferencedSile</methodName>
    <params>
        <param>
            <value xmlns:semdav="http://www.semdav.org/2008/07/xmlrpc/datatype
                ">
                <semdav:uri>
                    http://www.xmlrpc.com/spec
                </semdav:uri>
            </value>
        </param>
    </params>
</methodCall>
```

Listing 6.8: XML-RPC method call serialization example

ment must be specified for each paramter, while in the latter case, one `<param>` element must be present which contains an XML-RPC conformant array serialization using the `<array>` syntax described above. Listing 6.8 shows a full method call which creates a referenced sile with the specified URI in the repository.

A repository's response will, according to the XML-RPC specification, always be encapsulated by a `<methodResponse>` element; the return value must be wrapped by a `<params> <param><value>...</value></param></params>` structure. The serialization rules for return values are the same as for method parameters; if, according to the API specification, a method returns a collection (array) of values, then they must be encapsulated in an `<array>` element as described before.

6.3.3 Discussion

We have shown how elements of the sile model (siles, annotations, filters, spects) can be serialized into a XML representation, and can be transported over a network in order to remotely execute operations on a sile repository. The serialization rules presented in this chapter represent an alternative to the RDF serialization that was discussed in

Section 5.2.

Although RDF is a reasonable choice for the representation of semantically enriched data, and it was designed to be a representation for information on the Web, it has the significant drawback that it requires a two-step serialization and deserialization process. Several serialization formats for RDF exist; e.g., RDF/XML, N3, Turtle, or N-Triples. However, regardless of which format is used, application data must undergo a two-step serialization: first, objects have to be converted in some intermediate RDF graph representation (e.g., an in-memory graph); and second, this graph has to be serialized into the desired format. The message recipient must perform the same two-step deserialization: first, the RDF serialization has to be parsed into an in-memory model; then, the first class objects can be generated by iterating over this model's statements.

We have opted for the usage of XML-RPC over other, more light-weight architectures (like e.g., the REST architecture [Fie00]) because the characteristics of XML-RPC communication (especially its call-response structure, which directly represents the semantics of method calls in object-oriented languages, and the relatively straightforward style of information encoding) help to create lightweight client adapters that bind the SemDAV/XMLRPC protocol to concrete programming languages.

This design helps to integrate different, distributed services that all operate on a unified data model (the sile abstract model), and follow a shared operation semantics (the method calls defined in the `Repository` interface). Consider Figure 6.4(a), which shows a typical instantiation of a distributed sile system: a client software (e.g., a to-do list manager) uses the sile model to represent information and uses a *connector*, which implements the repository interface, to communicate with a remote server. On the server machine, a lightweight component translates incoming XML-RPC requests to native calls, while the actual server component again implements the same interface. If the user switches to a local sile repository instance, only the XML-RPC connectors have to be removed; no further modifications to the architecture or the single components have to be made (Figure 6.4(b)).

In this architecture, the *method call semantics* are retained through the entire execution process: the user performs an action in the client application's user interface, which is interpreted by the application and implies a number of API calls. These calls are directly translated into XML-RPC calls and executed by the repository. In contrast to architectures that focus on data (like the REST architecture mentioned above), this

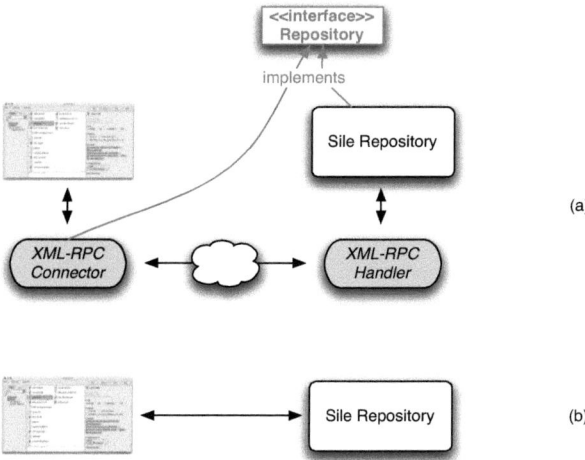

Figure 6.4: Distributed connector/handler architecture

design allows the executing party (the repository) to interpret the semantics of calls (e.g., *"add tag t to sile s"*). This interpretation can take place on many levels: for instance, the repository may apply security mechanisms to calls and forbid certain actions for certain users, or certain entities. Additionally, the repository may log method calls and, by combining them and integrating them with existing data, use these logs to infer implicit sile annotations [Oko08].

6.4 Enriching WebDAV with Sile Annotations

In the previous sections, we have discussed how we can encapsulate sile data as files using silepacks, and how we can serialize repository API calls over a network using an extension to XML-RPC. These two methods cover a wide range of application scenarios that require distributed sile systems. However, both of them require that any participating agent has full knowledge of the sile model, the semantics of repository calls, and the meaning of spects and filters.

We can observe a wide acceptance of hierarchical file systems: they are used on every desktop computer, represent a core foundation of operating systems, and are imitated in numerous ways (e.g., in IMAP accounts). Even one of the basic building blocks of the World Wide Web architecture, namely Unique Resource Identifiers (URIs) include the notion of hierarchical naming (cf. Section 1.4 of [BLFM05]), although this specification does not imply that the serving entity physically represents resources in a hierarchical structure.

The sile model aims to extend files with semantic annotations and, in principle, makes hierarchical organization structures obsolete. By attaching annotations like tags, attributes, and categories to siles, and by interconnecting siles via slinks, it establishes an *information graph*. However, to allow integration with the many systems in place that are based on hierarchical trees, it is desirable to find a way to represent sile data in hierarchical form. At first sight, such a representation must inevitably be a compromise, since a graph structure cannot be mapped to a tree without information loss. However, the way file systems are normally used disburdens us from the need to find a static tree representation of the sile graph: usually end users *interact* with file systems by browsing through folders; i.e., at a given point in time they only percept a subset of the entire tree. This allows us to employ a *dynamic* mapping, i.e., a mapping where the representation is constantly adapted to the user's navigation steps. Additionally, such a dynamic mapping is able to avoid the information loss described above up to a certain degree.

As we have described in the previous section, it is preferable to distribute sile systems; this applies also to any hierarchical representation of sile data. One basis technology for this purpose are the *HTTP Extensions for Distributed Authoring*; also called *WebDAV* [GWF+99]. This protocol uses a hierarchical data model that is similar to file systems, and data sets exposed via WebDAV can be mounted on desktop machines (all common desktop operating systems support this protocol off-shelf), whereby they appear as normal directories and files to the user. Additionally, WebDAV allows to annotate resources with metadata properties [WG04] and thus provides a lightweight annotation mechanism.

In the following we present an approach how we expose the graph structure represented by the sile model via WebDAV. The basic idea of this approach is to transform WebDAV collection URIs to sile filter expressions, and return the results of the filter execution as WebDAV resources. In the following we give a short introduction to WebDAV, before we describe the details of our mapping approach.

6.4.1 Introduction to WebDAV

WebDAV [GWF+99] is a protocol that was originally designed for distributed authoring of digital resources on the Web. WebDAV is designed on top of HTTP [FGM+99] and extends said protocol with a number of features. As HTTP, WebDAV is stateless, and it is defined in terms of *methods* that are sent from a client to a server, and are answered by a server response.

The WebDAV data model consists mainly of *resources* and *collections*. Resources are digital objects whose representation can be transmitted over a network. Collection resources are hierarchically nested structures that may contain other resources, including collections. Thus, a WebDAV repository exposes a structure similar to a hierarchical file system, whereas resources correspond to files and collections correspond to directories. Furthermore, WebDAV introduces *properties*, which are name/value pairs that describe the state of resources. WebDAV uses XML to encode server responses and properties, and uses URIs to identify resources, collections, and their properties.

In addition to the methods defined by HTTP, WebDAV defines operations that deal with the creation and manipulation of collections and properties. Most notably, WebDAV introduces the `PROPFIND` and `PROPPATCH` methods, which are used to read and manipulate resource properties, and `MKCOL` to create new collections[4]. It also introduces `COPY` and `MOVE` operations for resources. The details for all WebDAV methods can be found in Section 8 of [GWF+99].

The `PROPFIND` method, applied to a collection resource, allows the client to retrieve properties of this collection and properties of the collection's members, if there are any. Thus this method can be used by the client to retrieve information about which resources are contained in a collection. WebDAV uses a hierarchical URI syntax for resources and uses the slash character ("/") to delimit hierarchy levels. The fact that the hierarchical URI syntax for WebDAV resources implies also a collection membership (cf. [GWF+99], Section 5.2) allows us to define a mapping from hierarchical path expressions (i.e., WebDAV collection URIs) to sile filter expressions, and to create *virtual collections* that are populated by the results of the filter execution. In the following section we describe the details of this mapping.

---

[4]The HTTP method `DELETE` has been extended so that it can be applied to resources of all kinds, including collections.

6.4.2 Mapping Algorithm

A hierarchical WebDAV path (i.e., a WebDAV URL of which the protocol, hostname, and port parts have been omitted) can be interpreted as a sequence of *tokens* that are delimited by the slash character "/". We can define a set of *predefined tokens*, for each of which we define a corresponding filter that is instantiated whenever this predefined token appears in the WebDAV path. For each predefined token, we also define a set of rules how to map a number of subsequent tokens to parameters for the respective filter. The set of filters that can be derived from this analyzation of the WebDAV path are AND-combined and executed against the sile repository. For each sile in the result set, a *virtual child resource* is returned to the client.

Let us demonstrate this approach by an example. For instance, let us define the predefined token `!tag`. Let us define that for each `!tag` token a `TagFilter` is instantiated, which consumes one token (the one that follows the `!tag` token) and interprets it as parameter for the tag filter, i.e., as tag label. Thus, the WebDAV request

```
PROPFIND /!tag/important HTTP/1.1
```

would lead to the instantiation of a `TagFilter` with a tag label = `"important"`[5]. Similarly, the WebDAV request

```
PROPFIND /!tag/important/!tag/new
```

would lead to the instantiation of an `AndFilter` that contains two child filters, `TagFilter ("important")` and `TagFilter("new")`. With this technique, we can construct arbitrarily complex AND-combined filter expressions.

When a WebDAV `PROPFIND` request is executed, the repository searches for siles that match the specified criteria which are derived from parsing the request path. The result siles are returned as *virtual resources* which, by definition, have to have a URL that is derived from their containing collection's URL. Thus we instantiate a *virtual URL* that can be used to access the sile, as in the following example. This virtual URL consists of the path that is predetermined by the virtual collection URL plus an identifier for the sile. For example, for the request depicted above, the following virtual resources would be returned:

```
/!tag/important/!tag/new/sile1
```

---

[5]Note that the `HTTP/1.1` parameter is required by the HTTP protocol specification.

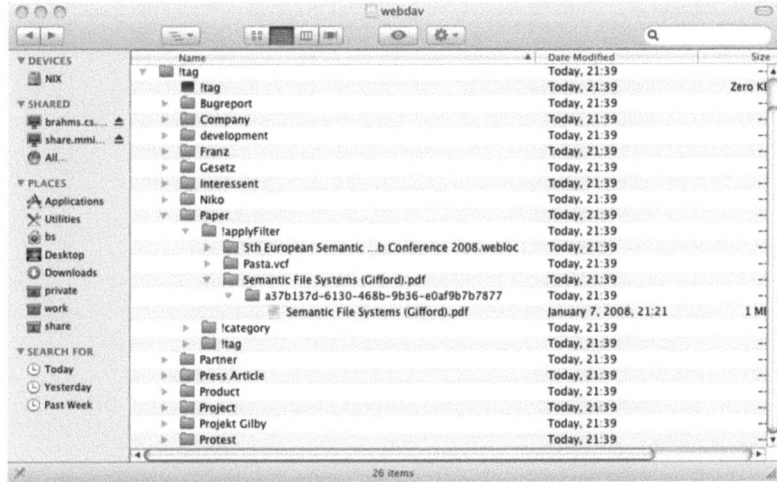

Figure 6.5: Sile repository mounted as WebDAV folder

/!tag/important/!tag/new/sile2
/!tag/important/!tag/new/sile3

However, we need a way to uniquely identify the siles, as WebDAV URLs must be unique. In principle, each sile has a "natural" unique identifier, its URI. However, the sile URI will often be created automatically by a repository (e.g., in the form of a UUID) and thus will be often not suitable for human consumption. Thus we use the value of the sile core property `sile:sile-label` (cf. Section 5.1), which is meant to contain a human-readable label for the sile, as identifier, and append it to the collection URL. However, the sile label is not required to be unique, i.e., two or more siles may have the same `sile:sile-label`. To resolve this problem, we add another *virtual collection resource* per distinct sile label which contains all instances that are annotated with this label. To distinguish the instances, we use the sile URI as an additional intermediate layer which contains the actual resource, this time safely identified by the sile label.

This design is illustrated in the following example. Consider three siles that have equal labels and are the result of a tag filter query. These siles are represented by the following resources:

```
/!tag/important/Important_Document.txt/
    urn%3Auuid%3A0e323733-11d5-4aa2-a772-000277d3bf03/Important_Document.txt
/!tag/important/Important_Document.txt/
    urn%3Auuid%3A29ab77fb-7d7d-48c8-942b-0f0f148e5b7c/Important_Document.txt
/!tag/important/Important_Document.txt/
    urn%3Auuid%3A6d550f69-9aa5-4d4a-87e8-9ba7c3e20576/Important_Document.txt
```

In this case, the URIs of the three siles are UUIDs, and each sile is represented as a virtual sub-collection of the `Important_Document.txt/` collection. This design has several advantages:

1. It reflects the design principle to uniquely identify siles by their URI, not by their "name".

2. The actual resource can be accessed by its label, not by its URI. This is especially important if the user wants to copy a resource to her local file system; in this case the label, not the sile URI, is used as the duplicate's file name, which is usually more meaningful to the user than the URI.

3. The sile label can be changed without modifying the URI. The repository can reject requests that would require to change the sile URI, however it can accept requests that aim to change the sile label.

4. Additional information regarding a sile can be represented. The repository can use the virtual collection that represents a sile (i.e., one of the collections named by a UUID in the above example) to include not only the sile itself as a member, but also additional information, like related siles:

```
/!tag/important/Important_Document.txt/
    urn%3Auuid%3A6d550f69-9aa5-4d4a-87e8-9ba7c3e20576/!slinked/
```

This path expression could be interpreted as a query for all siles that are connected via slinks with the sile under consideration.

As described before, the feature of mounting WebDAV repositories as virtual file system is implemented by all modern desktop operating systems. Thus, if a sile repository

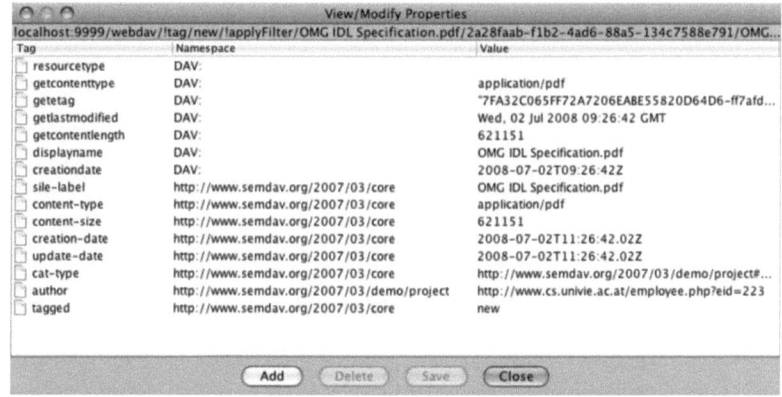

Figure 6.6: WebDAV representation of sile annotations

supports WebDAV access, one can connect to this repository and search and browse siles as if they were files in a hierarchical file system, using the standard file browser. A screenshot of such a browsing session is depicted in Figure 6.5.

As mentioned above, WebDAV resources can be annotated with properties. In our implementation, we have used this feature to represent all annotations that are attached to a sile as WebDAV properties. The WebDAV property design [WG04] perfectly matches the design of sile annotations, as both use URIs to identify the type of annotation. This information can be accessed by WebDAV-compliant client software and may be used to establish interoperability on a semantic and structural level between systems. Unfortunately these attributes are not used by typical file browsers; however, they can be displayed by dedicated WebDAV clients. An example of such a client, that renders all annotations of a WebDAV resource in tabular form, is depicted in Figure 6.6.

As we can see in this figure, sile annotations are represented as WebDAV properties. This includes attributes like content-type, content-size, and creation-date, but also slinks to other siles (author), categories (cat-type) and tags (tagged). As WebDAV only defines properties to represent resource annotations, all types of sile annotations are mapped to this construct; hence their type cannot be distinguished based only on the WebDAV representation.

Figure 6.6 also shows that as far as possible, sile annotations are also mapped to standard WebDAV properties. WebDAV defines several properties that are required or recommended for attributes (cf. [GWF+99], Section 13). Most of them coincide with the sile core attributes that also have to be present and thus can be generated by directly mapping them; e.g., the attribute `sile:content-size` is mapped to `DAV:getcontentlength`, the attribute `sile:content-type` is mapped to `DAV:getcontenttype`, and so forth.

6.5 Summary

In this section, we have introduced various approaches how sile data can be serialized, which address different needs that occur in different application contexts. First, we have introduced silepacks, which are a way to encapsulate objects from the sile model (siles, annotations, filters, and specs) into a single, self-contained unit that can be represented as file and thus be easily transferred over a variety of channels, including e-mail, instant messaging, or removable devices. Because they are based on well-documented formats and standards, silepacks additionally enable simple archiving or publishing of annotated sile data. Second, we have discussed how data represented in a sile repository can be exposed under consideration of the principles posted by the Linking Open Data initiative.

Since these guidelines do not permit write access on publish data, we have further described how we can distribute access to sile repositories by encoding method calls defined in the sile API using the XML-RPC standard. We have described an extension to the XML-RPC protocol that allows for semantically complete serialization of sile objects. Fourth, we have described how we can represent sile data and annotations as a file system-like hierarchical structure, and how we map this representation to the WebDAV protocol. This allows us to access sile repositories using standard software, like file browsers and other applications, which establishes interoperability on a very broad basis.

Chapter 7

Case Studies of Sile Repository Implementations

If we don't succeed, we run the risk of failure. —
Anonymous

After having presented the sile model and its elements in various levels of abstraction, we now discuss prototypical implementations of this proposed data structure. These implementations greatly differ in their functionality and their technological realization; this is by intent, since we want to show the flexibility of the sile model and its applicability in entirely different scenarios. We discuss three implementations:

1. the *SemDAV Server*, which is a sile repository based on Semantic Web technology and supports advanced services like reasoning, data integrity validation, and integration of external data sources;

2. *silefiles*, a lightweight repository that interprets hierarchical file systems as sile data; thus it becomes possible for the user to annotate and to relate them through the Repository interface, but at the same time it is possible to continue to use the files directly; and

3. *SileMail*, a wrapper for IMAP servers which exemplarily shows how data sources

that are relevant for personal information management can be represented as siles.

In the following, we outline the architecture and important implementation aspects of each of these prototypes.

7.1 The SemDAV Server: A Triple Store-based Sile Repository

7.1.1 Architecture Overview

We have implemented a fully-functional sile repository based on Semantic Web technologies. This implementation has been developed using the Java 1.6 platform; it uses plain files to store sile content, and it utilizes the Jena Semantic Web framework[1] with the Pellet OWL DL reasoner[2], backed by a PostgreSQL database[3], to store and manage sile annotations, which are internally represented using RDF [KC04]. Its main functionalities w.r.t. sile storage and management are

1. *storage* of sile data, including storage of content and annotations;

2. *handling of updates* to content and annotations;

3. *query processing*, including the conversion of filter expressions to SPARQL queries, and the transformation of result graphs to sile objects;

4. *ontology management* for performing reasoning and consistency checks on sile metadata;

5. *request handling* according to the specification of the SemDAV/XMLRPC protocol (see Section 6.3), the WebDAV-sile mapping (Section 6.4), and the SPARQL Protocol for RDF [CFT08];

6. *Interaction logging* for subsequent analysis and automatic generation of sile annotations [OS09].

---

[1] http://jena.sourceforge.net
[2] http://pellet.owldl.com
[3] http://www.postgresql.org

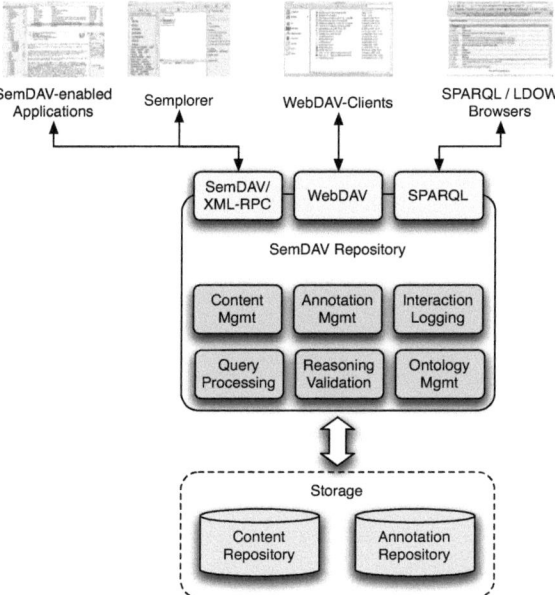

Figure 7.1: SemDAV server architecture overview

The architecture of the repository implementation is depicted in Figure 7.1. The implementation is highly modular, and any component can be exchanged without modifications to other ones. For instance, we have also implemented an experimental adapter for the Sesame RDF storage system[4]. In the following, we briefly describe the main components of the SemDAV server.

Content Management The binary contents of hosted siles are stored in plain files in a designated server directory. The current implementation uses a flat naming scheme, where the URI of siles is directly mapped to file names. This is done by encoding all URI characters that are not allowed in file names (like \, :, |, and so forth) so that they can be used as file names[5].

---

[4] http://www.openrdf.org
[5] The same mapping between URIs and file names is used within silepacks, cf. Section 6.1

Annotation Management As described above, we use the Jena Semantic Web framework as storage backend for sile annotations. The representation of siles within the repository is conformant to the mapping described in Section 5.2. The annotation management component is designed to support multiple named graphs [CBHS05a], although currently only the default graph is used[6].

Interaction Logging The manual creation of annotations is expensive, and often users are not willing to do such annotations because the immediate benefit of doing so is not apparent. In this case, methods for automatic annotation generation are required. One possible strategy to derive such annotations is to analyze the interactions (i.e., the requests that the server receives) with siles and annotations [SK06]. For this purpose, the interaction logging component traces all read and write requests that are issued to the server for subsequent analysis. The discussion of the analysis component is out of the scope of this work; we refer the reader to [OS09].

Query Processing The server receives filter expressions (cf. Section 4.1.3) via its XML-RPC interface; however these filters must be converted to SPARQL expressions so that they can be executed on the stored annotation data. The algorithms for this conversion are described in Section 5.3. The query processing component implements these algorithms and executes the resulting SPARQL CONSTRUCT query against the RDF database. Similarly, all SemDAV/XMLRPC operations that deal with annotations (for instance, getAttributes()) are internally transformed to SPARQL queries, and the results are re-converted to sile annotation objects. Currently all existing graphs are included in queries; however this may be restricted to subsets of all graphs in future versions.

Reasoning and Spect Management The server can be configured to load an arbitrary number of spects in the form of OWL-DL ontologies, which can be used for inferencing and consistency checks over the database. Every ontology is loaded into a separate named graph. The repository is implemented so that reasoning and consistency validation can easily be disabled to increase the overall system performance, which is a major issue in a system with dynamically changing data (cf. requirement *R8* in [WLL+07]).

---

[6]In later versions the repository may be extended, e.g., to support multi-user annotations; in this case each user's model could be stored in a separate graph.

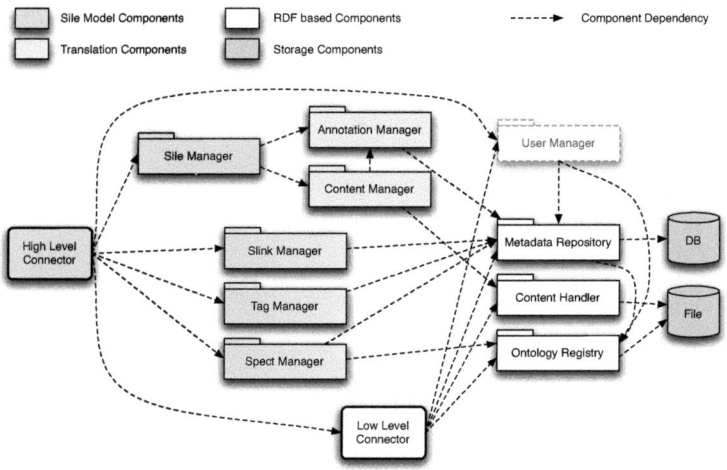

Figure 7.2: SemDAV server components

7.1.2 Request Handling

The server implementation is designed in a highly modular manner; the main components are depicted in Figure 7.2. This design allows for a strict separation of functionalities, and enables us to replace components if the internal structure of the server needs to be changed, or if external data sources should be integrated into the system (cf. Section 7.1.3).

We can roughly distinguish four groups of components, depending on their level of abstraction; these groups are indicated by different colors in Figure 7.2:

1. *Sile Model Components* are operating on objects of the sile API (which includes annotations and filters) and entirely abstract over any serialization of siles.

2. *Translation Components* implement the mapping between the sile API objects and the concrete RDF representation, as described in Section 5.2, between filters and SPARQL queries (cf. Section 5.3); and handle raw sile content.

3. *RDF based Components* work only with the RDF data model, i.e., they provide

functionality that is independent from the abstract sile model. These components could be reused for other RDF-based systems.

4. *Storage Components* are responsible for the actual physical storage of data. These components perform their individual mapping of low-level data, like RDF graphs and byte arrays, to physical representations (in our case, to a relational database and to files in a server directory).

The translation components, depicted in the left area of Figure 7.2 transform request data from the sile model to RDF and SPARQL and forward them to the underlying components. There, the requests are processed by using the storage components, which abstract over the actual data storage backend. The result data is processed by the storage components and re-converted into the sile model by the appropriate manager components. As an illustrative example, the workflow of a `searchSiles()` request is depicted in Figure 7.3.

All these components are referenced by a number of *connectors* that expose actual functionality to the outside. Currently we have implemented two connectors: first, the *High Level Connector* implements the `Repository` interface described in Section 4.1 and provides access to sile data on a high level. Through this interface, siles and annotations can be manipulated, and filter queries can be issued. It does not expose implementation details to the outside and is thus entirely independent from the RDF- and SPARQL-based representation of siles and filter expressions within the server. Second, via the *Low Level Connector* clients can directly access the raw data stored within the server. This connector provides methods to access RDF triples, to upload and download binary content, and to issue SPARQL queries.

The connectors are wrapped by *servlets* that provide protocol-specific access to the methods exposed by the two connectors. We have implemented two servlets based on XML-RPC [Win99], one that serializes binary Java objects, and another one that uses the platform-independent, generic XML serialization rules described in Section 6.3 to provide platform-independent access to objects in the repository.

7.1.3 External Data Integration

The modular architecture of the implementation described above allows for the easy integration of external data sources by replacing certain system components with other ones that communicate with external systems. By doing so we can instantiate a *sile*

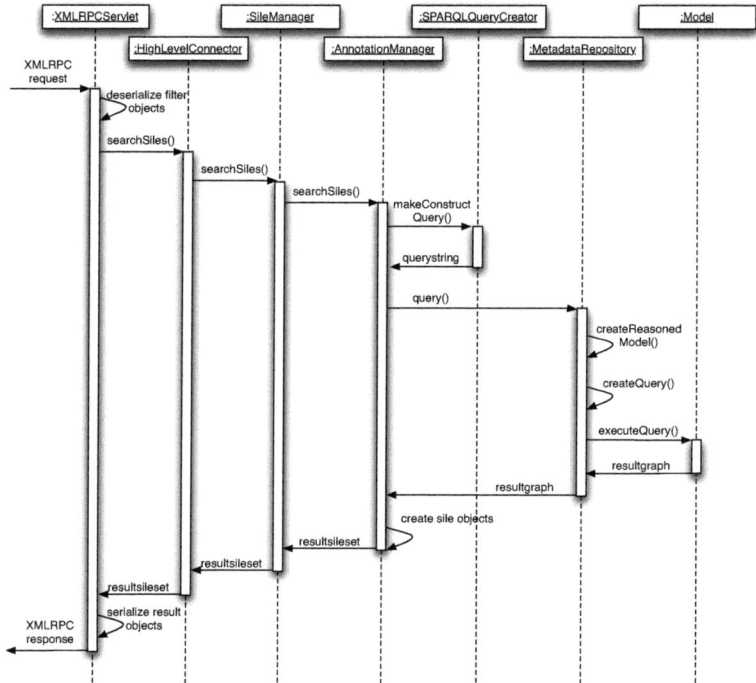

Figure 7.3: Sequence diagram for searchSiles() requests

facade for external systems, and thus integrate data of arbitrary form and structure into a semantic desktop environment. It is out of the scope of this work to discuss integration scenarios in more detail; however in this section we indicate starting points towards such work.

The selection of components to be replaced depends on the type and level of integration that should take place. For instance, for any data source that can be exposed as RDF and uses a suitable vocabulary (e.g., relational databases [BS04]), one could implement a corresponding MetadataRepository component. The interface of MetadataRepository is based on the RDF and SPARQL languages, thus in this scenario the data would not have to be converted in other formats. However, depending on the vocabularies used in the external source, it could be necessary to perform a schema mapping, which includes query rewriting, in order to transform the external RDF data sets into a representation that conforms to the sile and annotation representation rules discussed in Section 5.2 (for siles and annotations) and Section 5.3 (for filter expressions). An example for an integration architecture that performs such mapping on RDF instance data is discussed in [Has08].

If such a conversion cannot take place, one could consider replacing the entire `AnnotationManager` component. This component instantiates the mapping between the elements of the abstract sile model and the concrete RDF representation. Its interface does not expose any RDF-specific elements, and thus a manager component can be implemented that uses no RDF data model at all. For instance, on this level one could directly wrap information stored in online services or in relational databases[7].

In certain integration scenarios it may be necessary to refer only to externally hosted content; for instance, to content that resides in a file system, or to web resources that do not provide the means for semantically rich annotations. In such situations, it may be sufficient to replace the `ContentHandler` component. It is the task of this component to provide read and write access to binary content objects. In our reference implementation all binary content access operations are mapped to files that reside within a directory hierarchy on the server, but a different implementation could e.g., choose to redirect these requests to BLOBs stored in a RDBMS, or to remote content repositories.

7.2 silefiles: A Semantic File System Extension

In the previous section we have discussed a reference implementation of a sile repository that provides a large set of functionality, including ontology-based reasoning and validation. To demonstrate the versatileness of the sile model, we have also implemented a functionality-restricted, purely file-based prototype repository. This implementation builds on top of an existing hierarchical directory structure, and one of its main design goals was to allow users to continue working with files and directories, but to provide additional support for unstructured annotations; in this case, for tagging.

Our system implements a lightweight annotation tool for hierarchical file systems. It uses the same RDF-based representation for siles and annotations as the full repository implementation described in the previous section; however it does not employ a full

---

[7]For an initial discussion on the mapping between the relational model and the sile model refer to Section 5.4.2.

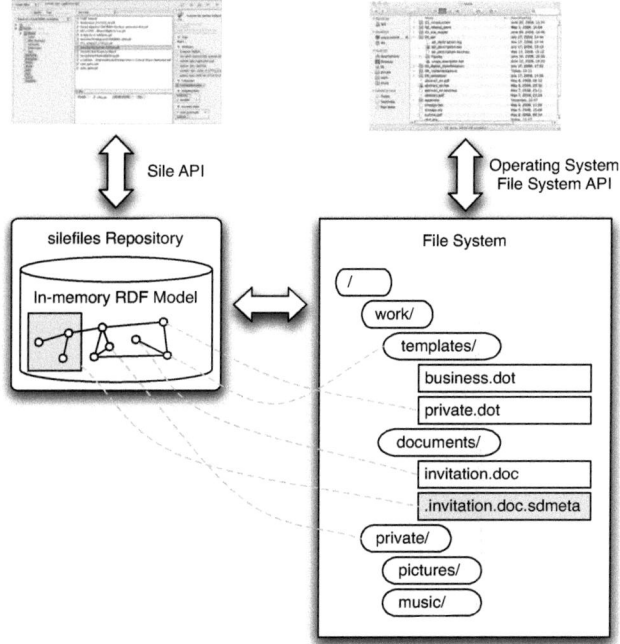

Figure 7.4: silefiles architecture

triple store or a relational database to store sile content and annotations. Instead, it holds an in-memory RDF model of the file system, and references actual files via their URIs. This in-memory model contains *implicit* and *explicit annotations*, which are described in the following. This design allows the user to continue to work with the hierarchical file system and its semantic extensions in parallel; hence the tools that the user is familiar with can be used further on, but additionally it is possible to semantically annotate and interrelate files.

- *Implicit Annotations* are derived from data that already exists in the file directory tree. These annotations include the file name, file size, and the dates of creation and last update (which are represented by attribute annotations), but also the

```
1  <http://www.semdav.org/2007/03/tag-class#important>
2      <http://www.w3.org/2000/01/rdf-schema#subClassOf>
3          <http://www.semdav.org/2007/03/core#Tagged> ;
4      <http://www.w3.org/2000/01/rdf-schema#label>
5          "important"^^<http://www.w3.org/2001/XMLSchema#string> .
6
7  <local:local>
8      <http://www.semdav.org/2007/03/core#tag-type>
9          <http://www.semdav.org/2007/03/tag-class#important> ;
10     <http://www.semdav.org/2007/03/core-annotation#derived-from>
11         <http://my.host/repository/work/templates/business.dot>
```

Listing 7.1: Example of a silefiles metadata file

file path, whereas this string is split into its parts (i.e., each subdirectory name is considered separately) and attached to the file as tags. Furthermore, a special category File is implicitly attached to all siles. Implicit annotations are generated on-the-fly and are never persisted to the file system.

- *Explicit Annotations* are annotations that can not be derived from information present in the file system. All sile annotations (tags, attributes, categories, slinks) are converted into their RDF representation, and are written to a hidden metadata file in the same directory as the file resides. The file is named as its reference file, and a .ttl suffix is added. Within this RDF model the file is referenced not via its URI but via a special resource local:local. This design increases the system's flexibility w.r.t. changes in the file system. As the connection between a file and its persisted annotations is established via the file name, redundancy is avoided by repeating the name within the metadata file. A typical metadata file is depicted in Listing 7.1. It shows a tag annotation and a slink to another file that resides in a different directory.

The URIs of siles that are exposed via the repository interface are minted by combining a repository-specific prefix (e.g., http://my.host/repository) with the path of the file, relative to the repository's root directory. Thus the mapping between RDF annotations and files is always unambiguous. However if a file is moved or renamed, the annotations (including slinks that point to this file) are lost. We have not yet implemented a solution for this problem; however it would be possible to hook into the underlying file system and trace corresponding events[8]. Then we can use this event information to keep the RDF model up-to-date. However, several problematic aspects of synchronization between underlying file systems and overlay metadata systems remain, as described in Section 3.1.

7.3 SileMail: Semantic Extensions to E-Mail

Similar to the silefiles implementation described in the previous chapter, we have developed a wrapper component for mail messages that reside in an IMAP server [Cri03]. Alongside files, e-mails are probably the most important manifestation of digital personal information [DB01] and are therefore of high interest to be integrated into a semantic desktop environment.

The structure of IMAP accounts is very similar to the structure of file systems: objects (in this case, mail messages) are arranged within a hierarchical structure. However, mail messages expose one alleviation in contrast to files: a unique `Message-ID` is generated by the mail system where the mail message is created; this id can be used for unambiguous reference. We have implemented a component similar to the system presented in the previous section. The idea is again to enable a parallel use of traditional e-mail clients and semantic PIM tools.

In contrast to files, e-mail messages provide a standardized way to store arbitrary describing data in the form of *headers*. A number of headers are already defined in the various standards that define e-mail message formats and communication protocols, and the information found therein (e.g., `From:`, `To:`, `Subject:`, `Priority:`, and so forth) can be exposed as attributes or slinks within the sile model as *implicit annotations*. If a message is unread, we can automatically attach a corresponding tag to the sile. The `References:` header, which contains message id's of previous mail messages within a conversation, is mapped to slinks. Additionally, custom headers can be used to store additional information, e.g., tag annotations or slinks to other siles. This information can be stored directly within the message on an IMAP server and is thus available through the IMAP protocol, which allows an e-mail client application to retrieve this

---

[8]All current desktop operating systems provide functionality to hook into file system events; for instance, on Mac OS X the *FSevents* framework can be used for this.

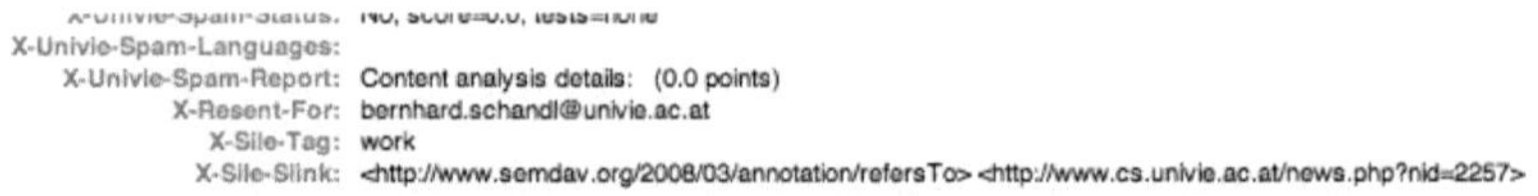

```
X-UIIIVIe-Spain-Status:    INU, SCUIe=U.U, tests=none
X-Univie-Spam-Languages:
    X-Univie-Spam-Report:  Content analysis details:  (0.0 points)
           X-Resent-For:   bernhard.schandl@univie.ac.at
              X-Sile-Tag:  work
           X-Sile-Slink:   <http://www.semdav.org/2008/03/annotation/refersTo> <http://www.cs.univie.ac.at/news.php?nid=2257>
```

Figure 7.5: An annotated e-mail message as displayed in an off-the-shelf e-mail client

information (cf. Figure 7.5).

The IMAP protocol defines a `SEARCH` command (cf. Section 6.4.4 of [Cri03]) which can be used to search for e-mails based on a number of criteria, including contents of custom headers, across the entire set of messages. By translating the generic sile filter algebra (cf. Section 3.3) to corresponding IMAP search expressions we can execute sile queries against e-mail repositories. For demonstration purposes we have implemented a mapping of tag filters to the `X-Sile-Tag:` header (cf. Figure 7.5).

7.4 Summary

In this section we have showed three different system implementations that are capable of representing sile and annotation data, and (to a certain extent) execute sile filter queries and return corresponding results. The range of implementations (from plain file systems to high-end RDBMS-backed repositories) shows that the sile model is able to adequately represent very diverging kinds of information. We have outlined the advantages of the modular design of our RDF-based repository implementation, which allows one to extend or replace certain components and connect to external data sources on various levels.

In the next section we will discuss a prototypical implementation of a client application, the *Semplorer*, which is a generic utility to browse and manipulate sile repositories. It uses the sile API to communicate with a sile repository and has been successfully tested with all three repository implementations presented in this chapter.

Chapter 8

The Semplorer: A User Interface for Sile Management

"Where did you put it?"
"Put what?"
"You know?"
"Where do you think?"
"Oh." — Nicholas Negroponte, Director of the MIT Media Lab, stating his ideal model of human-computer interaction

The vocabularies used to describe siles (i.e., the possible names for categories, attributes, and slinks) are extensible, and often they are not specified in a formal way, especially in the semantic desktop domain. While this fact is one of the greatest strengths of this data model, it also imposes severe consequences for application design and development: tools must be designed so as to accommodate changing and developing data models and data formats.

This issue becomes especially apparent in the context of user interfaces. Most "traditional" applications use a closed-world data model: the structure and semantics of the processed data is known at design time, and appropriate user interfaces can be designed, evaluated, and optimized—a rigid data model is a solid basis for user interface design. On the contrary, an application that operates with an open data model can only guess what the data it operates on will look like. Often the only known factor is the underlying meta model, thus the user interface for such an application must be designed sufficiently generic, yet suitable and understandable for the end user.

One example of such a generic interface is the file browser, of which we have analyzed several implementations in Section 2.1.6. Typical file browsers, as found in modern desktop operating systems, provide functionality for generic management of files, but do not consider the inner semantics of file contents and directory hierarchies. File browsers are used for both manual annotation (e.g., when saving a file within an application, a file browser window is opened to select a storage location and enter a file name) and retrieval (by navigating through the directory structure, or in an application's *Open File* dialog). File browsers can also be used to arbitrarily manipulate the file system structure (and, if not prevented by access control mechanisms, also to corrupt it). However it is not possible to edit file contents using a standard file browser, since the inner structure of files remains hidden.

In a generic information system, like the sile data model, the possible annotation and retrieval operations are more manifold; still, a generic user interface for search, retrieval, and manipulation is desirable.

We have developed the *Semplorer* [SAPT07], a generic interface for browsing, searching, and manipulating siles. In the following we give an overview on the design considerations, and describe the interaction mechanisms that we have realized in this implementation.

8.1 Design Considerations

In the design and implementation of the Semplorer, we focused on three main design objectives that we consider as important for a novel desktop data management paradigm; *familiarity*, *simplicitiy*, and *modularity*. We justify the emphasis of these three objectives in the following.

Familiarity

As mentioned above, we consider it important that a tool for annotation and retrieval of semantic data assets (siles) is—as far as possible—immediately familiar to end users. We respect the results of research in novel user interfaces and interaction metaphors, both for traditional file systems (cf. Section 2.1.6) and semantic systems[1]. However we believe that for the time being it is important not to force users to adopt to new interfaces, but to develop interfaces that adopt to what users are familiar with.

Such adoption takes place on multiple levels, including *metaphors*, *appearance*, *vocabulary*, and *interaction*. Metaphors subsume the abstract concepts that the user and the machine are collaboratively working with; they can be regarded as the bridge between the mental models in the human brain and the binary representation in the computer's memory.

The *metaphors* used on desktop computers (mainly files and directories) are, whether they actually adequately represent a human's mental model or not, well understood by end users[2]. The concept of single, self-contained logical information units seems to reflect—to a certain extent—the human view of the world. The sile model extends this concept by externalizing describing information for these units, and adds mechanisms to represent *semantic relationships* between them.

Consequently, the Semplorer can be seen as an extension of file browsers, where these extensions are also applied to *appearance* of the user interface. The classic rendering of files using a combination of a symbol icon and a textual label is retained in our design. We also keep the familiar representation forms of lists in various forms, although we add the possibility to represent siles in new ways that become possible only because of the underlying semantic data model; e.g., time-based views or customizable tabular views. The representation of organizational structures, however, is a different issue: while file systems provide only one dimension of structure (hierarchical directories), siles offer a variety of semantic annotations with various degrees of semantic expressivity, and these different types of annotations require different visualization renderings.

The question of the *vocabulary* used in user interfaces for semantic systems is very difficult to answer. On the one hand, users are familiar to certain terms, like "file", "folder", or "file name". The direct application of these terms to semantically rich concepts may cause confusion, since the concepts significantly differ on many levels: a sile is not a file, and vice versa. On the other hand, we should not expect users to become familiar with terminology from semantic systems, like "ontology", "data type property", or "disjoint classes", since these terms are loaded with certain, possibly unclear or diffuse interpretations; e.g., in science or in marketing; and are therefore hard to learn and

---

[1] Recent research in this field has been published, for instance, in the Semantic Web User Interaction Workshop series [msGD+08].

[2] We can observe that the term "file" often used as a synonym for "data" by computer users.

understand for end users.

Users face also a common set of *interaction* mechanisms in typical file browsers. The WIMP interface paradigm (cf. Section 2.1.6) exposes certain mechanisms that have been adopted by all desktop operating systems. We consider it important for a semantic user interface *(1)* to inherit interaction mechanisms, as far as possible, and apply them to the semantically rich concepts as far as possible, and *(2)* to integrate with external or legacy interfaces that are further used. In Section 8.2 we describe how we apply one of the most common interaction mechanisms, *drag and drop*, to our semantic user interface, and how we integrate this interface with the operating system's native user interface.

We believe that by implementing familiar user interface concepts and slightly adapting them to the semantic data management paradigms, we can ease the migration path for end users and increase the acceptance and efficiency of interactive semantic systems.

Simplicity

Semantic technologies and models expose a high level of complexity, especially when one considers the modelling and representation of complex ontologies. This complexity should be hidden from the user by the user interface, which should provide a simplified, yet comprehensive view on data, and interaction mechanisms that hide complex queries or processing procedures.

Naturally, the requirement of simplicity collides with the requirement of full functionality. Certain aspects of a semantic object model can only be accessed through a higher level of complexity; a good example for such a conflict are *search interfaces*. A simple keyword search can be transported through a highly reduced and simplified interface; however, a complex search query that possibly incorporates nested boolean expressions needs an advanced and thus more complex user interface. To overcome this problem, we followed an approach that is often successfully used for web search engines [TL05]; namely, to offer a *standard interface* with restricted functionality but simple appearance, and an *advanced interface* that provides full access to all features through a more sophisticated interface that, however, requires more experience and knowledge to use.

Modularity

A semantic data model like the one envisioned in this thesis can represent a wide variety of information, ranging from highly structured data sets that are backed by a relational database to the unstructured collections of files that can be found on an end user's desktop. Depending on her current context, different information aspects may be of relevance to the user. Naturally, one user interface cannot cover all possible application scenarios, and it is in fact one major goal of the sile model to provide a data abstraction layer that can be used by applications that bring their own, specialized and highly focused interface for specific tasks. Nevertheless, we believe that even a generic-purpose interface like the Semplorer should provide the possibility to change the user's view on information.

This becomes especially apparent when we consider the Semplorer as a kind of *user interface library*, which provides widgets and window components to be reused within other applications. The benefit of such generalized libraries can be seen by the means of the standardized *Open File* and *Save File* dialogs that are provided by operating systems: first, application developers do not need to re-implement the functionality provided by such components within their own applications; and second, users are always presented the same interface for the same task; i.e., to open or save files. The same advantages can be realized through interface components provided by the Semplorer: for instance, applications could reuse tag widgets so that they have equal appearance across a system, or they could reuse drag and drop implementations for object annotation.

Even if the functionality of a graphical user interface is highly modularized and de-coupled, one must guarantee that the user always percepts the system as a single unit; i.e., one must avoid visible or tangible gaps in the usage flow. For instance, the user should not notice a point of rupture when she synchronously interacts with loosely coupled components, or should be able to use the same interaction mechanisms regardless of which data view she is working with. Within the Semplorer we have implemented several interface variants for searching and browsing, and although they expose different views on information they share a common set of graphical widgets and interaction metaphors, as described in Section 8.2.

8.2 Interface Design

In the following we describe the main elements of the Semplorer UI design: the *main window* which contains the visual rendering of the interactive elements, and the *entity*

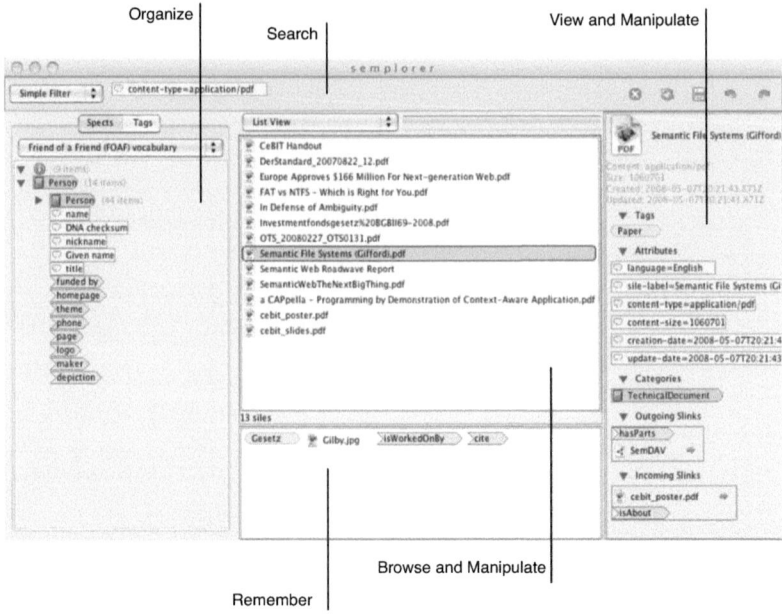

Figure 8.1: Semplorer main window structure

widgets which are small graphical units that represent elements of the sile data model and constitute the interactive elements of the system. Then, we sketch the interaction mechanisms through which a user is able to search, navigate, and manipulate siles.

The Semplorer Main Window With our design of the structure of the Semplorer main window, we follow the two design principles of familiarity, by designing the window's structure and appearance similar to common file browsers, and modularity, by separating the window into different parts, each of which can be considered as an individual component. A screenshot of a typical browsing session with the semplorer is depicted in Figure 8.1; the individual window parts and their purposes are described in the following.

1. *Organize* — With the Semplorer the user can navigate and manipulate the dif-

ferent organizational metaphors provided by the sile model (i.e., tags, attributes, categories, and slinks). Currently we have implemented a *spect browser* to navigate elements of a spect (cf. Section 3.2); i.e., a restricted view on an ontological model; and a *tag browser* through which tags can be created, searched, manipulated, and attached to siles.

2. *Browse* — The siles in the repository are displayed according to the currently loaded view implementation and can be browsed accordingly. We have implemented three different views on siles which are discussed in Section 8.2.1.

3. *Search* — Users can employ the annotations visible on screen to incrementally build search filters (cf. Section 4.1.3) which restrict the set of displayed siles. We have implemented a number of different search interfaces that expose different levels of complexity and expressivity w.r.t. modeling of complex filter queries; these are discussed in Section 8.2.2.

4. *View* — Detail information for the currently selected sile is displayed in the rightmost area of the window. This includes a sile label, core attributes like the sile's creation date and the date of its last update (cf. Section 5.1), and its associated annotations. Annotations are spatially grouped by their type, and each group can be collapsed and expanded. This area can also be used to manipulate sile annotations (see below).

5. *Manipulate* — Both the *browse* and the *view* area can be used to manipulate annotations; i.e., to edit, add, or remove annotations. These actions are initiated by simple mouse-based interactions; the detailed interaction mechanisms are discussed in Section 8.2.3.

6. *Remember* — Regularly used objects of all types can be remembered by the Semplorer and are kept in the bottom area of the screen. Items of any type can be "pinned" in this area, and since the remember area is not affected from filters, pinned items remain to stay there until the user explicitly removes them by selecting the widget's *remove* mark (see below).

The Entity Widget Concept The Semplorer provides a set of *widgets* to represent elements of the sile data model. The widgets for different annotation types differ in form and color in order to allow the user to immediately and unambiguously recognize and

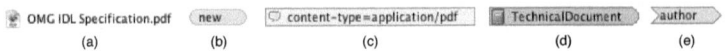

Figure 8.2: Entity widgets: sile (a), tag (b), attribute (c), category (d), slink (e)

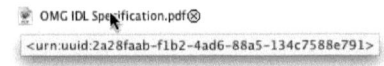

Figure 8.3: Widget with tooltip and delete button

identify the represented information. The five widget types are depicted in Figure 8.2 and described in the following.

- *Siles* are represented as an icon and a text, whereas the icon represents the sile's content type and the text is derived from a sile's `sile-label` attribute[3]. When the mouse hovers over the sile widget, the sile's URI is displayed in the form of a tooltip (see Figure 8.3).

- *Tags* are represented by blue rectangles with rounded vertexes on the left and right side. Tags are labelled with the tag's textual representation, which can contain an arbitrary sequence of characters including spaces.

- *Attributes* are represented by yellow rectangles with an icon in the form of a stylized speech bubble. The widget shows both the attribute name (in an abbreviated form) and the value, separated by an equivalence sign. The widget's tool tip shows more information about the attribute annotation, including the full name URI, the value, and the value data type.

- *Categories* are represented by green rectangles with a rounded right vertex, which slightly resembles the letter *C*. It contains a rendering of the category name and

---

[3]A sile may have multiple, different `sile-label` attributes; however we do not specify an algorithm how to select one in this case. Currently the Semplorer selects an arbitrary attribute instance, if many are present, and displays the sile's URI if no `sile-label` attribute is present. Future versions may use additional information (e.g., language tags) to select a sile label, or render all existing instances of the attribute.

a book icon, which indicates that there may be more information about this category "behind the scenes". Similar to attributes, the icon of the category may be overruled by the spect definition in future versions.

- *Slinks* are symbolized by a pink shape that points from the left to the right. It is labelled with the (abbreviated) slink name, and the slink URI is displayed when the user hovers over the widget. The arrow points from the slink's source sile to its target sile; hence the slink's source is always be displayed to the left of the widget, while the target is displayed to the right of the widget.

As described before, each widget can be dragged and dopped to perform various operations. In general, whenever an annotation is dropped onto a sile, this sile is annotated with the dropped annotation (cf. Section 8.2.3). When the user hovers over an annotation or a sile, a small "X" button is displayed which can be used to remove the object from its current context. Finally, all widgets can be used as search criteria by dragging them into the filter area (cf. Section 8.2.2).

8.2.1 Navigation

The Semplorer itself offers a restricted set of navigation methods. Usually the center area of the Semplorer window (the *Browse and Manipulate* area in Figure 8.1) displays siles from the repository that match the restrictions defined by the current set of filters (cf. Section 8.2.2). It depends on the selected rendering component how the siles are actually displayed. We have implemented three different views on siles (cf. [Tod08]) that may be helpful in different usage scenarios:

1. a *List View* (Figure 8.1) that arranges siles, sorted by their label, in a list. This is the default view and is useful for small numbers of items;

2. a *Table View* (Figure 8.5) displays selected information about siles in tabular form. The table view can be customized by the user by dragging annotations, e.g., attributes, into the table header; then, the according information is displayed in the column. The columns can also be re-arranged and removed by drag and drop operation;.

3. a *Timeline View* (Figure 8.4) that arranges siles along a one-dimensional axis, according to one user-selected attribute value. Siles are arranged along the x-axis

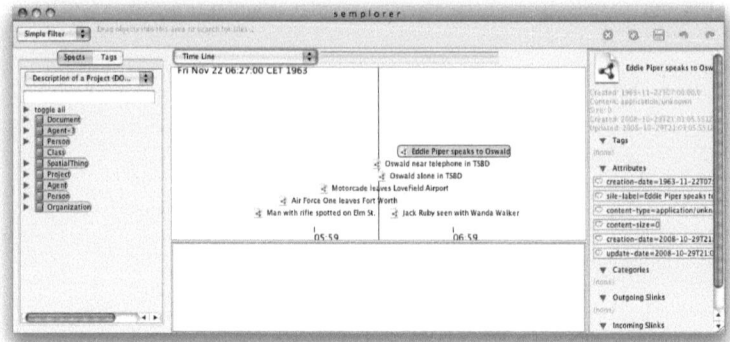

Figure 8.4: Semplorer timeline view [Tod08]

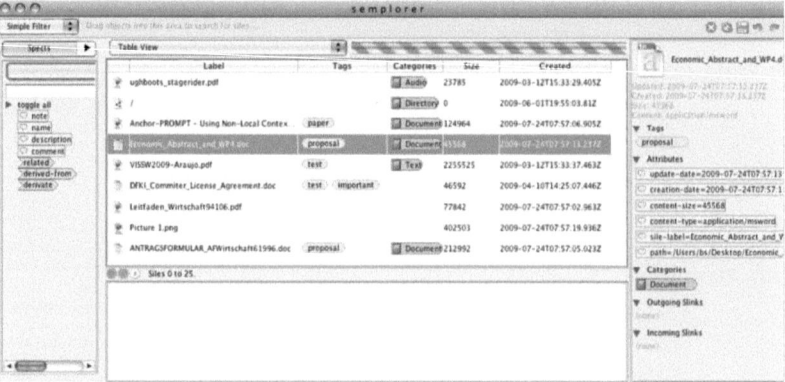

Figure 8.5: Semplorer table view

according to the value of this attribute, and are stacked along the y-axis if their rendering would collide. Using the left mouse button the user can scroll along the x-axis, and using the right mouse button the user can zoom in and out.

These components provide different view on information, and as the Semplorer is designed in a modular way it is possible to plug-in new views that integrate seamlessly into the user interface.

8.2.2 Search

The Semplorer wraps the generic sile filter framework (cf. Section 3.3 and Section 4.1.3) with a graphical query language. The basic idea in this design is to give the user the possibility to use every widget on screen as filter criterion. Thus we do not separate the tasks of *viewing* and *browsing* from the task of *searching*; instead we integrate them into a unified mechanism for interaction with available information.

We implemented this unified mechanism by providing an interface section called the *Filter Bar*, which is situated in the top section of the Semplorer window. Any widget can be dropped onto this bar and immediately extends the currently active filter (the *filter context*). This non-separation allows the user to define filter criteria very quickly and without the need to leave her current context. Instead of selecting a designated "Search" window, the user can—at any time—pick any widget from the screen and use it to narrow her view on the sile repository. Widgets are removed from the filter bar by clicking the "X" sign that appears when the user moves the mouse pointer over one filter element.

All elements in the filter bar are AND-combined. The filter that is added to the current filter context created depends on the type of the dropped widget and, in certain cases, on its state. A detailed enumeration of this behaviour is given in Table 8.1.

Notice that only a subset of all existing filters in the API (cf. Section 4.1.3) are accessible through this method. Currently there exists no visual representation for more elaborate filter types like `AttributeValuerangeFilter` or `SileSlinkFilter`; we choose to keep the UI mechanisms for searching simple instead of comprehensive.

As described above, all filters that are added to the filter bar are AND-combined. We have also implemented two alternative representations of the filter bar; one to model complex filter combinations using Venn diagrams—which, in principle, can be used to graphically represent combinations of large numbers of filters [RSW06]; however in our implementation we have restricted the maximum number of filters to three. Another

Annotation Type	Widget	Created Filter
Tag	`new`	`TagFilter`
Attribute with value	`content-type=application/pdf`	`AttributeNameValueFilter`
Attribute without value	`name`	`AttributeNameFilter`
Category	`TechnicalDocument`	`CategoryFilter`
Slink	`author`	`SlinkInOutboundFilter`
Sile	`OMG IDL Specification.pdf`	`SileInOutboundFilter`

Table 8.1: Conversion of entity widgets to sile filters

variant of the filter bar can be used to iteratively construct CNF filters by visually grouping them.

More details on these advanced interfaces for searching and browsing of semantically enriched data is out the scope of this work; for a more detailed discussion the reader is referred to [Tod08].

8.2.3 Manipulation

One main goal of the interaction mechanism design for the manipulation of siles and annotations was *consistency*: the same type of action should always have the same effect, regardless of the context wherein it was executed. Thus we choose the following basic types of interaction:

- *Drag and drop* operations establish a relationship between two entities; e.g., between a sile and a tag, or between two siles. The details of the action (e.g., the name of the slink with which two siles should be connected) are selected from a pop-up menu that appears after the drag and drop operation has been completed.

- A *mouse click* on an entity allows one to select edit the entity. In the browsing area, siles can be selected to view further details; a click on an attribute in the detail view area allows the user to change the value of an attribute, and so forth.

- A *remove icon* in the form of an "X" appears when the user moves the mouse over an entity (cf. Figure 8.3); by clicking on this icon the entity is removed from its current context. For instance, if a tag is deleted in the *organize* area in the left window part, it is removed from the repository; if it is deleted in the detail view of one sile, it is removed from this particular sile, but not from other ones..

However several manipulation actions cannot be carried out by these operations. For instance it is currently not possible to change the data type of an attribute (cf. Section 3.2), or to annotate a sile with an arbitrary category that is not defined in one of the specs, although the execution of such operations is possible by the definition of the sile API. Again, this design decision is a tradeoff between the user interface's complexity and expressivity: more advanced features would require a deeper understanding of the concepts of the sile model by the user. For instance, creating a new category would require understanding about their internal representation and how to integrate the category into existing specs in order to relate them to other categories, attributes, and slinks.

8.3 Summary

In this section, we have presented the Semplorer, a graphical user interface for sile repositories. The Semplorer is designed as a generic user interface without focus on a specific application, and resembles similarity to typical file browsers that can be found in desktop operating systems. We have discussed the rationales that led to the design of the Semplorer, and described how it applies simple interaction mechanisms, like drag and drop operations, to the complex data structures that underly the system. Finally, we have described our generic design that we consider as a basis for subsequent development of enhanced applications.

Part IV

Conclusions

Chapter 9

Discussion and Experimental Results

> *Statistics: The only science that enables different experts using the same figures to draw different conclusions.* — Evan Esar

In the following we discuss the results we have obtained during our research. We present a qualitative comparison to the Semantic Desktop approaches presented in Section 2.3, and we present experimental quantitative results that indicate the performance of our reference implementation of an RDF-based sile repository, which was presented in Section 7.1.

9.1 Comparison and Differentiation

In Section 2.3.4 we have analyzed a number of research projects in the field of *Semantic Desktop*. We have defined a number of characteristics and criteria, and qualitatively compared the approaches. From this analysis we drew a number of requirements which influenced the design and development of our sile model.

Table 9.1 reproduces the comparison table from Section 2.3.4, with the work pre-

	Nepomuk	Haystack	Chandler	Semex	DeepaMehta	OpenIRIS	DBin	IMeMex	Siles
Data Model									
Meta Model	RDF / NRL (1)	RDF (7)	Items, Collections	RDF	Topic Maps (+ extensions), RDF	RDF	RDF	IDM (graph-based) (23)	Graph-based hybrid model
Storage Layer	RDF2Go / Sesame2	In-memory DB	BerkeleyDB, Lucene	Jena In-memory DB (10)	MySQL, HSQL	Jena DB (16)	Sesame2	Apache Derby (RDBMS)	RDF (alternatives possible)
Metadata Model									
Ontologies	Four level model (2) with predefined core ontologies	Predefined specific ontologies	Predefined ontology	Predefined domain model	Predefined high-level concepts (13)	Predefined high-level concepts (subset of CLIB) (14, 15)	Predefined ontology	No predefined schema	Predefined core ontology
Extensibility	Based on NIE (3)	Adenine (9)	Python data structures (21, 22)	Malleable Schemas (12)	Base Java class	OWL Ontologies	Brainlets (27)	IDM Resource View Classes (23)	Lightweight Ontologies (Spects)
Integration / Interoperability									
External Data Sources	Data wrapper/ crawler framework	Data Extractors (defined by demonstration) (26)	IMAP, ICal	File System	SQL, IMAP, SMTP, IMAP	Harvester for file system, e-mail	RDF import and export	File system, XML, IMAP, RDBMS, RSS	File system, IMAP, ...
Data Mapping	Alignment engine with user feedback (5)	-	-	Reference reconciliation (11)	-	Bayesian classifier	Resource matching	Incremental integration (planned) (24)	-
Application Programming Interface	Access via SOAP/REST, application plugins	-	CalDAV, WebDAV, HTTP	-	SOAP, EJB	XML-RPC	-	HTTP, WebDAV (25)	Generic API, XML-RPC, WebDAV, SPARQL
Operating System	Integration in KDE Core	-	-	-	-	-	-	File events (planned)	File events (planned)
User Interface									
Interface Metaphor	Knowledge Workbench	View Prescriptions, Lenses (7,8)	Tree- and list-based item browser	Tree-based search and navigation	Graph-based resource browser	Tree-based item browser	Tree-based topic browser	Tree-based resource browser	File browser-like, drag and drop
Implementation	Standalone (RCP)	Standalone (RCP)	Standalone (Python) + Web Interface	Standalone (Java)	Standalone (Java) + Web Interface	Standalone (Java)	Standalone (RCP)	AJAX Web Interface	Standalone (Java)
UI Extensibility	RCP plugins (GnoGno framework)	Declarative (Adenine) (9)	Python classes (21)	-	Java classes + Java Server Pages	Application plugin framework (Java Beans)	Brainlets (RCP Plugins)	-	Event model, widget library
Collaboration									
Data Sharing	P2P Infrastructure (GridVine) (4)	-	Client/Server Publish/ Subscribe Mechanism	-	Shared workspaces (13)	(planned)	RDFGrowth (17) / Semantic Web Pipes (19)	(planned)	Linking Open Data, Silepacks
Access Control	RMU-Cube (6)	-	Item-based	-	Type-based	-	Restricted P2P Groups (20)	-	-
Synchronization	P2P-based replication (2)	-	Via dedicated server	-	-	Jabber-based Sync Protocol	P2P-based resource exchange (18)	(planned)	-

(1) Sintek et al, 2007
(2) Reif et al, 2007
(3) http://www.semanticdesktop.org/ontologies/nie
(4) Aberer et al, 2004
(5) http://dev.nepomuk.semanticdesktop.org/wiki/LocalDataAll
(6) Ioannou et al, 2007
(7) Karger et al, 2005
(8) Quan and Karger, 2004
(9) http://groups.csail.mit.edu/haystack/developers/adenine.ht
(10) http://data.cs.washington.edu/semex/download/download.l
(11) Dong et al, 2005
(12) Dong and Halevy, 2005
(13) Richter andPoelchau, 2008
(14) Cheyer et al, 2005
(15) http://www.cs.utexas.edu/users/mfkb/RKF/tree
(16) http://www.openiris.org/downloads/IRIS-nightly/doc-current/doc/dev/pdf/iris-developer-guide.pdf
(17) Tummarello et al, 2006
(18) Tummarello et al, 2004
(19) Morbidoni, 2008
(20) Tummarello et al, 2007b
(21) http://chandlerproject.org/Projects/PluginsTutorial
(22) http://chandler.osafoundation.org/docs/0.7/parcel-schema-guide.html
(23) Dittrich and Salles, 2006
(24) Blunschi et al, 2007
(25) Dittrich et al, 2005
(26) Hogue and Karger, 2004
(27) Tummarello et al, 2006a

Table 9.1: Qualitative comparison of the sile model with other approaches

sented in this thesis added in the rightmost column. In the following, we reproduce the criteria that we applied in our survey and compare our approach and its implementation against the analyzed projects. We discuss to which extent our approach fulfils the requirements, and how it differentiates from other approaches.

Data Model The predominant data model used in most of the discussed approaches is the *Resource Description Framework* (RDF). Basically RDF represents data in the form of a graph, which we also adapt in our data model, the sile model. However, in contrast to RDF, where each node within the graph is an individual and equal entity, the sile model treats larger amounts of information as atomic units. RDF nodes do not carry inherent information: a node has no information value as long as it is not considered in the context of its graph. There exist proposals how to define groups of triples that form a logical unit; however these approaches cannot efficiently avoid the predominant role of the single triple in RDF.

In the sile model, although it can be represented as graph, we do not lift the graph structure into the main focus of the user (i.e., the software developer who writes applications that operates on sile data, or the end user). To mask the underlying graph structure, we define several types of first-class objects (siles, annotations, filters, and so forth) which can be treated individually and independent of any concrete representation. Additionally, we treat non-meta data (i.e., sile content) as an integral part of siles. In contrast to RDF, which merely deals with the *description of resources*, the sile model includes the resource itself—at the cost of renouncing the possibility to describe so-called "non-information resources".

Meta Data Model Our choice of a meta data model for siles is very much in line with the choice taken in related projects. A core ontology has been derived from the sile model; this core ontology represents the model's building blocks and entity types, as well as property types to represent relationships between them. However, the sile core ontology is not a domain ontology: it does not define domain-specific categories or attribute and slink names. Instead, the sile model provides a generic mechanism how ontological knowledge can be captured and represented, in the form of spects. We believe that in the field of the semantic desktop and personal information management, there is no need for highly complex, massively structured ontologies: they tend to overburden end users, and cause additional workload and performance loss in the underlying storage systems. Nevertheless, since the sile model (and, especially, spects) are defined in an abstract manner, the concept puts no restrictions on repository implementations w.r.t. the usage and application of ontological knowledge to sile data.

The ontology layer of the sile model can be extended by loading additional spects into a repository. Such spects can, for instance, be derived from existing ontologies. We have implemented a component that loads an OWL DL ontology, uses the rules defined therein to perform reasoning and consistency checks, and exposes all information that can be represented by the spect framework to client applications. This concept, again, allows for interoperability between systems: an RDF-based sile repository can continue to use its OWL or RDFS ontologies, while a sile repository implemented on top of an RDBMS can expose its relational schema in the form of a spect. From the client perspective, both systems appear to have equal data structures and can be treated in a unified way.

Integration and Interoperability One of the main goals behind the design of the sile model was to reach data interoperability on the desktop. In principle, we share this goal with many other approaches in this field, and lots of research has been conducted in the field of data source wrapping, transformation, and integration[1]. However it is not the main goal of our architecture to actually reach "perfect" integration in the sense that the borderlines between heterogeneous systems entirely disappear. We do not deal with algorithms or mechanisms that enable us, for instance, to specify how data that conforms to a specific schema can be transformed to another one. Instead our goal is to provide a unified view on different types of data, and allow applications to access them without knowing the details of the physical information representation. We have shown how we can integrate external data sources by two examples, IMAP servers and hierarchical file systems.

To provide such unified access, we have defined a generic application programming interface which can be implemented in arbitrary languages. We provide different mechanisms that distribute sile systems and enable interoperability in cases where the storage and the client components are operating on different machines or on different platforms. By using our mapping algorithm between the sile model and RDF, we are able to publish sile data on the web and thus interlink it with other open data sources. Also we provide a means to access sile repositories with traditional file browsers by providing a dynamic mapping to a tree representation, and by exposing this representation via the standardized WebDAV protocol.

---

[1] A comparative study of web-based mapping solutions is given in [Has08].

User Interface Although research on user interfaces is not the primary focus of this work, we have discussed one possible visualization and interaction metaphor for sile data. In comparison to the user interfaces found in other Semantic Desktop projects, we choose a very restricted and simplified representation of semantic information. The Semplorer user interface is oriented close towards file browsers, which represent digital objects (files and directories) as labelled icons, and allow the user to perform operations via mouse gestures (e.g., drag and drop). The Semplorer applies a similar design philosophy; one of the main differences to other approaches is that it allows the user to directly interact with every piece of information visible on the screen. In the current implementation of the Semplorer, the user is never required to manually enter URIs; instead she can work with drag and drop operations to annotate siles, or to modify search queries. One drawback of this approach is that the interface is not functionally complete (for instance, the majority of filter types cannot be used in the current implementation); however we tend to apply here the *Pareto principle*: we estimate that 80% of all user queries can be formulated by the 20% of filters that are available in the Semplorer. For more complex queries, we have implemented advanced representations that can be activated on demand.

Collaboration The sile model does not provide explicit support for collaboration; however it provides several means to exchange information between co-workers. Also because of its distributed nature, shared sile repository instances can be instantiated. However the sile model does currently not include mechanisms for access control, or for replication and synchronization, which are out of the scope of this work.

9.2 Experimental Results

The proposed data model for siles, its associated query framework, and the discussed directions towards physical representation of sile data are highly generic concepts. Its target domain, personal information management and desktop data management, is a very broad field, and the potential users, use cases, and implementation scenarios are manifold. Instead of performing a highly specialized evaluation under the assumption of a very limited usage scenario—which would bear the risk of being not representative for the general case—, we outline our preliminary experience with our proposed models and their implementations on two levels: first, we describe experience that we gained through the implementation of components that operate on the sile model. Second, we discuss several quantitative aspects of sile-based desktop data management that indicates research directions for the future performance improvement of semantic desktop data storage systems.

9.2.1 Implementation Experience

We have implemented several components that use different mechanisms to store and manage sile data; these are in detail described in Chapter 7. Because of the clear semantics and reduced complexity of the API types and repository method calls, only small effort is required to build systems on top of them.

In most cases, the sile model elements could be more or less directly mapped to elements of the native system, and the choice of annotation types was predetermined by the underlying system's structures. In all cases, it was possible to adequately represent elements of the base system's meta model using the mechanisms that are provided by specs, without significant information loss. Additionally, the transformation of filter expressions to search queries (or corresponding programmatic constructs) was possible. This experience shows that the sile model is able to cover many aspects of information that is found on desktops, and that it can be used to cover both information representation and retrieval needs.

However, in certain cases it was very expensive or, in certain cases, not even possible to map all filter types to the underlying system. For instance, the SemDAV server has been implemented with a triple store (Jena) based on a relational database backend (PostgreSQL). Thus, Jena translates incoming SPARQL queries to SQL queries and issues them against the database. However, in the version we used for our implementation, no direct translation of FILTER queries to SQL conditions is possible; hence, the filter criteria are applied after the data has been retrieved from the database, which causes significant performance loss. Another example is the IMAP-based implementation: the IMAP `SEARCH` command does not provide means to query for value ranges, which renders an efficient implementation of attribute value range filters impossible.

The sile model also gives developers the flexibility to choose between different implementation approaches; for instance, in the case of silefiles (cf. Section 7.2) we faced the two options of implementing search operations either on an in-memory cache that holds annotations of the entire file system tree under consideration, or to crawl for metadata files throughout the entire directory tree each time a search request is issued. Both approaches have advantages and disadvantages; however the sile model does not enforce or prefer one particular implementation architecture.

Regarding the implementation of client applications, we have already shown in the usage examples of the sile API (cf. Section 4.2) that working with sile repositories requires only few lines of code. Application developers are enabled to directly operate on siles, their annotations, and filters without additional overload. We see this as an important contribution towards the adoption of semantic technologies, and as an example of how the simplicity of existing structures (e.g., hierarchical file systems) can be retained while simultaneously the expressivity of the data model is significantly increased.

9.2.2 Quantitative Results

To evaluate the performance of our approach, we have analyzed the execution times of typical file system operations that were executed against a virtual file system implemented on top of the SemDAV Server (cf. Section 7.1), called *SileFS* [SH09]. To estimate a realistic amount of data, we crawled the home directories of our department's members, which includes scientific staff (7 persons) as well as technical and administrative staff (3 persons). We used only home directories in favor of scanning entire hard disks because personal data will be the target domain for a semantic file system, and there is little need to semantically annotate system- and application-internal file structures. We discarded files that were on a black list of files and directories that usually are present in users' home directories but are not directly accessed by end users; e.g., .svn, desktop.ini, and *.tmp. The resulting average size of the home directory was 38,000 files stored within 5,150 directories. We view these numbers as upper limits, since we assume that the home directories of computer scientists will typically contain more files (e.g., source code trees) than those of average end users.

To estimate the influence of the size of home directories on our system's performance, we artificially created three test data sets, which are described in Figure 9.2. To represent basic data about files and directories nine triples per object were created. Note that this does not include any additional descriptive triples (i.e., semantic annotations); these were not considered in our performance evaluation. Our implementation also requires loading a set of core ontologies, which add another ≈700 triples to the database.

We have analyzed the runtime performance of typical access patterns to file systems: navigation between directories, listing of directory contents, deletion, moving, and renaming of files. We have carried out the experiments on a high-end consumer

Dataset #	1	2	3
Hierarchy depth	2	3	4
Average no. of sub-directories per directory	5	6	7
Average no. of files per directory	12	15	15
Total number of siles (directories and files)	403	4,144	44,816
Total number of RDF triples	3,626	37,295	403,343
Total number of RDF triples incl. ontologies	4,361	38,030	404,078

Table 9.2: Datasets used for performance evaluation

notebook (MacBook Pro, Core 2 Duo, with 2 GB RAM) running Mac OS X 10.5 and JVM 1.5. We have used the command shell (/bin/bash) to perform our measurements and used only standard commands (cd, ls, rm, and mv). Because of our implementation architecture, each operation is processed by a number of external components (e.g., the FUSE kernel module; see Figure 9.1) which are not under our direct control. Hence we do not have influence on how shell commands are translated to file system driver calls; for instance, issuing a directory listing command (ls) causes the execution of four FUSE calls being passed to our implementation. Nevertheless, our goal was to measure the execution time as experienced by the end user, hence we tracked the total processing time of commands, including overhead caused by the operating system and the FUSE kernel module.

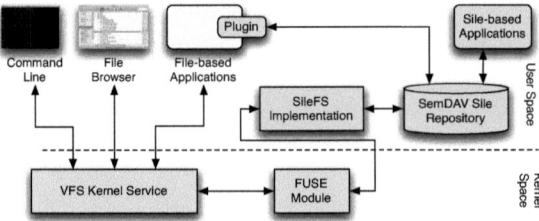

Figure 9.1: Architecture of a virtual file system, based on a sile repository

The operations we have evaluated involve read-only access (directory navigation

Dataset #	1	2	3
Total number of siles	403	4,144	44,816
cd	0.029	0.048	0.107
rm	0.063	0.142	0.879
ls	0.258	0.464	1.547
mv within directory	0.254	0.488	2.488
mv across directories	0.296	0.688	3.238

Table 9.3: Evaluation results for virtual file system access operations: average execution times in seconds

and directory listing) and read+write operations (deletion, moving, renaming). For the latter, the complexity of read and write operations differs: for a sile deletion, (*1*) the triples within the store that describe the object to be deleted have to be identified (read), and (*2*) these triples have to be removed from the store (write). Move and rename operations require in principle the same access operations, whereas a move across directories requires an additional read and write operation, namely the update of the relationship between the file and its parent directory. For our experiment, we have executed each of these operations 10 times in random order, and the entire experiment was repeated five times.

The results of our experiments are depicted in Figure 9.3. For the first two datasets (≈400 and ≈4,000 siles) we can observe very low execution times, which allow for uninterrupted interactive work with virtual file systems. For a dataset consisting of ≈40,000 siles, the response times for simple operations (change directory, remove file) are still in a reasonable range, and even operations that involve multiple, complex queries (directory listing, moving) are within a range comparable to accessing remote file systems via the Web. We did not evaluate the performance of actual read and write operations on the file content: the modifications to metadata caused by these actions are comparable to those of a move operation (i.e., an update of the content-length and update-time properties), and the actual file content is provided by the underlying file system and hence is out of the scope of our performance measurements.

Dataset #	1	2	3
Total number of triples	11,049	123,967	1,238,534
Search siles tagged with a specific tag	0.271	1.084	2.008
Search siles tagged with one out of three tags	0.734	1.182	2.304
Search siles that are related to a given sile	0.014	0.029	0.039
Retrieve all sile annotations	0.037	0.050	0.071
Create one sile and add one tag	0.158	0.187	0.205
Delete one sile	0.044	0.051	0.071

Table 9.4: Evaluation results for metadata access operations: average execution times in seconds

These numbers indicate that even a prototypical implementation of a virtual file system, based on our data model and built using an off-the-shelf RDF triple store, has acceptable performance for everyday usage on a typical consumer machine. A semantic file system and a more efficient triple store, more tightly integrated into the operating system, could achieve even better performance, since this would allow us to circumvent the rather inefficient architecture that we have chosen for the sake of implementation simplicity.

We have also evaluated the performance of typical access operations to sile metadata under comparable amounts of data. For this test, we have extended the datasets described before. We have annotated each sile in the repository with (in average) 3 tags, 4 categories, 8 attributes, and 5 slinks, which results in repositories containing up to 1.2 million triples. For the number of siles we have oriented us towards the numbers of files on typical user desktops as described before; additionally we have assumed numbers of annotations that we consider as easily manageable by end users.

We have loaded these data into our repository implementation, which we ran on a high-end laptop machine (Apple MacBook Pro, 2.53 GHz Intel Core 2 Duo with 4 GB RAM, running Mac OS X 10.5.7) using Java 6, Jena 2.5.5, and PostgreSQL 8.2.5. We tested a mix of API calls against this instance, including read and write access. These API calls are implemented in our repository prototype using different mechanisms; for instance, some are implemented using graph access through the Jena API (e.g., retrieval of sile annotations), others are realized through SPARQL queries (e.g., search for siles based on tags), and some involve write access to the graph. Each test session was repeated 10 times.

Table 9.4 shows the average execution times of the different calls. These numbers indicate that an RDF-based sile repository, as described in this paper, is able to handle the discussed data volumes with response times ranging from 14ms for simple queries (e.g., retrieving all attributes for a sile) to around three seconds for more complex queries (e.g., retrieval of siles that are tagged with one out of three given tags). Especially operations that are implemented using SPARQL queries (i.e., sile search operations) require longer execution times with increasing data amounts, hence we can identify the need to further improve triple stores and SPARQL execution engines so that they are applicable in desktop environments. Nevertheless we consider the average execution times of typical data access operations already as acceptable for interactive work with such a system.

Chapter 10

Conclusions and Future Directions

The best way to predict the future is to invent it. —
Alan Kay

10.1 Summary and Conclusions

This thesis introduces a novel concept for data management on the personal desktop, the *sile model*. It is the goal of the sile model to provide a core foundation for the management and handling of semantically annotated unstructured content. To accomplish this, we have combined model elements from file systems, semantic technologies, and the object-oriented paradigm, and have defined a formal model which can serve as a basis for the future development of systems that exhibit improved and more user-oriented characteristics w.r.t. personal information management.

We have founded our conceptualization on an analysis of the current situation in the domain of personal information management and the semantic desktop. We have analyzed the wide range of technologies, starting from simple organization metaphors that are in place today, like hierarchical file systems, to heavyweight semantic desktop solutions that provide full support for ontology-based modelling of personal data. From this analysis, we have derived requirements and design goals for a generic data model that offers a sufficiently high level of flexibility to be able to represent the different types of data that are found on typical desktops. This model, called the *sile model*, has been defined in an abstract model; i.e., independent from concrete representation syntaxes or implementations. The basic elements of this model are siles (i.e., discrete, identifiable units of information), annotations (that are used to describe siles), and spects (lightweight ontologies that describe valid annotation constellations). We have enriched this model with an abstract query language, which we call *sile filters*, that selects data objects based on their annotations. These models allow us to describe and process different kinds of data that are typically relevant in the context of personal information management.

In anticipation of concrete implementations, we have discussed a mapping from the sile model to a concrete representation which uses Semantic Web technologies (RDF, RDFS, SPARQL). This mapping can be used *(1)* to implement sile repositories which are backed by triple stores, and *(2)* to serialize sile data into self-contained files (so-called *silepacks*) and transmit them across different systems.

In addition to the RDF-based serialization mechanisms, we have shown a general method to provide remote access to repositories via XML-RPC requests, which allows us to distribute sile data across different systems and platforms. We have also discussed how we can represent sile data in a hierarchical, file system-like fashion. This representation is exposed via WebDAV so that it can be accessed from every common desktop operating system, as if it were a normal file system.

As proof of concept, we have discussed three different implementations of sile repositories. One is based on Semantic Web technologies and makes use of their full set of features, including inference and model validation. Because it is backed by a triple store, it provides direct access to sile data in the form of RDF triples and thus can be integrated with other data sources exposed on the Web of Data. Another prototypical implementation shows how another important class of personal information, e-mail, that is stored on an IMAP server can be wrapped and transformed to the sile model. This transformation allows us to interpret e-mail messages as siles, and to put them into a unified information context with other data sources. A further example for such an information system are file systems, for which we have implemented another prototypical wrapper. This wrapper stores file annotations *in-place*; i.e., in small chunks of RDF that are stored directly in the file system.

We have presented a prototypical implementation of a user interface, the Semplorer, that allows users to search, browse, and manipulate sile data in a way similar to file browsers. The Semplorer operates on the unified data structure that the sile model provides, and thus does not distinguish between the actual representation of siles. Hence the Semplorer enables the user to annotate files, mail messages, relational databases, or triple stores in the same manner.

Finally, we have concluded our work with a discussion of our approach, and an outline of commonalities as well as differences to other approaches in the semantic desktop research area.

10.2 Future Research Directions

The results of this thesis can be regarded as the basis for a number of future research directions, which we will outline in the following.

Extensions for the Sile Model and the Sile Filter Algebra The current specification of the sile model and its associated query algebra covers, in the author's opinion, a wide range of application needs. Many directions to extend them are conceivable, and we plan to specify additional annotation types and operator types. However we must ensure that implementations of the model and the algebra are still simple and straightforward to use.

Access Control Mechanisms for Graph-Based Data Structures One question we did not address in this thesis is how to efficiently manage access control in graph-based, open data structures. This functionality is required as soon as sile repositories are intended not only for personal use, but in collaborative environments. By "open data structures" we mean that the data do not adhere to predefined schemas or structure definitions (as it is the case, e.g., in relational databases). Similar to RDF, the sile model is designed to be extensible in terms of the vocabulary that is used to describe and relate entities. Spects can be loaded into the system, and repository implementations may use arbitrarily complex internal schemas. In contrast to hierarchical structures, no rights inheritance can take place in graph-based structures; thus, we need models and algorithms that allow for a fine-granular definition of access rights for graph structures that take into account constantly changing data, both on the instance and on the schema level.

Performance Optimization of Dynamic Triple Stores As we have seen in our prototypical implementation of the sile repository, triple stores still suffer from a significant performance drawback if the application requires reasoning and integrity validation in combination with frequent dynamic updates of data. In the personal information management domain, data is subject to constant change; this causes heavy load on the reasoning sub-systems, regardless of whether inference is performed during update time or during query time. We want to further investigate the question how triple stores can be designed and implemented more efficiently under these conditions.

Integration of Data Sources We have already outlined how systems that contain relevant data in the context of personal information management (e.g., e-mail servers) can be wrapped by adapters that transform the information into the sile model and vice versa. However we regard our work in this field only as initial step and preliminary proof of concept. We plan to investigate on the question how more complex data structures can be efficiently transformed to siles, and how sile filters can be executed on native data sets.

Integration of Desktop Applications Users carry out most of their daily productive work not on the basis of underlying data structures (like files, RDF, or siles), but by using applications. Applications and their user interfaces represent the direct connection between digital data and the user's mental model, and they possess detailed knowledge about the meaning and context of actions executed by a user. Thus, the application layer has the best knowledge about human factors; however, in current systems this information is often lost. Our goal is to work on algorithms how applications can capture and persist such knowledge in order to generate relevant annotations for personal data, which may help in subsequent search and retrieval tasks.

Sile Repository Mediation We have shown how different data sources, e.g., e-mail servers or file systems, can be wrapped and represented as siles. However in order to interrelate these distinct data sources, mediation components are required. Such components wrap an arbitrary number of sile repositories, but appear to the outside as a single sile repository. Internally, such a component would distribute incoming requests to the mediated repositories, and combine the results to a single, integrated view.

Replication and Synchronization Currently, the sile model does not provide mechanisms for repositories to synchronize or replicate their data. This is an open issue also for related technologies like RDF databases. With the increasing power of mobile devices in terms of computing power and memory, however, the importance of this question increases. In the future, we plan to investigate on efficient algorithms that allow users to "undock" subsets of their personal information space and re-synchronize them later on.

Analysis of Interaction Logs The manual generation of annotations is cumbersome, and often users are not willing to perform this task because they do not see an immediate benefit. Research on automatic generation of annotations is mostly focusing on content analysis algorithms. However these approaches are only in a limited manner applicable to our model, which is not restricted to certain media types. Thus we plan to investigate in algorithms for the analysis of user interaction logs, i.e., time series of actions that users and applications have executed on the existing data, for which the sile model and our implementations are a solid basis. We hope to derive context information out of these time series and can use these data to instantiate new annotations and relationships between siles.

Integration of Structured and Unstructured Annotations Semantically enriched personal information management, as it is envisioned by the Semantic Desktop idea, is situated in the area of conflict between unstructured, lightweight annotations (like tags) and complex, formally specified ontologies. The sile model and its implementations aim to be a kind of intermediator between these two worlds, which is reflected by the inclusion of annotations of different semantic expressivity in the sile model. However, the interdependencies between annotations on different semantic levels have not been fully studied, and are subject to further research.

List of Figures

2.1	Pseudo-ontological use of file names and directories in a media library	20
2.2	File management interface in Mac OS 1.1 and Mac OS X	23
2.3	File management interface in Windows XP and Red Hat Linux	24
2.4	Folder icons in Windows XP, Windows Vista, Apple Mac OS X, and Linux/KDE	25
2.5	Three-dimensional user interfaces for file systems	29
2.6	Multiple scattered hierarchies on a user's desktop computer	31
2.7	Typical file preview: no actual content	33
2.8	Typical file metadata: no information available	34
2.9	RDF graph example	37
2.10	RDF Turtle syntax example	38
2.11	Semantic Desktop user interfaces	58
3.1	Representation of mail messages and files using the sile model	77
3.2	A spect defining rules for the relationship between email categories and attributes	80
4.1	Sile type hierarchy	94
4.2	Annotation type hierarchy (abstract annotations)	96
4.3	Bound annotation type hierarchy	97
4.4	Annotation type hierarchy (complete)	98
4.5	Spect type	99
4.6	Filter type hierarchy (root types)	100
4.7	Attribute filter type hierarchy	102
4.8	Sile and slink filter type hierarchy	103
4.9	Mediator-wrapper architecture using the repository interface	105
4.10	Repository type	106

5.1	Sile ontology core classes	120
6.1	Structure of a silepack	148
6.2	The Linked Open Data cloud as of March 2009	152
6.3	Example XML-RPC communication	154
6.4	Distributed connector/handler architecture	165
6.5	Sile repository mounted as WebDAV folder	169
6.6	WebDAV representation of sile annotations	171
7.1	SemDAV server architecture overview	175
7.2	SemDAV server components	177
7.3	Sequence diagram for `searchSiles()` requests	179
7.4	silefiles architecture	181
7.5	An annotated e-mail message as displayed in an off-the-shelf e-mail client	184
8.1	Semplorer main window structure	190
8.2	Entity widgets: sile (a), tag (b), attribute (c), category (d), slink (e)	192
8.3	Widget with tooltip and delete button	192
8.4	Semplorer timeline view	194
8.5	Semplorer table view	194
9.1	Architecture of a virtual file system, based on a sile repository	208

List of Tables

2.1	Comparison of file system characteristics	15
2.2	Comparison of Semantic File Systems	21
2.3	Comparison of Semantic Desktop projects	54
5.1	URI prefixes for the sile ontology	118
5.2	RDF properties for core attributes	121
5.3	RDF properties for core slink names	121
5.4	RDF properties for spects	122
5.5	RDF properties for sile filters	123
6.1	Serialization of spect applicability rules	162
8.1	Conversion of entity widgets to sile filters	196
9.1	Qualitative comparison of the sile model with other approaches	202
9.2	Datasets used for performance evaluation	208
9.3	Evaluation results for virtual file system access operations: average execution times in seconds	209
9.4	Evaluation results for metadata access operations: average execution times in seconds	210

Listings

5.1	Example RDF representation of siles	127
5.2	Simple SPARQL query	128
5.3	SPARQL CONSTRUCT query	128
5.4	SPARQL triple pattern for a `TagFilter`	135
5.5	SPARQL representation of a negated `TagFilter`	136
5.6	SPARQL representation of two OR-combined `TagFilters`	137
5.7	SPARQL representation of a negated AND-combination of two `TagFilters`	138
6.1	Silepack `meta.ttl` file example	149
6.2	Sile serialization example	156
6.3	Tag serialization example	157
6.4	Tag array collection example	158
6.5	Content serialization example	159
6.6	Filter serialization example	160
6.7	Spect serialization example	161
6.8	XML-RPC method call serialization example	163
7.1	Example of a silefiles metadata file	182

Bibliography

[AAH06]   David Ahlstroem, Rainer Alexandrowicz, and Martin Hitz. Improving Menu Interaction: A Comparison of Standard, Force Enhanced and Jumping Menus. In *CHI '06: Proceedings of the SIGCHI Conference on Human Factors in Computing Systems*, pages 1067–1076, New York, NY, USA, 2006. ACM Press.

[AB06]   Anand Agarawala and Ravin Balakrishnan. Keepin' it Real: Pushing the Desktop Metaphor with Physics, Piles and the Pen. In *CHI '06: Proceedings of the SIGCHI Conference on Human Factors in Computing Systems*, pages 1283–1292, New York, NY, USA, 2006. ACM Press.

[ABDL07] Nitin Agrawal, William J. Bolosky, John R. Douceur, and Jacob R. Lorch. A Five-Year Study of File-System Metadata. In *Proceedings of the 5th Conference on File and Storage Technologies (FAST '07)*, San Jose, CA, 2007.

[ABG+06] Sasha Ames, Nikhil Bobb, Kevin M. Greenan, Owen S. Hofmann, Mark W. Storer, Carlos Maltzahn, Ethan L. Miller, and Scott A. Brandt. LiFS: An Attribute-Rich File System for Storage Class Memories. In *Proceedings of the 23rd IEEE / 14th NASA Goddard Conference on Mass Storage Systems and Technologies*, 2006.

[ABK+07] Sören Auer, Christian Bizer, Georgi Kobilarov, Jens Lehmann, Richard Cyganiak, and Zachary Ives. DBpedia: A Nucleus for a Web of Open Data. In *Proceedings of the 6th International Semantic Web Conference (ISWC 2007), Busan, Korea*, 2007.

[ABM04]   Riccardo Albertoni, Alessio Bertone, and Monica De Martino. Semantic Web and Information Visualization. In *Proceedings of the Semantic Web Applications and Perspectives Workshop (SWAP 2004)*, 2004.

[ACMHP04]   Karl Aberer, Philippe Cudré-Mauroux, Manfred Hauswirth, and Tim Van Pelt. GridVine: Building Internet-Scale Semantic Overlay Networks. In Sheila A. McIlraith, Dimitris Plexousakis, and Frank van Harmelen, editors, *International Semantic Web Conference*, volume 3298 of *Lecture Notes in Computer Science*, pages 107–121. Springer, 2004.

[Ado05]   Adobe Systems Incorporated. *XMP Specification*. Adobe Systems Incorporated, September 2005.

[Aga06]   Anand Agarawala. Enriching the Desktop Metaphor with Physics, Piles and the Pen. Master's thesis, University of Toronto, 2006.

[AL98]   Nicolas Anquetil and Timothy Lethbridge. Extracting Concepts from File Names: A New File Clustering Criterion. In *ICSE '98: Proceedings of the 20th International Conference on Software engineering*, pages 84–93, Washington, DC, USA, 1998. IEEE Computer Society.

[AMMH07]   Daniel J. Abadi, Adam Marcus, Samuel Madden, and Katherine J. Hollenbach. Scalable Semantic Web Data Management Using Vertical Partitioning. In *Proceedings of the 33rd International Conference on Very Proceedings of the 33rd International Conference on Very Large Database (VLDB 2007)*, pages 411–422, 2007.

[AMS07]   Kemafor Anyanwu, Angela Maduko, and Amit Sheth. SPARQ2L: Towards Support for Subgraph Extraction Queries in RDF Databases. In *WWW '07: Proceedings of the 16th International Conference on World Wide Web*, pages 797–806, New York, NY, USA, 2007. ACM Press.

[App93]   Apple Computer, Inc. *Inside Macintosh: Files*. Addison-Wesley Publishing Company, 1993.

[App00]   Apple Computer, Inc. *HFS Plus Volume Format*. Apple Computer, Inc., 2000.

[AR06] Nicole Alexander and Siva Ravada. RDF Object Type and Reification in the Database. In *ICDE '06: Proceedings of the 22nd International Conference on Data Engineering*, page 93, Washington, DC, USA, 2006. IEEE Computer Society.

[BB04] Hal Berghel and Natasa Brajkovska. Wading into Alternate Data Streams. *Communications of the ACM*, 47(4):21–27, 2004.

[BBMN06] Ofer Bergman, Ruth Beyth-Marom, and Rafi Nachmias. The Project Fragmentation Problem in Personal Information Management. In *CHI '06: Proceedings of the SIGCHI conference on Human Factors in computing systems*, pages 271–274, New York, NY, USA, 2006. ACM Press.

[BD04] Michael Balzer and Oliver Deussen. Hierarchy Based 3D Visualization of Large Software Structures. In *VIS '04: Proceedings of the Conference on Visualization '04*, page 598.4, Washington, DC, USA, 2004. IEEE Computer Society.

[BDG+07] Lukas Blunschi, Jens-Peter Dittrich, Olivier René Girard, Shant Kirakos Karakashian, and Marcos Antonio Vaz Salles. A Dataspace Odyssey: The iMeMex Personal Dataspace Management System. In *CIDR*, pages 114–119. www.crdrdb.org, 2007.

[Bec04] David Becket. *RDF/XML Syntax Specification (W3C Recommendation 10 February 2004)*. World Wide Web Consortium, 2004.

[Bec07] David Beckett. *Turtle – Terse RDF Triple Language*, 2007. Available at `http://www.dajobe.org/2004/01/turtle/`, retrieved 08-Aug-2008.

[BG04] Dan Brickley and R.V. Guha. *RDF Vocabulary Description Language 1.0: RDF Schema (W3C Recommendation 10 Februar 2004)*. World Wide Web Consortium, 2004.

[BGSV06] Stephan Bloehdorn, Olaf Görlitz, Simon Schenk, and Max Völkel. TagFS – Tag Semantics for Hierarchical File Systems. In *6th International Conference on Knowledge Management (I-KNOW'06)*, 2006.

[BHAR07] Chris Bizer, Tom Heath, Danny Ayers, and Yves Raimond. Interlinking Open Data on the Web. In *Poster at the 4th Europen Semantic Web Conference (ESWC 2007)*, 2007.

[BHLT06]   Tim Bray, Dave Hollander, Andrew Layman, and Richard Tobin. *Namespaces in XML (Second Edition) (W3C Recommendation 16 August 2006)*. World Wide Web Consortium, 2006. Available at http://www.w3.org/TR/REC-xml-names/.

[BKvH02]   Jeen Broekstra, Arjohn Kampman, and Frank van Harmelen. Sesame: A Generic Architecture for Storing and Querying RDF and RDF schema. In *Proceedings of the First International Semantic Web Conference (ISWC 2002)*, 2002.

[BL06a]   Tim Berners-Lee. *Linked Data*. World Wide Web Consortium, 2006. Available at http://www.w3.org/DesignIssues/LinkedData.html, retrieved 08-Aug-2008.

[BL06b]   Tim Berners-Lee. *Notation 3*. World Wide Web Consortium, 2006. Available at http://www.w3.org/DesignIssues/Notation3, retrieved 08-Aug-2008.

[BL07]   Tim Berners-Lee. *What do HTTP URIs Identify?*, 01 2007. Available at http://www.w3.org/DesignIssues/HTTP-URI2, retrieved 08-Aug-2008.

[BLCC+06]   Tim Berners-Lee, Yuhsin Chen, Lydia Chilton, Dan Connolly, Ruth Dhanaraj, James Hollenbach, Adam Lerer, and David Sheets. Tabulator: Exploring and Analyzing Linked Data on the Semantic Web. In *Proceedings of the 3rd International Semantic Web User Interaction Workshop*, 2006.

[BLFM05]   T. Berners-Lee, R. Fielding, and L. Masinter. *Uniform Resource Identifier (URI): Generic Syntax (RFC 3986)*. Network Working Group, January 2005.

[BLHL01]   Tim Berners-Lee, James Hendler, and Ora Lassila. The Semantic Web. *Scientific American*, 284(5):34–43, 2001.

[BN95]   Deborah Barreau and Bonnie A. Nardi. Finding and Reminding: File Organization from the Desktop. *SIGCHI Bull.*, 27(3):39–43, 1995.

[Boa01]   Richard Boardman. Multiple Hierarchies in User Workspace. In *CHI '01: CHI '01 Extended Abstracts on Human Factors in Computing Systems*, pages 403–404, New York, NY, USA, 2001. ACM Press.

[Boo03]   David Booth. *Four Uses of a URL: Name, Concept, Web Location and Document Instance*. World Wide Web Consortium, 2003.

[BS04]   Chris Bizer and Andy Seaborne. D2RQ - Treating Non-RDF Databases as Virtual RDF Graphs. In *Poster at the 3rd International Semantic Web Conference (ISWC2004)*, 2004.

[BS08]   Chris Bizer and Andreas Schultz. Benchmarking the Performance of Storage Systems that Expose SPARQL Endpoints. In *Proceedings of the 4th International Workshop on Scalable Semantic Web Knowledge Base Systems (SSWS 2008)*, 2008.

[BS09]   Christian Bizer and Andreas Schultz. The Berlin SPARQL Benchmark. *To appear in: International Journal on Semantic Web and Information Systems — Special issue on Scalability and Performance of Semantic Web Systems*, 2009.

[BSS03]   Richard Boardman, Robert Spence, and M. Angela Sasse. Too Many Hierarchies? The Daily Struggle for Control of the Workspace. In *Proceedings of HCI International 2003*, volume 1, pages 616–620, 2003.

[BSW02]   Benjamin B. Bederson, Ben Shneiderman, and Martin Wattenberg. Ordered and Quantum Treemaps: Making Effective Use of 2D Space to Display Hierarchies. *ACM Trans. Graph.*, 21(4):833–854, 2002.

[Bus45]   Vannevar Bush. As We May Think. *The Atlantic Monthly*, 176(1):101–108, July 1945.

[Byr93]   Michael D. Byrne. Using Icons to Find Documents: Simplicity is Critical. In *CHI '93: Proceedings of the SIGCHI Conference on Human Factors in Computing Systems*, pages 446–453, New York, NY, USA, 1993. ACM Press.

[CBHS05a]   Jeremy J. Carroll, Christian Bizer, Pat Hayes, and Patrick Stickler. Named Graphs. *Journal of Web Semantics*, 3(4), 2005.

[CBHS05b]   Jeremy J. Carroll, Christian Bizer, Pat Hayes, and Patrick Stickler. Named Graphs, Provenance and Trust. In *WWW '05: Proceedings of the 14th International Conference on World Wide Web*, pages 613–622, New York, NY, USA, 2005. ACM Press.

[CDD+04] Jeremy J. Carroll, Ian Dickinson, Chris Dollin, Dave Reynolds, Andy Seaborne, and Kevin Wilkinson. Jena: Implementing the Semantic Web Recommendations. In *WWW '04: Proceedings of the 13th International Conference on World Wide Web*, pages 74–83, New York, NY, USA, 2004. ACM Press.

[CFT08] Kendall Grant Clark, Lee Feigenbaum, and Elias Torres. *SPARQL Protocol for RDF (W3C Recommendation 15 January 2008)*. World Wide Web Consortium, 2008.

[CG06] Andy Cockburn and Andrew Gin. Faster Cascading Menu Selections with Enlarged Activation Areas. In *GI '06: Proceedings of Graphics Interface 2006*, pages 65–71, Toronto, Ont., Canada, Canada, 2006. Canadian Information Processing Society.

[Chi02] Robert Chin. Three-Dimensional File System Browser. *Crossroads*, 9(1):16–18, 2002.

[CJ09] Richard Cyganiak and Anja Jentzsch. *The Linking Open Data Dataset Cloud*, 2009.

[Cla02] Kendall Grant Clark. *Identity Crisis*, 2002. Available at http://www.xml.com/pub/a/2002/09/11/deviant.html, retrieved 08-Aug-2008.

[Cla05] Kendall Grant Clark. *RDF Data Access Use Cases and Requirements (W3C Working Draft 25 March 2005)*. World Wide Web Consortium, March 2005.

[Cla06] Kendall Grant Clark. SPARQL Protocol for RDF (W3C Candidate Recommendation 6 April 2006). Technical report, World Wide Web Consortium, 2006.

[Cod70] E. F. Codd. A Relational Model of Data for Large Shared Data Banks. *Commun. ACM*, 13(6):377–387, 1970.

[Con07] Dan Connolly. *Gleaning Resource Descriptions from Dialects of Languages (GRDDL) (W3C) Recommendation 11 September 2007*. World Wide Web Consortium, 2007.

[Cor] NudgeNudge Corp. Punakea – Make Tags come True.

[CPG05]   Adam Cheyer, Jack Park, and Richard Giuli. Iris: Integrate. relate. infer. share. In Stefan Decker, Jack Park, Dennis Quan, and Leo Sauermann, editors, *Proceedings of the 1st Workshop on The Semantic Desktop. 4th International Semantic Web Conference (Galway, Ireland)*, 2005.

[Cre07]   Anne Cregan. Symbol Grounding for the Semantic Web. In Franconi et al. [FKM07], pages 429–442.

[Cri03]   M. Crispin. *Internet Message Access Protocol (IMAP) (RFC 3501)*. Network Working Group, 2003.

[CW91]   Mark H. Chignell and John A. Waterworth. WIMPs and NERDs: An Extended View of the User Interface. *SIGCHI Bull.*, 23(2):15–21, 1991.

[Cyg05]   Richard Cyganiak. A Relational Algebra for SPARQL. Technical Report HPL-2005-170, HP Labs, 2005.

[DA07]   Sebastian Dietzold and Sören Auer. Integrating SPARQL Endpoints into Directory Services. In Franconi et al. [FKM07].

[DAK+06]   Andreas Dengel, Stefan Agne, Bertin Klein, Achim Ebert, and Matthias Deller. Human-Centered Interaction with Documents. In *HCM '06: Proceedings of the 1st ACM International Workshop on Human-Centered Multimedia*, pages 35–44, New York, NY, USA, 2006. ACM Press.

[DB99]   John R. Douceur and William J. Bolosky. A Large-scale Study of Filesystem Contents. In *Proceedings of the 1999 ACM SIGMETRICS International Conference on Measurement and Modeling of Computer Systems*, pages 59–70, New York, NY, USA, 1999. ACM Press.

[DB01]   Nicolas Ducheneaut and Victoria Bellotti. E-Mail as Habitat: An Exploration of Embedded Personal Information Management. *interactions*, 8(5):30–38, 2001.

[DELS99]   Paul Dourish, W. Keith Edwards, Anthony LaMarca, and Michael Salisbury. PRESTO: An Experimental Architecture for Fluid Interactive Document Spaces. *ACM Trans. Comput.-Hum. Interact.*, 6(2):133–161, 1999.

[DES03] Rosario De Chiara, Ugo Erra, and Vittorio Scarano. VennFS: A Venn-Diagram File Manager. In *Proceedings of the Seventh International Conference on Information Visualization (IV'03)*, 2003.

[DFJ+04] Li Ding, Tim Finin, Anupam Joshi, Rong Pan, R. Scott Cost, Yun Peng, Pavan Reddivari, Vishal Doshi, and Joel Sachs. Swoogle: A Search and Metadata Engine for the Semantic Web. In *CIKM '04: Proceedings of the 13th ACM International Conference on Information and Knowledge Management*, pages 652–659, New York, NY, USA, 2004. ACM Press.

[DH05] Xin Dong and Alon Y. Halevy. Malleable Schemas: A Preliminary Report. In *Proceedings of the 8th International Workshop on the Web & Databases (WebDB 2005)*, pages 139–144, 2005.

[DH06] Philip L. Davidson and Jefferson Y. Han. Synthesis and Control on Large Scale Multi-Touch Ssensing Displays. In *NIME '06: Proceedings of the 2006 Conference on New Interfaces for Musical Expression*, pages 216–219, Paris, France, France, 2006. IRCAM.

[DHM05] Xin Dong, Alon Halevy, and Jayant Madhavan. Reference Reconciliation in Complex Information Spaces. In *SIGMOD '05: Proceedings of the 2005 ACM SIGMOD International Conference on Management of Data*, pages 85–96, New York, NY, USA, 2005. ACM.

[Die05] Sebastian Dietzold. Generating RDF Models from LDAP Directories. In *Proceedings of the Workshop on Scripting for the Semantic Web (Co-located with ESWC 2005)*, 2005.

[DKD+05] Li Ding, Pranam Kolari, Zhongli Ding, Saikanth Avancha, Tim Finin, and Anupam Joshi. Using Ontologies in the Semantic Web: A Survey. Technical Report TR CS-05-07, University of Maryland Baltimore County, Department of Computer Science and Electrical Engineering, 2005.

[DMM00] Stefan Decker, Prasenjit Mitra, and Sergey Melnik. Framework for the Semantic Web: An RDF Tutorial. *IEEE Internet Computing*, 04(6):68–73, 2000.

[DS04]   Mike Dean and Guus Schreiber. *OWL Web Ontology Language Reference (W3C Recommendation 10 February 2004)*. World Wide Web Consortium, February 2004. Available at http://www.w3.org/TR/owl-ref/.

[DS06]   Jens-Peter Dittrich and Marcos Antonio Vaz Salles. iDM: A Unified and Versatile Data Model for Personal Dataspace Management. In *Proceedings of the 32nd International Conference on Very Large Data Bases, Seoul, Korea, September 12-15, 2006*, pages 367–378, 2006.

[DSKB05]   Jens-Peter Dittrich, Marcos Antonio Vaz Salles, Donald Kossmann, and Lukas Blunschi. iMeMex: Escapes from the Personal Information Jungle. In *VLDB '05: Proceedings of the 31st International Conference on Very Large Data Bases*, pages 1306–1309. VLDB Endowment, 2005.

[DWSK03]   Luping Ding, Kevin Wilkinson, Craig Sayers, and Harumi Kuno. Application-Specific Schema Design for Storing Large RDF Datasets. In *In First Intl Workshop on Practical and Scalable Semantic Systems*, 2003.

[EB04]   Sarah P. Everett and Michael D. Byrne. Unintended Effects: Varying Icon Spacing Changes Users' Visual Search Strategy. In *CHI '04: Proceedings of the SIGCHI conference on Human factors in computing systems*, pages 695–702, New York, NY, USA, 2004. ACM Press.

[EM07]   Orri Erling and Ivan Mikhailov. RDF Support in the Virtuoso DBMS. In Sören Auer, Christian Bizer, Claudia Müller, and Anna V. Zhdanova, editors, *CSSW*, volume 113 of *LNI*, pages 59–68. GI, 2007.

[Eng70]   Douglas C. Engelbart. *X-Y Position Indicator for a Display System (Patent No 3541541)*. United States Patent Office, 1970.

[FFG96]   Scott Fertig, Eric Freeman, and David Gelernter. "Finding and Reminding' Reconsidered. *SIGCHI Bull.*, 28(1):66–69, 1996.

[FGM+99]   R. Fielding, J. Gettys, J. Mogul, H. Frystyk, L. Masinter, P. Leach, and T. Berners-Lee. *Hypertext Transfer Protocol – HTTP/1.1 (RFC 2616)*. Network Working Group, 1999.

[FGSSB06]   Norberto Fernandez-Garcia, Leo Sauermann, Luis Sanchez, and Ansgar Bernardi. PIMO Population and Semantic Annotation for the Gnowsis

Semantic Desktop. In *Proceedings of the Semantic Desktop and Social Semantic Collaboration Proceedings of the Semantic Desktop and Social Semantic Collaboration Workshop at the ISWC*, 2006.

[FHM05] Michael Franklin, Alon Halevy, and David Maier. From Databases to Dataspaces: A New Abstraction for Information Management. *SIGMOD Rec.*, 34(4):27–33, 2005.

[Fie00] Roy Thomas Fielding. *Architecture Styles and the Design of Network-based Software Architectures*. PhD thesis, University of California, Irvine, 2000.

[FKM07] Enrico Franconi, Michael Kifer, and Wolfgang May, editors. *The Semantic Web: Research and Applications, 4th European Semantic Web Conference, ESWC 2007, Innsbruck, Austria, June 3-7, 2007, Proceedings*, volume 4519 of *Lecture Notes in Computer Science*. Springer, 2007.

[FM04] Leah Findlater and Joanna McGrenere. A Comparison of Static, Adaptive, and Adaptable Menus. In *CHI '04: Proceedings of the SIGCHI conference on Human factors in computing systems*, pages 89–96, New York, NY, USA, 2004. ACM Press.

[FNB06] Jennifer Ferreira, James Noble, and Robert Biddle. A Case for Iconic Icons. In *AUIC '06: Proceedings of the 7th Australasian User interface conference*, pages 97–100, Darlinghurst, Australia, Australia, 2006. Australian Computer Society, Inc.

[Gar03] L. M. Garshol. *Living With Topic Maps and RDF*. Ontolpia, 2003. Available at http://www.ontopia.net/topicmaps/materials/tmrdf.html, retrieved 08-Aug-2008.

[GEP04] Gunnar Astrand Grimnes, Pete Edwards, and Alun D. Preece. Learning Meta-Descriptions of the FOAF Network. In Sheila A. McIlraith, Dimitris Plexousakis, and Frank van Harmelen, editors, *The Semantic Web - ISWC 2004: Third International Semantic Web Conference,Hiroshima, Japan, November 7-11, 2004. Proceedings*, volume 3298 of *LNCS*, pages 152–165. Springer, 2004.

[GG95]   Nicola Guarino and Pierdaniele Giaretta. Ontologies and Knowledge Bases: Towards a Terminological Clarification. In N. J. I. Mars, editor, *Towards Very Large Knowledge Bases: Knowledge Building and Knowledge Sharing*, pages 25–32. IOS Press, Amsterdam, 1995.

[GHM04]   Claudio Gutiérrez, Carlos A. Hurtado, and Alberto O. Mendelzon. Foundations of Semantic Web Databases. In Alin Deutsch, editor, *Proceedings of the 23rd ACM Symposium on Principles on Database Systems*, pages 95–106. ACM, 2004.

[GHM+07] Tudor Groza, Siegfried Handschuh, Knud Moeller, Gunnar Grimnes, Leo Sauermann, Enrico Minack, Cedric Mesnage, Mehdi Jazayeri, Gerald Reif, and Rosa Gudjonsdottir. The NEPOMUK Project - On the Way to the Social Semantic Desktop. In Tassilo Pellegrini and Sebastian Schaffert, editors, *Proceedings of I-Semantics' 07*, pages pp. 201–211. JUCS, 2007.

[GHM+08] Bernardo Cuenca Grau, Ian Horrocks, Boris Motik, Bijan Parsia, Peter Patel-Schneider, and Ulrike Sattler. OWL 2: The Next Step for OWL. *Web Semantics: Science, Services and Agents on the World Wide Web*, 6(4):309 – 322, 2008. Semantic Web Challenge 2006/2007.

[Gia99]   Dominic Giampaolo. *Practical File System Design with the Be File System*. Morgan Kaufmann Publishers, 1999.

[GJSJ91] David K. Gifford, Pierre Jouvelot, Mark A. Sheldon, and James W. O'Toole Jr. Semantic File Systems. In *SOSP '91: Proceedings of the 13th ACM Symposium on Operating Systems Principles*, pages 16–25, New York, NY, USA, 1991. ACM Press.

[GN96]   Don Gentner and Jakob Nielsen. The Anti-Mac Interface. *Commun. ACM*, 39(8):70–82, 1996.

[Gra04]   Bernardo Cuenca Grau. A Possible Simplification of the Semantic Web Architecture. In *WWW '04: Proceedings of the 13th international conference on World Wide Web*, pages 704–713, New York, NY, USA, 2004. ACM Press.

[Gra06] Bernardo Cuenca Grau. *OWL 1.1 Web Ontology Language Tractable Fragments (W3C Member Submission 19 December 2006)*. World Wide Web Consortium, 2006.

[Gre07] Mark Greaves. Semantic Web 2.0. *IEEE Intelligent Systems*, 22(2):94–96, 2007.

[Gri04] Richard Grimes. Code Name WinFS: Revolutionary File Storage System Lets Users Search and Manage Files Based on Content. *MSDN Magazine*, 19(1), 2004.

[Gru93] T.R. Gruber. A Translation Approach to Portable Ontology Specifications. *Knowledge Acquisition*, 5(2):199–220, 1993.

[GWF+99] Y. Goland, E. Whitehead, A. Faizi, S. Carter, and D. Jensen. *HTTP Extensions for Distributed Authoring – WebDAV (RFC 2518)*. Network Working Group, 1999.

[Has08] Bernhard Haslhofer. *A Web-based Mapping Technique for Establishing Metadata Interoperability*. PhD thesis, University of Vienna, 2008.

[Hay04] Patrick Hayes. *RDF Semantics (W3C Recommendation 10 February 2004)*. World Wide Web Consortium, 2004.

[HBEV04] Peter Haase, Jeen Broekstra, Andreas Eberhart, and Raphael Volz. A Comparison of RDF Query Languages. In *Proceedings of the Third International Semantic Web Conference, Hiroshima, Japan, 2004.*, NOV 2004.

[HH07] Olaf Hartig and Ralf Heese. The SPARQL Query Graph Model for Query Optimization. In Franconi et al. [FKM07], pages 564–578.

[HHPS01] Ian Horrocks, Frank Van Harmelen, and Peter F. Patel-Schneider. *DAML+OIL*. Joint US/EU ad hoc Agent Markup Language Committee, 2001.

[HK04] Andrew Hogue and David Karger. Wrapper Induction for End-User Semantic Content Development. In *First International Workshop on Interaction Design and the Semantic Web*, 2004.

[HK08]   Bernhard Haslhofer and Wolfgang Klas. A Survey of Techniques for Achieving Metadata Interoperability. *ACM Comput. Surv.*, 2008. Accepted for publication.

[HMPR04]   A. R. Hevner, S. T. March, J. Park, and S. Ram. Design Science in Information Systems Research. *MIS Quarterly*, 28(1):75–105, 2004.

[HRS07]   Harry Halpin, Valentin Robu, and Hana Shepherd. The Complex Dynamics of Collaborative Tagging. In *WWW '07: Proceedings of the 16th International World Wide Web Conference*, pages 211–220, New York, NY, USA, 2007. ACM Press.

[IAD06]   Jon Iturrioz, Sergio Fernández Anzuola, and Oscar Díaz. Turning the Mouse into a Semantic Device: The seMouse Experience. In York Sure and John Domingue, editors, *The Semantic Web: Research and Applications, 3rd European Semantic Web Conference, ESWC 2006, Budva, Montenegro, June 11-14, 2006, Proceedings*, volume 4011 of *Lecture Notes in Computer Science*, pages 457–471. Springer, 2006.

[ICK+07]   Ekaterini Ioannou, Juri De Coi, Arne Koesling, Daniel Olmedilla, and Wolfgang Nejdl. Access Control for Sharing Semantic Data across Desktops. In Tim Finin, Lalana Kagal, and Daniel Olmedilla, editors, *Proceedings of the Workshop on Privacy Enforcement and Accountability with Semantics (PEAS2007) at ISWC/ASWC2007, Busan, South Korea*, November 2007.

[JCS+04]   Andrew Josey, Donald W. Cragun, Nicholas Stoughton, Mark Brown, and Cathy Hughes. *IEEE Standard 1003.1, 2004 Edition*. IEEE and The Open Group, 2004 edition, 2004.

[JEI02]   JEITA. *Exchangeable Image File Format for Digital Still Cameras: EXIF Version 2.2*. Japan Electronics and Information Technology Industries Association, April 2002.

[Jon04]   William Jones. Finders, Keepers? The Present and Future Perfect in Support of Personal Information Management. *First Monday*, 9(3), 2004.

[Jos06]   S. Josefsson. *The Base16, Base32, and Base64 Data Encodings (RFC 4648)*. Network Working Group, October 2006.

[JW05] Ian Jacobs and Norman Walsh. *Architecture of the World Wide Web, Volume One (W3C Recommendation 15 December 2004)*. World Wide Web Consortium, 2005. Available at http://www.w3.org/TR/webarch/.

[Kar07] David R. Karger. Haystack: Per-User Information Environments Based on Semistructured Data. In Victor Kaptelinin and Mary Czerwinski, editors, *Beyond the Desktop Metaphor*, pages 49–100. Massachusetts Institute of Technology, 2007.

[Kat07] Phil Katz. *ZIP File Format Specification*. PKWARE Inc., 2007.

[KBH+03] David Karger, Karun Baksxhi, David Huynh, Dennis Quan, and Vineet Sinha. Haystack: A Customizable General-Purpose Information Management Tool for End Users of Semistructured Data. In *Proceedings of the 2nd Biennal Conference on Innovative Data Systems Research (CIDR 2005)*, 2003.

[KC04] Graham Klyne and Jeremy J. Carroll. *Resource Description Framework (RDF): Concepts and Abstract Syntax (W3C Recommendation 10 February 2004)*. World Wide Web Consortium, 2004.

[KHL+07] Akrivi Katifori, Constantin Halatsis, George Lepouras, Costas Vassilakis, and Eugenia Giannopoulou. Ontology Visualization Methods – A Survey. *ACM Comput. Surv.*, 39(4):10, 2007.

[LM99] Stephen Laurence and Eric Margolis. Concepts and Cognitive Science. In Eric Margolis and Stephen Laurence, editors, *Concepts: Core Readings*, chapter 1, pages 3–81. MIT Press, July 1999.

[LMS05] P. Leach, M. Mealling, and R. Salz. *A Universally Unique IDentifier (UUID) URN Namespace (RFC 4122)*. Network Working Group, 2005.

[LT07] Stefan Leitich and Martin Topf. Globe of Music - Music Library Visualization Using GeoSOM. In *8th International Conference on Music Information Retrieval (ISMIR 2007)*, Vienna, Austria, 9 2007. Österreichische Computer Gesellschaft (OCG).

[Mal83] Thomas W. Malone. How do People Organize their Desks? Implications for the Design of Office Information Systems. *ACM Trans. Inf. Syst.*, 1(1):99–112, 1983.

[Mar06]   Ben Martin. The World is a libferris Filesystem. *Linux Journal*, April 2006.

[Mas98]   L. Masinter. *The "data" URL Scheme (RFC 2397)*. Network Working Group, August 1998.

[MB05]   Alistair Miles and Sean Bechhofer. *SKOS Simple Knowledge Organization System Reference (W3C Working Draft 25 January 2008)*. World Wide Web Consortium, 2005.

[MH07]   Knud Möller and Siegfried Handschuh. Towards a Light-Weight Semantic Desktop. In Siegfried Handschuh and Gerald Reif, editors, *Proceedings of the Semantic Desktop Design Workshop at ESWC 2007*, pages 36–46, 2007.

[MM04]   Frank Manola and Eric Miller. *RDF Primer (W3C Recommendation 10 February 2004)*. World Wide Web Consortium, February 2004.

[msGD+08]   m.c. schraefel, Jennifer Golbeck, Duane Degler, Abraham Bernstein, and Lloyd Rutledge, editors. *Proceedings of the Semantic Web User Interaction Workshop at CHI 2008: Exploring HCI Challenges*, 2008.

[MSSvE07]   Antoni Mylka, Leo Sauermann, Michael Sintek, and Ludger van Elst. NEPOMUK Ontologies. Technical report, NEPOMUK Project Consortium, 2007. Available at http://www.semanticdesktop.org/ontologies.

[MTCP04]   Aimilia Magkanaraki, Val Tannen, Vassilis Christophides, and Dimitris Plexousakis. Viewing the Semantic Web through RVL Lenses. *Journal of Web Semantics*, 1(4):359–375, 2004.

[MvH04]   Deborah L. McGuinness and Frank van Harmelen. *OWL Web Ontology Language Overview (W3C Recommendation 10 February 2004)*. World Wide Web Consortium, 2004.

[NH02]   Quang Vinh Nguyen and Mao Lin Huang. Improvements of Space-Optimized Tree for Visualizing and Manipulating Very Large Hierarchies. In *VIP '02: Selected papers from the 2002 Pan-Sydney workshop on Visualisation*, pages 75–81, Darlinghurst, Australia, Australia, 2002. Australian Computer Society, Inc.

[NH04] Quang V. Nguyen and Mao L. Huang. Visualising File Systems Using ENCCON Model. In *VIP '05: Proceedings of the Pan-Sydney area workshop on Visual information processing*, pages 61–65, Darlinghurst, Australia, Australia, 2004. Australian Computer Society, Inc.

[NHT+06] Lev Novik, Irena Hudis, Douglas B. Terry, Sanjay Anand, Vivek Jhaveri, Ashish Shah, and Yunxin Wu. Peer-to-Peer Replication in WinFS. Technical Report MSR-TR-2006-78, Microsoft Research, 2006.

[NL06] Olaf Noppens and Thorsten Liebig. Interactive Visualization of Large OWL Instance Sets. In *Proceedings of the 3rd International Semantic Web User Interaction Workshop*, 2006.

[ODC+08] Eyal Oren, Renaud Delbru, Michele Catasta, Richard Cyganiak, Holger Stenzhorn, and Giovanni Tummarello. Sindice.com: A Document-oriented Lookup Index for Open Linked Data. *Internal Journal of Metadata, Semantics and Ontologies*, 3(1):37–52, 2008.

[OG92] James W. O'Toole and David K. Gifford. Names Should Mean What, Not Where. In *Proceedings of the 5th ACM SIGOPS European Workshop on Models and Paradigms for Distributed Systems Structuring*, pages 1–5, New York, NY, USA, 1992. ACM Press.

[Oko08] Adaora Chinelo Okoli. Extraction of Contextual Metadata from File System Interactions. Master's thesis, University of Vienna, 2008.

[OS09] Adaora Okoli and Bernhard Schandl. Extraction of Contextual Metadata from File System Interactions. In *Workshop on Exploitation of Usage and Attention Metadata (EUAM 09) Workshop on Exploitation of Usage and Attention Metadata (EUAM 2009)*, 2009.

[OVBD06] Eyal Oren, Max Völkel, John Breslin, and Stefan Decker. Semantic Wikis for Personal Knowledge Management. *Database and Expert Systems Applications*, pages 509–518, 2006.

[PAG06a] Jorge Pérez, Marcelo Arenas, and Claudio Gutierrez. Semantics and Complexity of SPARQL. In Isabel F. Cruz, Stefan Decker, Dean Allemang, Chris Preist, Daniel Schwabe, Peter Mika, Michael Uschold, and Lora Aroyo, editors, *International Semantic Web Conference*, volume 4273 of *Lecture Notes in Computer Science*, pages 30–43. Springer, 2006.

[PAG06b] Jorge Pérez, Marcelo Arenas, and Claudio Gutiérrez. Semantics of SPARQL. Technical Report TR/DCC-2006-17, Universidad de Chile, October 2006.

[PBKL06] Emmanuel Pietriga, Christian Bizer, David Karger, and Ryan Lee. Fresnel: A Browser-Independent Presentation Vocabulary for RDF. In Isabel F. Cruz, Stefan Decker, Dean Allemang, Chris Preist, Daniel Schwabe, Peter Mika, Michael Uschold, and Lora Aroyo, editors, *International Semantic Web Conference*, volume 4273 of *Lecture Notes in Computer Science*, pages 158–171. Springer, 2006.

[PH03] Jeff Z. Pan and Ian Horrocks. RDFS(FA) and RDF MT: Two Semantics for RDFS. In Dieter Fensel, Katia P. Sycara, and John Mylopoulos, editors, *International Semantic Web Conference*, volume 2870 of *Lecture Notes in Computer Science*, pages 30–46. Springer, 2003.

[Pow03] Shelley Powers. *Practical RDF*. O'Reilly, Beijing, Cambridge, 2003.

[PPS04] Bijan Parsia and Peter F. Patel-Schneider. Meaning and the Semantic Web. In *WWW Alt. '04: Proceedings of the 13th international World Wide Web conference on Alternate track papers & posters*, pages 306–307, New York, NY, USA, 2004. ACM Press.

[PS03a] Steve Pepper and Sylvia Schwab. *Curing the Web's Identity Crisis: Subject Indicators for RDF*. Ontopia, 2003. Available at http://www.ontopia.net/topicmaps/materials/identitycrisis.html, retrieved 08-Aug-2008.

[PS03b] A. Pras and J. Schoenwaelder. *On the Difference Between Information Models and Data Models (RFC 3444)*. Network Working Group, 2003.

[PS08] Eric Prud'hommeaux and Andy Seaborne. *SPARQL Query Language for RDF (W3C Recommendation 15 January 2008)*. World Wide Web Consortium, 2008.

[PSH06] Peter F. Patel-Schneider and Ian Horrocks. Position Paper: A Comparison of Two Modelling Paradigms in the Semantic Web. In *WWW '06: Proceedings of the 15th international conference on World Wide Web*, pages 3–12, New York, NY, USA, 2006. ACM Press.

241

[RP08]   Jörg Richter and Jurij Poelchau. Deepamehta — another computer is possible. In Jörg Rech, Björn Decker, and Eric Ras, editors, *Emerging Technologies for Semantic Work Environments: Techniques, Methods, and Applications*. Idea Group Inc., 2008.

[Roh05] Jean Rohmer. Lessons for the Future of Semantic Desktops Learnt from 10 Years of Experience with the IDELIANCE Semantic Networks Manager. In Stefan Decker, Jack Park, Dennis Quan, and Leo Sauermann, editors, *Proc. of Semantic Desktop Workshop at the ISWC, Galway, Ireland*, November 6, volume 175, November 2005.

[RGH+07] Gerald Reif, Tudor Groza, Siegfried Handschuh, Mehdi Jazayeri, and Cédric Mesnage. Intermediate Nepomuk Architecture. Technical Report NEPOMUK D6.2.A, NEPOMUK Project Consortium, 2007.

[Res01] P. Resnik. *Internet Message Format (RFC 2822)*. Network Working Group, 2001.

[RCCR02] George Robertson, Kim Cameron, Mary Czerwinski, and Daniel Robbins. Polyarchy Visualization: Visualizing Multiple Intersecting Hierarchies. In *CHI '02: Proceedings of the SIGCHI conference on Human factors in computing systems*, pages 423–430, New York, NY, USA, 2002. ACM Press.

[QHSK02] Dennis Quan, David Huynh, Vineet Sinha, and David Karger. *Adenine: A Metadata Programming Language*. Massachusetts Institute of Technology, 2002.

[PSR06] Yoann Padioleau, Benjamin Sigonneau, and Olivier Ridoux. Lists: A logical information system as a file system. In *Proceeding of the 28th International Conference on Software Engineering (ICSE 2006)*, pages 803–806, New York, NY, USA, 2006. ACM Press.

[PSH07] Peter F. Patel-Schneider and Ian Horrocks. *OWL 1.1 Web Ontology Language Overview (W3C Member Submission 19 December 2006)*. World Wide Web Consortium, 2007. Available at http://www.w3.org/Submission/owl11-overview/, retrieved 08-Aug-2008.

[RSK04] Pamela Ravasio, Sissel Guttormsen Schär, and Helmut Krueger. In Pursuit of Desktop Evolution: User Problems and Practices with Modern Desktop Systems. *ACM Transactions on Computer-Human Interaction (TOCHI)*, 11(2):156–180, 2004.

[RSW06] Frank Ruskey, Carla D. Savage, and Stan Wagon. The Search for Simple Symmetric Venn Diagrams. *Notices of the American Mathematical Society*, 53(11):1304–1311, 2006.

[RVH05] Jörg Richter, Max Völkel, and Heiko Haller. DeepaMehta — A Semantic Desktop. In Stefan Decker, Jack Park, Dennis Quan, and Leo Sauermann, editors, *Proceedings of the 1st Workshop on The Semantic Desktop. 4th International Semantic Web Conference (Galway, Ireland)*, volume 175. CEUR-WS, NOV 2005.

[SAPT07] Bernhard Schandl, Arash Amiri, Stefan Pomajbik, and Diman Todorov. Integrating File Systems and the Semantic Web. In *Demo at the 3rd European Semantic Web Conference (ESWC 2007)*, 2007.

[SBD05] Leo Sauermann, Ansgar Bernardi, and Andreas Dengel. Overview and Outlook on the Semantic Desktop. In Stefan Decker, Jack Park, Dennis Quan, and Leo Sauermann, editors, *Proceedings of the 1st Semantic Desktop Workshop*, volume 175, Galway, Ireland, November 2005. CEUR Workshop Proceedings.

[SBLH06] Nigel Shadbolt, Tim Berners-Lee, and Wendy Hall. The Semantic Web Revisited. *IEEE Intelligent Systems*, 21(3):96–101, 2006.

[Sch06] Bernhard Schandl. SemDAV: A File Exchange Protocol for the Semantic Desktop. In *Proceedings of the Semantic Desktop and Social Semantic Collaboration Workshop*, volume 202, Athens, GA, USA, November 2006. CEUR Workshop Proceedings.

[SDvE+06] Leo Sauermann, Andreas Dengel, Ludger van Elst, Andreas Lauer, Heiko Maus, and Sven Schwarz. Personalization in the EPOS Project. In *Proceedings of the Semantic Web Personalization Workshop at the ESWC 2006*, 2006.

[Sea04] Andy Seaborne. *RDQL - A Query Language for RDF (W3C Member Submission 9 January 2004)*. World Wide Web Consortium, 2004.

[SSB+08] Markus Stocker, Andy Seaborne, Abraham Bernstein, Christoph Kiefer, and Dave Reynolds. SPARQL Basic Graph Pattern Optimization Using Selectivity Estimation. In *WWW '08: Proceeding of the 17th international conference on World Wide Web*, pages 595–604, New York, NY, USA, 2008. ACM.

[SS08] Simon Schenk and Steffen Staab. Networked Graphs: A Declarative Mechanism for SPARQL Rules, SPARQL Views and RDF Data Integration on the Web. In *WWW '08: Proceeding of the 17th international conference on World Wide Web*, pages 585–594, New York, NY, USA, 2008. ACM.

[SS94] Andrew Sears and Ben Shneiderman. Split Menus: Effectively Using Selection Frequency to Organize Menus. *ACM Trans. Comput.-Hum. Interact.*, 1(1):27–51, 1994.

[SM07b] Lucia Specia and Enrico Motta. Integrating Folksonomies with the Semantic Web. In Franconi et al. [FKM07], pages 624–639.

[SM07a] Andy Seaborne and Geetha Manjunath. *SPARQL/Update: A Language for Updating RDF Graphs*. Hewlett-Packard, 2007.

[SK06] Bernhard Schandl and Ross King. The SemDAV Project: Metadata Management for Unstructured Content. In *CAMA '06: Proceedings of the 1st International Workshop on Contextualized Attention Metadata: Collecting, Managing and Exploiting of Rich Usage Information*, pages 27–32, New York, NY, USA, 2006. ACM Press.

[Sir05] John Siracusa. *Mac OS X 10.4 Tiger. ars technica - the art of technology*, 2005.

[Shn92] Ben Shneiderman. Tree Visualization with Tree-Maps: 2D Space-Filling Approach. *ACM Trans. Graph.*, 11(1):92–99, 1992.

[SH09] Bernhard Schandl and Bernhard Haslhofer. The Sile Model – A Semantic File System Infrastructure for the Desktop. In *Proceedings of the 6th European Semantic Web Conference (ESWC 2009)*, Heraklion, Greece, 2009.

[SH08] Leo Sauermann and Dominik Heim. Evaluating Long-Term Use of the Gnowsis Semantic Desktop for PIM. In *The Semantic Web — ISWC 2008*, volume 5318 of *LNCS*, pages 467–482. Springer, 2008.

[Ta03] Marcelo Tallis. Semantic Word Processing for Content Authors. In *In Workshop Notes of the Knowledge Markup and Semantic Annotation Workshop (SEMANNOT 2003), Second International Conference on Knowledge Capture (K-CAP 2003)*, October 2003.

[TH06] Yannis Tzitzikas and Jean-Luc Hainaut. On the Visualization of Large-sized Ontologies. In *AVI '06: Proceedings of the working conference on Advanced visual interfaces*, pages 99–102, New York, NY, USA, 2006. ACM Press.

[TJB06] Jaime Teevan, William Jones, and Benjamin B. Bederson. Introduction to the Special Issue on Personal Information Management. *Commun. ACM*, 49(1):40–43, 2006.

[TL05] Heikki Topi and Wendy Lucas. Searching the Web: Operator Assistance Required. *Information Processing and Management*, 41(2):383–403, March 2005.

[TM07] Giovanni Tummarello and Christian Morbidoni. Collaboratively Building Structured Knowledge with DBin: From del.icio.us Tags to an "RDFS Folksonomy". In *Workshop on Social and Collaborative Construction of Structured Knowledge (CKC 2007) at WWW 2007*, Banff, Canada, 2007.

[TMN06] Giovanni Tummarello, Christian Morbidoni, and Michele Nucci. Enabling Semantic Web Communities with DBin: An Overview. In *Proceedings of the 5th International Semantic Web Conference (ISWC 2006)*, pages 943–950, Springer, 2006.

[TMNP06] Giovanni Tummarello, Christian Morbidoni, Michele Nucci, and Onofrio Panzarino. Brainlets: "Instant" Semantic Web Applications. In Sören Auer, Chris Bizer, and Libby Miller, editors, *Proceedings of the ESWC'06 Workshop on Scripting for the Semantic Web*, volume 183 of *CEUR Workshop Proceedings ISSN 1613-0073*, June 2006.

[Tod08] Dimau Todorov. User Interface Concepts for Semantic Information Systems. Master's thesis, University of Vienna, 2008.

[TPM07] Giovanni Tummarello, Axel Polleres, and Christian Morbidoni. Who the FOAF knows Alice? A Needed Step Toward Semantic Web Pipes. In Proceedings of the First International Workshop "New forms of reasoning for the Semantic Web: scalable, tolerant and dynamic". CEUR Workshop Proceedings, 2007.

[vD97] Andries van Dam. Post-WIMP User Interfaces. Commun. ACM, 40(2):63–67, 1997.

[vHvW02] Frank van Ham and Jarke J. van Wijk. Beamtrees: Compact Visualization of Large Hierarchies. In INFOVIS '02: Proceedings of the IEEE Symposium on Information Visualization (InfoVis '02), page 93, Washington, DC, USA, 2002. IEEE Computer Society.

[VS06] Max Völkel and Sebastian Schaffert, editors. Proceedings of the First Workshop on Semantic Wikis - From Wiki to Semantics (Co-located with ESWC 2006), volume 206. CEUR-WS.org, 2006.

[vWvHvdW03] Jarke J. van Wijk, Frank van Ham, and Huub van de Wetering. Rendering Hierarchical Data. Commun. ACM, 46(9):257–263, 2003.

[Wal05] Carsten Waldeck. Liquid 2D Scatter Space for File System Browsing. iv, pages 451–456, 2005.

[Wat07] Andrew Watt. Professional Windows PowerShell. Wrox Press Ltd, Birmingham, UK, 2007.

[WG04] E. James Whitehead and Yaron Y. Goland. The WebDAV property design. Softw. Pract. Exper., 34(2):135–161, 2004.

[WGM95] C.E. Wiils, D. Giampaolo, and M.S. Mackovitch. Experience with an Interactive Attribute-based User Information Environment. In Computers and Communications, 1995. Conference Proceedings of the 1995 IEEE Fourteenth Annual Phoenix International Conference on, pages 359–365, Mar 1995.

[Win99] David Winer. XML-RPC Specification. UserLand Software, Inc., 1999. Available at http://www.xmlrpc.com/spec, retrieved 08-Aug-2008.

[WLHW08] Gang Wu, Juanzi Li, Jiangiang Hu, and Kehong Wang. System Π: A Native RDF Repository Based on the Hypergraph Representation for RDF Data Model. In *WAIM '08: Proceedings of the 2008 The Ninth International Conference on Web-Age Information Management*, pages 62–69, Washington, DC, USA, 2008. IEEE Computer Society.

[WLL+07] Timo Weithöner, Thorsten Liebig, Marko Luther, Sebastian Böhm, Friedrich W. von Henke, and Olaf Noppens. Real-World reasoning with OWL. In Franconi et al. [FKM07], pages 296–310.

[WWDW06] Weixin Wang, Hui Wang, Guozhong Dai, and Hongan Wang. Visualization of Large Hierarchical Data by Circle Packing. In *CHI '06: Proceedings of the SIGCHI conference on Human Factors in computing systems*, pages 517–520, New York, NY, USA, 2006. ACM Press.

[XC05] Huiyong Xiao and Isabel F. Cruz. A Multi-Ontology Approach for Personal Information Management. In Stefan Decker, Jack Park, Dennis Quan, and Leo Sauermann, editors, *Proc. of Semantic Desktop Workshop at the ISWC, Galway, Ireland, November 6*, volume 175, November 2005.

Die VDM Verlagsservicegesellschaft mbH vertritt

**Die VDM Verlagsservicegesellschaft sucht für wissen-
schaftliche Verlage abgeschlossene und herausragende
Dissertationen, Habilitationen,
Diplomarbeiten, Master Theses,
Magisterarbeiten usw.**
für die kostenlose Publikation als Fachbuch.

Sie verfügen über eine Arbeit, die hohen inhaltlichen und formalen Ansprüchen genügt, und haben Interesse an einer hono-
rarvergüteten Publikation?

Dann senden Sie bitte erste Informationen über sich und Ihre
Arbeit per Email an *info@vdm-vsg.de*.

Sie erhalten kurzfristig unser Feedback!

VDM Verlagsservicegesellschaft mbH
Dudweiler Landstr. 99   Telefon +49 681 3720 174
D - 66123 Saarbrücken   Fax   +49 681 3720 1749

www.vdm-vsg.de

Printed by Books on Demand GmbH, Norderstedt / Germany